Soul Food & Living Water

Soul Food & Living Water

Spiritual Nourishment and Practical Help for African-American Families

Yolanda Powell & William J. Powell

A Focus on the Family book
published by Moody Publishers, Chicago, Illinois

Focus on the Family books are available at special quantity discounts when purchased in bulk by corporations, organizations, churches, or groups. Special imprints, messages, and excerpts can be produced to meet your needs. For more information, contact: Resource Sales Group, Focus on the Family, 8605 Explorer Drive, Colorado Springs, CO 80920; or phone (800) 932-9123.

Editor: Shana Murph
Cover Design: Solid Roxx Media
Cover Photo: Generations by Corbis

Library of Congress Cataloging-in-Publication Data

Powell, Yolanda, 1961-
  Soul food & living water : spiritual nourishment for African American
families / by Yolanda Powell & William J. Powell.
    p. cm.
Includes bibliographical references and index.
  ISBN 0-8024-1757-4
  1. African American families—Religious life. 2. Christian life—United States. I.
Title: Soul food and living water. II. Powell, William J., 1955- III. Title.
  BR563.N4 P69 2003
  248.4'089'96073—dc21
                          2002012769

Printed in the United States of America
1 2 3 4 5 6 7 8 9 / 08 07 06 05 04 03 02

We dedicate this labor of love to two great African-American patriarchs:

The late Alfred Thomas White,
our dad and father-in-law,
who taught us the meaning of sacrificing for the family,
and
the late Alexander Anderson,
our brother and mentor in Christ,
who openly modeled the deep and abiding love of a
husband, father, and elder of the faith.

Contents

Acknowledgments

This book was birthed out of a deep soul struggle and heart cry. We are indebted to the help of many brothers and sisters in Christ who served and aided us in this great delivery.

Faithful nursemaids and midwives include Karla Hall, Wilhelmina Harris, Judy Plater, Carolyn McCalvin, Pearl Williams, and Sandra Friend, who called periodically to encourage us. A "hallelujah high five" goes to Charles Harris, Charles Day, Ken Plater, Henry Moore, and other men in William's accountability group who remembered us in prayer. Renee Groff, our humble intercessor, prayed daily through the endless process of writing, rewriting, and editing. We were honored by her perserverance.

Treasured feedback came from friends and colleagues like Pastor Dennis Blackwell, Sharmayn Stoves, Kandie Harris, Charlotte Collins, Warren Mosby, and Norm Rohrer at the Christian Writers' Guild, who provided early comments that kept me on a proper writing path. And yet, I could not have endured the rigors of "pioneer writing" without the help of Jocelyn Drakeford, an armor bearer extraordinaire—chosen of God for such a time as this!

Two teaching priests—Ira and Delita Jacobs—challenged us greatly in our passion for this project and kept a prophetic light before us in dark times. Special thanks goes to Pastor Michael Jones and Harvest Community Church, where we first taught these principles in a weekly Bible study. Their gracious support has sustained us in numerous ways.

I am grateful to literary agent Christine Bolley, who first told me that a book for the African-American family was needful in the Christian marketplace and primed me to pursue this vision with tenacity; Linda McGinn, who gave me the "ins and outs" of excellence in public ministry; and Marlene Bagnull, of the Greater Philadelphia Christian Writers' Fellowship, who encouraged me to speak and write—during a season when I was still unsure of doing either well.

Much thanksgiving goes to my editing assistant, Kim Booker Savage, who read tons of text and provided critical insights; Bob Lessig, our astute Bible researcher and authority on Greek and Hebrew; and my colleagues at the College of Southern Maryland, where surrogate office space was erected when our computer crashed two weeks before our deadline.

Great appreciation is extended to the editorial and marketing teams at Focus on the Family, Lift Every Voice, and Moody Publishers. These publishing professionals supported our "new voice" in the marketplace with incredible vigor. We applaud the untiring dedication of Shana Murph, Mick Silva, Dyxie Lincoln, Karen Waddles, and Cynthia Ballenger.

The underlying foundation of this book was fortified by the revelatory preaching of our pastor, Bishop Donald Anthony Wright of Jabbok International Fellowship, where the Word of God is graciously served as our only true sustenance. We are strengthened by this continuous feast!

As parents, we applaud the patience of our sons, Joseph, Jeremy, and Jordan, who supported us through four straight seasons of non-stop writing—when a sense of normalcy left our humble abode and never returned. May our elongated efforts become your great reward.

Our most triumphant ovation goes to the Delivering Physician, our Lord and Savior Jesus Christ, who thwarted the "stillborn" threats of the Enemy and brought this "book baby" to full term despite all hindrances. May all that we have birthed here bring You glory as Your bounty and provision fills each home.

Introduction

The Powell family has weathered many storms—numerous "floods," and a dozen "droughts"—over the last eighteen years. Out of each one, we have come through alive and magnifying the Lord our God! Today, we lift our voices and give testimony to the awesome power of God to deliver.

During times of trouble, the Lord always shows up with soul food and living water to personally nurture those who trust in Him. Sadly, it takes some of us a long time to realize what an awesome God we serve—and an even longer time to return the praise due His name.

Seeing the reality of our spiritual hunger and thirst, our family cried out to the Lord, asking Him to fill us with the sustaining nutrition that flowed only from Him. In many ways, we feel we have "crossed over the Jordan," and now the Lord has sent us back to tell other families how they can find their way into the land of promise. This book is our report on the promised land sent to sustain you and your family as you journey to victorious Christian living!

Once we had tasted the milk and honey of God's promises, we peered back over our former wanderings and saw the startling realities of family life for the first time. Our hearts grew heavy with desire to assist those, like us, who had been trapped in the house of bondage. Sadly, spiritual famine and drought runs rampant throughout the American landscape, increasingly finding its way into each and every home. As God-conscious families, we all struggle to maintain a vibrant faith in the midst of such conflicting morals and declining social values. For African-American families, marital commitment, child rearing, and financial integrity are problems that have become intensely magnified in recent years. Whether in urban centers or suburban sprawls, African-American families are under enormous pressures, from marital conflict and financial lack, to public school safety and racial injustice. It seems we are troubled on every side!

Yet we are never forsaken! The same God who delivered Daniel out of the den of lions, brought the Israelites across the Red Sea, and set our ancestors free from slavery will indeed bring us bodily into all His spiritual promises in a new century. But we have a responsibility to hold fast to His unchanging hand! What we must possess—now more than ever—is an intense love for the "God of our weary years, the God of our silent tears"! This love is realized by a renewed commitment to the daily discipline of God's unfailing Word and the practical application of His timeless truths to family life. For a great number of us, "churchin'" is great, but the sermons and studies we hear each week don't always carry over into how we live every day. We are often powerful in the *church house,* but powerless on the *home front!* And the twain must become one!

Many of us are so busy with social activities, business pursuits, parenting dilemmas, and community concerns that we have not stopped to realize our own spiritual hunger and thirst! We've got a lot. We go a lot. We even give a lot. But the quiet place on the inside where we commune with a personal Savior is often a dry, dark, and dreary sanctuary. If we are willing to slow our pace, we will see the deep need in our own face and in the faces of our family.

The real famine and drought is spiritual, and it is *within.* Oh, how we need an *internal* Holy Ghost revival! How desperately we need soul food and living water from the God who created us and knows us intimately. We need a personal touch from the Lord to bring life, health, and strength to the family . . . God's *first* institution! We need a restoration of godly values and biblical wisdom. And we need it right now!

As an African-American family in Christ, we have had times of spiritual hunger and thirst—and we have partaken of God's bountiful provision. We've had little and we've had much, but neither place meant anything unless Jesus was Lord of the house. And it is this principle of the life-changing reign and rule of Christ that we have the privilege of sharing with you on these pages. Here, our failures as a family will be transparent, and our triumphs will be boldly shared to empower you and your family. With liberty we open unto you our most treasured life lessons on loving God and cherishing one another.

Soul Food & Living Water has been published in a partnership between Focus on the Family, an international Christian organization with a heartfelt mission to strengthen the family, and Moody Publishers, also an international ministry, committed to teaching the uncompromising truths of the Bible. These organizations are being mightily used of God to get the "glad streams" of the water of the Word flowing into historically barren places. With great joy, African-American families now have a specialized and targeted resource to assist them on the home front and in the trenches—where we live and work every day!

We've designed this book for quick and easy reading: Each chapter is compact and hard-hitting! You'll even find real-life examples and practical aids running through the chapters like streams to keep you nourished and refreshed—and to help you put Christ at the center of family life.

As you will see, *Soul Food & Living Water* is a scriptural oasis designed to strengthen the Christian family where we are weak and lacking. It is written to bring relief as a savory meal in the wilderness and a cool spring in the desert. In essence, *Soul Food & Living Water* is a personal invitation to "come and dine" at the

Lord's table, to be comforted in His presence, and to feast upon His words. So eat well and drink deep!

Be deeply strengthened and encouraged! The fresh manna of God is falling down, and the reservoirs of His boundless grace are flowing in. Our Father has heard your cry in the late-night hour! He has seen your marriage grow more difficult over the years and your children lose interest in spiritual and family things. *Soul Food & Living Water* is a direct response from a God who sees and knows all things! He peers into our private quarters and knows the help we desperately need!

With *Soul Food & Living Water,* you'll find joyful pathways back into the presence of God and fun activities to bring the whole family along! So, open wide the doors of your home: Spiritual nourishment is sent priority status and special delivery from our heart and home to yours! Be richly blessed!

PART ONE

Our Personal Relationship with God

❶

Spiritual Nourishment
Without Cash or Credit

William's eyes were moist as he fought back the tears. Unless he completed his dissertation in thirty days, his contract would not be renewed at the university where he had just been hired a year prior. Our well-laid plans to prosper had come crashing in on us like a truck speeding out of control. In that moment, we stood broken and paralyzed in one another's reflection. Only the lifting of our eyes *upward* gave us any relief.

As a family, we had committed to support William's pursuit of higher education. Our three boys and I had uprooted numerous times and sacrificed tremendously to garner what we called "the family doctorate." Even though William was earning the degree, each of us became private stockholders anticipating the dividends that would inevitably come out of the family's sacrificial investment.

But over time, we all had grown weary living on sparse

stipends and lean loans that kept us pinned under the federal poverty line. Our eyes grew dim looking to the distant future when we'd be able to afford more than the bare essentials. So when the offer came "out of the blue" for William to leave school a year early and take a teaching position as a junior professor, we all leaped at the opportunity! He would simply teach during the day, work on his dissertation at night, and earn those long-awaited funds. All of us rejoiced at our anticipated lot! It would be nice to have a biweekly income and be able to do the "normal" things that families do, like drive a decent car, purchase adequate health insurance, and save for summer vacations.

Now, having those things meant little to understanding our present trial. What had gone wrong? How could we have let this happen? Where was God our Savior? We had known about the deadline for William's dissertation for a full year but refused to discipline our lives. Our focus was so distracted and our energies so diverted that we had hardly noticed that our current livelihood and long-anticipated dreams were swaying aimlessly in the wind. The barrenness of busyness had so invaded our lives that it took a proverbial Mack truck to awaken us to this reality: *Our days are numbered!*

None of us have as much time as we imagine to accomplish the special things God has promised us—both individually and as a family. The years go fast, children grow up, interest rates rise, deadlines arrive, and before we know it, little time remains to be as fruitful and productive as we had hoped. The urgent swallows up the essential, and we are left oblivious as to why our marriage is broken, how our children got into so much trouble, and whether our dreams will ever take flight. Compromising thoughts of "ho hum," "oh, well," "someday," and "maybe later" soon lead us astray—away from the awesome paths God has prescribed. Before we know it, we end up in crazy situations, doing unbelievable things that in no way glorify the Lord.

After William lost his job and we were unable to pay our bills for a length of time, we painstakingly had to face the fact that we were spiritually malnourished, biblically bankrupt, and internally deficient! During our years of financial lack, our family had remained faithful to God in prayer and the study of His Holy Word—enjoying extended together times around the simplicities of life. We were lean on the outside but rich on the inside. Christ was uncompromisingly the central focus of our home, and our total dependency was upon Him to provide our daily bread and meet our every need. But with a good bit of disposable income in our pockets and the joys of numerous luxuries at our fingertips, we became too busy and grand for God our Savior. We still went to church, said grace over meals, participated in ministry activities, and even shared the Gospel with others from time to time; but we failed to uphold Christ as "Lord of the home front," where He had always reigned supreme. Our reverence and adoration for His daily presence waned from day to day, and we failed to recognize our selfish preoccupations. The special communion we had shared with the Lord around the dinner table or during bedtime routines had nearly diminished; everyone was moving to a different beat. With the increased movement and activities of our schedules, we didn't have time to meditate and contemplate on the Word or seek the Father's counsel on the intricacies and details of the day. We were Christians dedicated to a natural agenda instead of a living Lord, and we were in big trouble!

The 5-5 Family Plan of Spiritual Bounty

The Lord is completely aware of our spiritual deficit—and He patiently awaits our return to His bounty! As we cried out to the Lord, He spoke gently to William and me and led us to an oasis of spiritual nurture in His Holy Word. Isaiah 55 became a spiritual reservoir to our family as we pulled off the weight of worldly pursuits and sat down at the streams of God to regain our strength and direction.

In verses 1–3, the Lord spoke strong words to His people, the Israelites, attempting to encourage and challenge them as they languished in Babylonian exile. Speaking to Israel then (and to us today), Isaiah 55 is a timeless message of God's care and concern for our spiritual nourishment. We see it as God's 5-5 plan for families that have been exploited and depleted by the bondage of overindulgence and natural entanglements. Since five is considered the number of grace in Holy Writ, it's clear that through these verses of restoration, God is heaping grace upon grace over those who willingly respond. That's exactly what He did for our family. Grace met us at each line of text and revived our aching souls word by word. "Ho! Everyone who thirsts, come to the waters; and you who have no money, come, buy and eat. Yes, come, buy wine and milk without money and without price. Why do you spend money for what is not bread and your wages for what does not satisfy?" (verses 1–2a).

While the Lord's words spoken through the prophet are full of hope, the power of Isaiah 55 unveils the anguish of God's own heart. Just as we were experiencing, His people had suffered the tragic consequences of their own sinfulness because they had turned away from Jehovah. So He pleads with them in earnestness to return. The Lord's words are dripping with grave concern and loving-kindness: "Listen carefully to Me, and eat what is good, and let your soul delight itself in abundance. Incline your ear, and come to Me. Hear, and your soul shall live . . ." (Verses 2b–3a).

Listening to divine direction is a vital skill when a family is undergoing spiritual renovation and restoration. The Lord must be able to speak to us, correct us, and guide us from leanness into spiritual bounty. Consider the condition of your own soul right now and that of your family. Are stressful issues, bad news, and difficult decisions all around you? Remember, the Lord is the same yesterday, today, and forever. He is still beckoning us to come to Him.

So often we find ourselves tripping and running from one

"spiritual marathon" to another, pulling our hair out on never-ending issues, or spending our hard-earned dollars on desires that do nothing but create more debt and despair! Consider our friends John and Sherrie, who run three businesses out of their home and are always juggling ringing phones, constant FedEx deliveries, dining room clutter, and mental fatigue. Can you relate? Or how about my neighbor Janice, who is always complaining about her roller-coaster schedule: "Girl, I'm up at 5:30 running! I put kids on the bus by 6:30 and inch through morning traffic all the way to work. Yet, I'm always running late for early meetings and staying late for conference calls." She's constantly murmuring about life's many demands of errands to run, bills to pay, meals to cook, and clothes to wash. Then there's the church schedule of weekly Bible studies, youth groups, and choir rehearsals. It appears to be a never-ending roller coaster. "Child, I'm so exhausted at the end of the day! I can't hardly look at a Bible, let alone read one! I know the Lord understands."

Do you hear the Master insisting that enough is enough? He will never sympathize with lavish itineraries of spiritual neglect. He beckons us to change our ways and come to Him! Surely He has a better way for all of us! The Lord our God offers us His peace and provision for change. The *real* good news is that this generous offering is extended to you today without a down payment or a credit application. It's a 5-5 plan that you cannot deny and is always available.

"Come, Buy and Eat!"

What Jesus has secured for you and your family is *truly* paid in full! You merely accept His invitation by faith and reach out to receive all that you need to *really* live! Are you parched, dry, and thirsty? Drink from the fountain of Living Water. Are you concerned about where your next meal is coming from and how you are going to "make groceries"? *Come, buy and eat without money!*

Are you missing the wine of merriment and the milk of strength in your family life? *"Come, buy wine and milk without money and without price."* Are you spending much and gaining little? Is your soul still empty after you've expended almost everything? The Lord admonishes you to change your ways and *"eat what is good."*

We know about God's provision firsthand. While William was pursuing his doctorate in upstate New York, we lived on his $680 monthly stipend. I was working a couple of hours at a Christian radio station by night and staying home all day with our boys (who were all under age six at the time). The rent and car note consumed nearly all of our meager income each month, and food was a rare commodity. I shall never forget our first white Christmas. We were "broke, busted, and disgusted," as one preacher phrased it. With our family so far away and times so lean, the joy and merriment of the season seemed galaxies away, until two friends blew in with the north wind and blessed us with gift certificates for food and toys. It was the first time we had ever encountered our God as Jehovah Jireh, the God who sees and provides!

This provision caused us to grow by leaps and bounds as a family. We embraced God as our heavenly Father and realized that even when nobody else knows our natural needs, He does! And just as He performs those natural miracles of bringing meat and toys for Christmas, He will do the same in meeting our spiritual needs.

As a person who loves the Lord, you must put emphasis on your soul's sustenance, even at the expense of your fleshly desires. Make a decision to delight yourself in what will truly satisfy. And what might that be? Only the Lord Himself! "Incline your ear, and come to Me," says the Lord. "Hear, and your soul shall live" (Isaiah 55:3). Life is not found in the substance of the things we possess. Abundant life may be found in one person. It's all very simple. "He who has the Son has life" (1 John 5:12). Jesus looks squarely at our bleak circumstances and grave needs and still summons gently, "Come to Me" (Matthew 11:28; John 7:37).

Taking Spiritual Inventory

There are many issues affecting the African-American family and community that keep us from "coming fully" to the Lord and really partaking of His spiritual bounty. Either we're too busy trying to make ends meet or keeping our businesses afloat, or we're burdened about the safety of our children or the security of our jobs. Somewhere in between, we may consider our spiritual destiny and wonder whether God is pleased with our mundane worship and our stale routine. However, our lives are so stretched across miles and minutes that we can never find the space and time to take a personal spiritual inventory. We move so fast and so much that we never have time to "stop and smell the flowers."

Just as it's important to take inventory of our physical belongings for insurance records (in case of a robbery or fire), we also must take inventory of our own family's spiritual needs for those times when we must confront the Enemy that comes to "steal, and to kill, and to destroy" (John 10:10). When many of us hear this verse, our first thought is to think of a tragedy or natural disaster—physical death, car accident, forest fire, massive hurricane, etc. But it was a good friend and home-schooling mother who enlarged my understanding of this verse. "Do you know that the Enemy stole three months of my life last year?" she shared during some serious "sister-girl" time.

"Three months?" I questioned in a baffled tone. "How did he accomplish that?"

"I was depressed about my marriage and angry at my husband for having an extramarital affair. But instead of seeking counseling and healing, I pushed on with my daily routine," she said matter-of-factly.

"From March 1 to June 1, I don't remember going grocery

shopping, changing any bed linen, or reading a single magazine. I certainly didn't teach my children anything or correct them on bad behavior or laugh at their jokes," she said regrettably.

"Ninety-two days went by me, and I don't recall one of them. They appeared like a gray dream. Time was stolen from me as I walked around in bitter pain," my friend reflected.

I was awed by the reality of her story. My thoughts were racing: *Satan can steal literal days, kill personal dreams, and destroy family time! He's a spiritual robber, a liar, and a murderer!*

At this point, perhaps it would be helpful to take a quick inventory of the spiritual items that reflect a healthy Christian home. The first time I took spiritual inventory of my family, I wept in godly sorrow. We were lean and lacking or negligent and deficient in ten critical areas:

- Christ as HMIC (Head Master in charge)

- Individual Bible reading and quiet meditation

- Family prayer and devotion

- Corporate fasting with a unified purpose

- Shared meals with stimulating conversation

- Family gatherings and recreation

- Marital intimacy and periodic getaways

- Household orderliness and cleanliness

- Financial management and spending maintenance

- Sabbath rest and reflection

It was obvious that some sort of theft or negligence had invaded our home life. William was on the other side of town, trying desperately to adjust to a new career path as a professor. Yet the rigors and pressures of a new teaching schedule kept invading his spiritual focus, family time, and doctoral energy. As his helpmeet, I should have been able to assist my husband and help keep him on track, but I was too busy dealing with my own issues.

Personal ambition had blinded me to the importance of keeping both my natural and spiritual world in order. I was publishing and coauthoring my first book and soon became consumed by the process of creating a "winning product." My coauthor, the first African-American licensed auctioneer in the state of Alabama, had been featured in *Essence* and *Black Enterprise* magazines, and a small taste of worldly fame crossed my lips. I had gotten caught up in the world of publishing, and my spiritual compass had become foggy. But God was letting me know that the natural is the best indicator of the spiritual.

Also during that time intimacy became casual between my husband and me due to enormous fatigue, family prayer was completely nonexistent, and dinner was often prepared by short order or, as my mother calls it, "Everybody for themselves and God for us all!" My hectic book schedule left little time for life-giving relationships with my church family or friends. The barrenness of extreme busyness was devouring the meaningful aspects of my life.

Our house was always disheveled and out of order, bills were strewn about and constantly behind, and our spending was extravagant and out of control. There was little attention given to corporate fasting or family outings, and the television served as our live-in babysitter. We were in a spiritual mess!

I was so consumed with publishing, products, and publicity that my call to minister to family and friends was totally depleted. I was on a high-speed, circling merry-go-round, and I couldn't seem to find a good spot to jump off! I kept telling myself that this was "ministry," and that I was helping others who needed to discover "historical riches through auctions, antiques, and collectibles." But in my heart I knew that I was far from my known spiritual path; and, unfortunately, I had dragged my family along into this desolate place.

By honest confession, I still had "a form of godliness, but [was] denying the power thereof" (2 Timothy 3:5 KJV). What Jesus desires to pour out to others through us must flow first in us. We are to be first partakers of the good fruit that Jesus is growing on the branches of our lives.

William and I quickly recognized that we didn't need a family therapist; rather, we needed the Counselor profiled in Isaiah 9. We had to repent and refocus our attention and affection upon the Lord. As a family, we had to learn all over again to come closer to the One who knows us best and to trust Him to breathe new life into us individually and corporately. And that's what began to happen! Not overnight, but day by day unexplainable peace and clearer priorities began to infiltrate our home again.

First, we opened our Bible to engage in personal study. Reading the Word of God and a weekly family night became uncompromising commitments. The television was turned off so that we could engage in quiet reading and intimate conversation. William and I learned to take a $20 bill and treat ourselves to what we jokingly coined "a just-gotta-get-away." Our special time would often take place on a Saturday morning. We'd start with breakfast at McDonald's, then travel to Annapolis (the closest metropolitan town) to pick up a coveted (used) item or two from the thrift store and end with a midday retreat at Barnes and Noble bookstore (browsing through new books and reading "hot off the press" magazines). This time refreshed us deeply and renewed our affection for the things we loved—even with very little money. Putting things in the proper order gave us a reassuring wink that our spiritual lives had once again become pleasing to our Lord.

A Day Early and a Dollar Over

Being raised in an African-American community, you surely have heard the well-worn phrase, "A day late and a dollar short!" It's one of those familiar sayings that characterize our inability to pull it all together. Despite our best efforts, time runs short and money runs dry just before we can realize our dreams and make significant progress. Yet, I believe that Christ can change such bitter dilemmas, and breathe fresh air into our circumstances. He removes the constant strain of lost time and little money and empowers us to succeed. By the Lord's grace and mercy we can always arrive "a day early and a dollar over!" Our lives don't have to become a sad museum of "wish I coulda-woulda-shoulda!" Christ is the change agent who can broker our lives and yield increasing dividends of fresh abundance.

From a historical perspective, the African-American family is extremely resilient! We have endured tremendous hardships and difficulties. When we crossed the threshold of the twenty-first century, we had a collective testimony on our tongues and unified praise on our lips!

But this overcoming tenacity can also be disguised as one of our greatest weaknesses. We can be *too strong!* We can do *too much!* We can push *too hard!* And we can reason *too long!* As a people, our survival training often has conditioned us to try to fake it until we can make it! Instead of crying out for help, we tend to wallow in a wide mess or languish in a deep ditch, while trying to "pull ourselves up by our own bootstraps." This behavior is contrary to the ways and teachings of Christ. Such times reveal how untrusting and unfaithful we really are in believing God and taking Him at His Word. With Jesus Christ, all relationships between our heavenly Father and His earthly children are reconciled. We can inquire *swiftly* of our Father and He has promised to *swiftly* answer us. As the elder mothers used to say, "He may not come when you want Him, but He's always on time!"

There is not a situation under our roofs, within our bedrooms, hidden in our closets, or existing in our communities that the true and living God cannot adequately address. We must seek His wisdom and call upon His name with confident boldness! Isaiah 55: 6–7 (NASB) invites us to

Seek the Lord while He may be found;
Call upon Him while He is near.
Let the wicked forsake his way,
And the unrighteous man his thoughts;
And let him return to the Lord,
And He will have compassion on him;
And to our God,
For He will abundantly pardon.

If I can be completely honest, sometimes it seems our religious fervor can become personally abusive and spiritually unproductive when we try to appear saved, whole, and free, and attempt to convince others that we are "okay with God." Jesus is not most interested in our works of righteousness, but in our surrender to His help. We don't have to "fake it till we can make it." He knows our framework and He pursues us *anyway!* The life Christ has granted us must be *real!* Jesus Christ came down to wrestle inadequacy off our backs, to renew our minds with faith, and to lift the weights of guilt and shame from our remembrance. He alone will replace our former days of being late and lean with future days of divine favor and overflow. So live. And live well! We are not victims, but victors—because of Him who loves us and gave Himself for us!

Jesus Paid It All

Jesus is the only One who can feed our hungry souls and quench our thirsty spirits. He doesn't ask a lot of questions or make immediate demands, nor does He require an application or ID card in order to nourish us. Spiritual nourishment flows instantly out of His being to fill every barren and lacking place— just for the asking!

When I'm ministering God's Word to children, I always tell them that the Lord God is the world's greatest chef and that I'm His waitress! He prepares for people exactly what they need, and He does it with succulent flair! All I do is serve each exquisite dish with a servant's heart. And I'm always astonished at the scrumptious dishes He can whip out to replenish the famished or fortify the weak.

There's a special thrill in receiving an unexpected dinner invitation to your favorite ritzy restaurant from a cherished friend. For one night, you toss the pots and pans in the cupboard and throw fast food to the curb. On this exciting evening, you have the luxury of ordering your favorite appetizer, entrée, and dessert from the pricey menu. You feast on fabulous cuisine and enjoy great conversation without worrying about your *own* cash flow or credit card limits. It's all taken care of—carte blanche! By the time the cappuccino arrives, you are feeling thoroughly satisfied and richly blessed from head to toe.

Times like these don't have to be rare at all, because the true and living God is our cherished Friend and well-equipped Savior! He *always* picks up the tab for our spiritual dining. Never forget that we were created to feast on both natural *and* spiritual food. Our heavenly Father, who formed us in His own image and likeness, knows we need "spiritual nourishment" to sustain our spiritual well-being. Jesus taught that "Man shall not live by bread alone, but by every word that proceedeth out of the mouth of God" (Matthew 4:4 KJV).

There is more to human beings than an outer shell. As many Bible teachers explain, humanity was created as a tripart being with distinct elements that comprise our makeup. We live in a *body* (that needs physical food like baked chicken, collard greens, and potato salad); we have a *mind* (that feeds on the intellectual food of books, poetry, and technology); but our essence is *spirit* (requiring the daily spiritual food of God's living Word). In order for us to mature in a dynamic relationship with the Lord of life, we must learn to feast heartily on the sustenance of His Holy Scripture.

African-American culture is known for its superb soul food recipes, delicious baked cakes, and mouthwatering pies. We bring a spirit of excellence to the traditional Soon-as-Church-Is-Over-Sunday-Dinner, Friday-Night-Fish-Fry, and Down-Home-Bar-B-Cue. These meals are always prepared well and presented with all the trimmings! Yet the same expertise and flawless preparation that we bring to "feeding our faces" must also be applied to communing with our God. We can only grow and increase *spiritually* by learning to "enter in" and "sup" with the Master in His private chambers.

How can we live as the bride of Christ (fully adorned without spot, wrinkle, or blemish) unless *time* in the Word and prayer become daily practice, just like eating? Christ alone is our soul sustainer! He is fresh food for the soul and living water for the spirit!

I believe you are an overcomer in Christ. So, as one of the redeemed of the Lord, "say so" by the way you live your faith! Lift your head, clean your house, love your spouse, and train your children. Jesus paid your tab and cleared up all your debts. So don't let anything keep you from accepting His special dinner invitation. You must come boldly and confidently to the banquet table of God! A place is set for you right now. The dinner bell is ringing, and a linen card is set with your name on it. Enjoy the splendor of the moment and the special meal the Master has prepared just for you. And receive all of the spiritual nourishment He has to offer you day by day. Come and dine alone with Him.

2

An Invitation
to Come
and Dine

C hildren, have you any food?"

Christ already knows the answer; yet, He still asks such loaded questions. He is well acquainted with our innermost needs, both natural and spiritual. Yet He asks us directly in order to show His true love and concern and to make welcome His supernatural ability to provide.

Jesus supplies every substance and sustenance of life. Whenever you hear this simple inquiry, *watch out!* Supernatural provision is coming! Whet your appetite and loosen your belt, because enormous bounty is on its way!

The testimony of the disciples confirms this. The Master poses this same question in John 21:5 as He sits seaside watching His disciples fish early one morning. They are expert fishermen who had left the toil and labor of the sea to become fishers of men. But despite the charge given to them by Jesus in a postresurrection appearance, the disciples have returned to their fishing boats. Despite their calling, they resume their former vocations, perhaps thinking it will return some degree of normalcy to their lives.

When the Lord asks the disciples if they have any food, He already knows they have nothing. He is whetting their appetites for more than *natural food*. He is preparing a feast of the *spiritual* kind that will bring them back to the mission to which He has called them.

The disciples' plight is so much like our own. We know that we are called to walk with Jesus into difficult places (the morning light as well as the dark night), but our humanity is often weak and frail. At times when we should stand and show His glory in a corrupt world, we often seek to retreat and lick our wounds in despair instead. Even with all we know about Jesus—His miracles and His teachings—there are moments when our pride gets in the way and we forget the true meaning of grace. Sometimes just staying married, raising children, and earning a living becomes too great a burden, and we attempt to pull away, desperate to find *ordinary* relief when only spiritual nourishment will truly satisfy.

If we are earnest in our desire for the Master's help, a closer look at His invitation to the disciples may provide enlightenment for our own circumstances.

Fatigued Fishermen

"Let's go fishing!"

Peter can see that the other disciples need something to lift their spirits. In the span of a single week, their entire world has been tossed upside down. Painfully, they have come face-to-face with their own human failure, the agonizing reality of Calvary, and the amazing yet confusing appearances of a resurrected Deity. These men are emotionally spent and spiritually foggy after the life-changing realities of the previous week. In an uncertain time, they do what most of us would do—they return to the comfort of the familiar. A fishing trip on the Sea of Tiberias is the perfect getaway. Surely that will take their minds off their weariness and reconnect them to the less stressful lives they once knew.

But after fishing all night long they have produced no evidence that they are any kind of fishermen, must less professionals. Their night of toil has produced nothing. Not a single fish! Imagine the frustration! What was supposed to lift them up and calm their spirits has only served to frustrate them, reminding them of how utterly incapable, empty, and useless they really are without the Lord.

We all have this experience at times: Our best efforts and most advanced training employed—and still we produce *nothing!* We sacrifice blood, sweat, and tears in order to find comfort in being able to "make it," but come up empty-handed again, and again, and again. Is there a worse feeling?

We need the Master to offer His invitation to come and dine. "Come to Me, all who are weary and heavy-laden, and I will give you rest" (Matthew 11:28 NASB).

The Lord Jesus arrives at the seaside while the disciples fish in the early light of dawn. He observes the failure and fatigue of these fishermen, His beloved disciples. He starts a fire and stands watching them, seeing them as they truly are: *victorious fishers of men who ultimately will turn the world right side up again.* And He smiles.

Isn't this the ultimate contrast? The disciples are mentally worn, dripping wet, and shivering cold, while the resurrected Christ is positioned ashore with breakfast already prepared! This scene is mind-blowing because we find ourselves in a similar place today. At this very moment, we may be dazed and perplexed, hungry and cold, and empty and needy in many areas of our lives. To gain comfort, we keep returning to the familiar—going back to past appetites and revisiting previous affections—hoping to find significance and comfort where there is none to be found. Once

God calls us to live in His kingdom and ordains us to be "fishers of men," we discover that the former things of our lives will never satisfy or bring us lasting joy.

And while we toss and turn on our own sea of Tiberius, Jesus views us from a nearby position of provision and power. Christ stands patiently at the shoreline of our lives, waiting for just the right moment when we will be hungry and open to the nourishment He offers. He watches as we flounder about trying to make ends meet, handling multiple tasks, and maintaining a Christian presence in the world. He sees our endless family struggles over faith, forgiveness, and finances. So He asks us now the same spiritual question He has asked the disciples: "Children, have you any food?"

Deliverance at Daybreak

There's something spectacular about God and mornings. Perhaps it has something to do with the fact that He is the Dayspring and "the Bright and Morning Star" (Revelation 22:16), the comforting light of God in a dark world. "When the morning had now come, Jesus stood on the shore; yet the disciples did not know that it was Jesus" (John 21:4). How often is this the case for us? We come through a soul struggle or difficult situation, not realizing that Jesus has been right there all along. He alone plays the starring role in our miraculous transformation from night to day and from empty nets to overflowing boats.

Christ Jesus *always* shows up in the light of a new day, bringing just the right word of instruction to help us overcome the obstacles that have kept us bound in darkness. In the disciples' case, their answer to the Lord's inquiry, "Have you any food?" is a resounding, "No!" They aren't trying to fake a fishermen's feast. There is no food! There's something about this type of honest response that moves the heart of God. When we tell him *exactly* where we are, He will tell us *exactly* what we need to do next.

Honesty is still the best policy for getting your needs met by the Master. William and I had to be brutally honest with the Father on many occasions. It takes a lot for a family to admit that its members are spiritually malnourished, poverty-stricken, and deficient. But only then can we have access into the bounty of God and partake of His spiritual provisions.

Next, while His identity is still undisclosed, Jesus speaks prophetically into these fishermen's lives. It is a sovereign statement requiring faith on their part and aiding them in ascertaining His lordship. Confidently, He shouts from the seashore, "Cast the net on the right side of the boat, and you will find some [fish]" (verse 6). And these distraught fishermen listen and obey. He knows their toil and labor as He knows ours! God provides bountiful blessings for those who obey Him without a "but," a "what-if," or a "we've already tried that." The disciples simply throw the net of their faith in the direction the Lord has instructed. Immediately their miracle unfolds in the morning light. "And now they were not able to draw it in because of the multitude of fish" (verse 6). Your miracle will come the same way—through self-abandonment and quick obedience!

Our nets of faith must be cast when and how He directs! There is no room for human interference or carnal thinking. This is the only way we can realize the present help of God in times of trouble.

The One from Whom All Blessings Flow

Bountiful blessings flow into the disciples' boat in the dawn light, and Jesus' trademark fingerprints are all over that miraculous morning. The presence of Christ immediately quickens John's spirit. He knows that only the Lord can do this kind of deep-sea fishing from the shoreline! Everything about the moment unveils the Messiah—the manner, the bounty, and the splendor of taking what was empty and filling it to abundance. John has seen Him do it too many times before. Who else but Christ the Lord can command such a reversal of the dreary circumstances of life? Who else can take an all-night struggle and transform it into a morning of joy? Only One. The realization is a familiar one to John; he recognizes the Master's touch.

"It is the Lord!" John says to Peter. And, without words, Peter turns and plunges into the sea, his mind bent on being with his risen Savior. God's miracle handout is not enough for Peter—he wants to behold Him face-to-face.

African-American Christians can exercise this same level of self-abandonment to see Jesus. Just think about it: Too many wonderful things happen in the course of the day for us not to recognize God's watch and care for us. His sovereign fingerprints are all over our lives, even when we aren't aware of them. Can we deny God's provision? We have a roof over our heads, reliable transportation (even if it is a "hoopty"), food in the refrigerator, and growing children to nurture in Christ. Our health is good and we can thank God, as our forebears did, for "a *reasonable portion of health and strength*." And we have minds to serve Him—even when we stumble in submitting to His Holy Word. So what keeps us from plunging into the sea and getting wet in worship to praise the One from whom all blessings flow?

Our negativity in the face of a good God can cause us to miss out on many good things. "Nothing good ever happens to me"; "Everybody is doing better than we are"; "Our family just can't seem to get ahead." If your situation has any hint of goodness (and it does if you are still here and alive), to God be the glory! And if you have a heart longing for spiritual nourishment, know that that too comes from Him. *"Alleluia! Thank You, Jesus!"* He is the only One who can sustain life, bringing deliverance through countless blessings. The very thing you ache for right now, He already sees and knows; and He longs to provide it for you!

The God Who Sees and Knows

As Peter swims ashore, the other disciples follow in the boat, dragging their net of fish—approximately 153 big ones! Jesus tells them to bring some of their miracle catch to His "seaside breakfast." This scene is mesmerizing; it shows that Jesus is always where we need Him to be, with the very thing we are longing for most. As my pastor, Bishop Donald Wright, explains, "The Lord our God does not walk *beside* us; He is the Sovereign God who always goes *before* us. When we arrive at our destination, Jesus is already present—ready to give us the very thing that we have been desperately seeking all along."

The impossible is made possible through the power of *El Shaddai*. The Lord God Almighty is more than enough. He is the "giver and sustainer of life." Yet He is also *El Roi*. The Hebrew word for *roi* means "the One who sees." The Lord God Almighty sees us in our need. He knows our every thought, word, and deed. He is acquainted with every detail of our lives because He is a loving Father who aches to supply our need from His overflowing abundance. In John 21, He knows that a fishing trip is not what the disciples need. They long to be close to Him and bask in the fullness of His presence.

Does God know your present condition, your hurting circumstances, your crippling struggles? Of course He does! He is *El Roi*. The psalmist testifies to this intimate knowledge that God had over his life (and ours):

Where can I go from Your Spirit?
Or where can I flee from Your presence?
If I ascend into heaven, You are there;
If I make my bed in hell, behold, You are there.
If I take the wings of the morning,
And dwell in the uttermost parts of the sea,
Even there Your hand shall lead me,

And Your right hand shall hold me.
If I say, "Surely the darkness shall fall on me,"
Even the night shall be light about me;
Indeed, the darkness shall not hide from You,
But the night shines as the day;
The darkness and the light are both alike to You. (Psalm 139:7–12)

Let the fact that the Lord sees and knows all things be your deepest encouragement. He knew exactly where His disciples were at 5:00 A.M. almost two thousand years ago, as well as the frustration they were experiencing. Likewise, He also knows where you are at every hour of the day and night. His eyes run "to and fro throughout the whole earth" (2 Chronicles 16:9) looking to show Himself strong on our behalf. Because the "darkness and light are both alike" to our God, we do not have to worry about being taken advantage of, or being left high and dry, or having no food to eat. God is watching, His wonders to perform!

A Hot Fish "Sammich"

My good friend Jocelyn is usually fatigued on Fridays after a week of teaching middle school youngsters. As soon as the bell rings, she always calls with a bubbly voice, "After prayer tonight, you wanna go get a hot fish sammich?" It's become our way of reviving ourselves after a hard workweek. Many an evening we've sat with two gigantic, hot, fried whiting fillets, doused in hot sauce, and nestled between two pieces of potato bread—smacking our lips and glorifying God with unintelligible murmurs. The combination of fish and fellowship serves to remove our fatigue at the end of a long week. Our weekly ritual of food and fellowship provides just a hint of the way Jesus revives us when we are hungry and tired. He invites us to come and dine on a hot fish "sammich" that can never be finished!

Now that's an open invitation you can't refuse!

Jesus' simple words, "Come and dine" (verse 12, KJV), are so warm and inviting. As I speak them aloud, they give me goose pimples! The disciples are standing before Jesus on the seashore, hungry and fatigued, and the Lord of the universe knows exactly what to do for them. Verse 13 says, "Jesus then came and took the bread and gave it to them, and likewise the fish." They start out hungry and tired, but seaside dining with the Master makes a tremendous difference!

These men receive three specific provisions from the Lord that morning.

- Spiritual: the assurance of His resurrected presence

- Emotional: a warm fire for an intimate reunion

- Physical: a hot fish sandwich on which to feast!

Jesus provided everything they needed. As I meditate on this passage, I can almost hear the disciples munching on their seaside breakfast. Their lip-smacking, finger-licking refrain rises out of the text, letting us know this was a meal they definitely would never forget!

Family and Fish Galore

As a child growing up in sunny West Palm Beach, Florida, I enjoyed all types of seafood dishes—from fish and crabs to conch and scallops. In our community, family and friends were always having fish fries and crab parties, and fixing shrimp salad and conch fritters. And anybody could (and would!) just drop by and get a plate.

My mother was the undisputed queen of fried fish. Hers was an art form so perfect (crunchy on the outside, yet juicy on the inside) that even when folks were bursting at the seams, they always took one more for the road.

Our family ate fried sand perch every Friday night with a Bahamian dish called Pigeon Peas and Rice, again the following Saturday morning with grits, eggs, and toast, and later Saturday night with homemade French fries and coleslaw. My father had my sister Cheryl and me convinced that fish was "brain food," and we should eat lots of it to be smart. Of course, he simply loved Mom's fried fish and didn't want to eat anything else. Fish was his true soul food. Cheryl and I finally rebelled when we became teenagers, occasionally ordering a pizza on Friday nights. But we never strayed far from the family table. Fish has been the tried-and-true staple of our family for as long as I can remember.

There's just something special about it for our family. Somehow it seems to nourish us at the core of our being, providing a lot more than just physical sustenance. For our family, eating fried fish together is a spiritual encounter that lifts the soul. As I think about those times even now, I can hear the Lord again inviting us to "come and dine."

Will you take the plunge into the sea and meet the Master in the place of provision? He's inviting you to leave the frustration of your own labor and meet Him on the morning shore.

Seaside Dining with the Master

Yet none of the disciples dared ask Him, "Who are You?"—knowing that it was the Lord. (John 21:12)

As the sun rises on this seashore scene, there is a quiet satisfaction filling the open air. Jesus is serving the disciples from His own substance, and they are truly thankful. There's only one problem—He never announces Himself as Christ the Messiah. He must have looked somewhat different after the Resurrection because the disciples do not easily recognize Him. They just know who He is.

42

He does not brag about His conquests over hell, death, and the grave, or share secrets of His triumphant resurrection. His identity is not verbalized. He simply is the Lord! And when He's your God, He doesn't have to announce Himself with pomp and circumstance or worldly fanfare. You will easily recognize His sovereign touch. His fingerprints are all over every gift you've ever received. That unexpected $500 check wasn't from Aunt Betty; it was drawn on a heavenly bank account. Those extra meats your neighbor couldn't fit in her freezer, the vegetables from your coworker's garden, the increase in your paycheck that covered your son and daughter's college tuition, the peace you felt after your grandmother passed; all of these are our divine assurances that everything will be all right. Oh, how the Lord wants to nurture and nourish us in times of despair and pain! The Father seeks just one thing: that we cease our own labor and receive the awesome wonder of His provision. The entire family will benefit from this dining—from the infants to the elders. Such provision flows out of a covenant relationship with the possessor of heaven and earth.

Therefore, we should never have to ask, "Lord, is that You?" When we come to Him, His supply begins to fill our lives. Jeremiah prophesied that God would establish His laws in our inward parts and then write them on our hearts. He promised that He would be our God and we would be His people: "No more shall every man teach his neighbor, and every man his brother, saying, 'Know the Lord,' for they shall all know Me, from the least of them to the greatest of them, says the Lord" (Jeremiah 31:34).

"Children, have you any food?" When He inquires this of you and your family, be honest. Jesus not only knows the answer; He's packing much more than you can ask for or even conceive. Just get ready to receive from the Lord! He is sitting close by and knows everything you need—spirit, soul, and body!

3

All-You-Can-Eat Buffet of the Word

Jesus gave us the scoop on this spiritual truth almost two thousand years ago. "Man does not live on bread alone, but on every word that comes from the mouth of God" (Matthew 4:4 NIV). Without the solid food of the Word, we will become weak and beggarly about spiritual things, and far removed from the nature of Christ.

The human body can only fast from natural food for so long before becoming weak or ill. Nutritionists inform us that the human body cannot go without water for any extended period without suffering severe dehydration. We must have food and water to nourish and replenish our bodies. And so it is with spiritual food. If we nourish ourselves with the Word and squeeze life from its truths, we will grow and mature in the likeness of Christ.

Daily Bread and Springwater

Clearly the soul food we're sharing is not a Southern delicacy but a person! We are sharing the life-giving nutrition of Christ the Lord, who is our *true* sustenance. In the gospel of John, our Lord is recorded as saying,

> *"I am the bread of life. He who comes to Me shall never hunger, and he who believes in Me shall never thirst . . . He who believes in Me has everlasting life. . . . Your fathers ate the manna in the wilderness, and are dead. This is the bread which comes down from heaven, that one may eat of it and not die. I am the living bread which came down from heaven. If anyone eats of this bread, he will live forever; and the bread that I shall give is My flesh, which I shall give for the life of the world." (John 6:35, 47–51)*

Bread is often used as a general term for life-sustaining nourishment. Here Jesus boldly proclaims Himself as the "bread of life," or the daily substance that we need to live and thrive in this present world.

In looking at the Old Testament provision of daily manna for the children of Israel, we can begin to understand with new eyes the necessity of having Christ as our living bread. Manna was a food supernaturally supplied to the Israelites during the forty years of their wilderness wanderings. God supplied the manna when the Israelites grumbled about a lack of food (Exodus 16:3). But when they first saw this white, fine, flakelike thing appear as a residue after the early morning frost evaporated, they wondered, *What is it?* It was simply heaven's version of fresh bread!

The daily supply of manna not only provided for the physical needs of God's people; it was also a symbol of His provision for their spiritual needs as well. In the same way, Jesus has provisions to supply humankind's most essential needs and arrest our deepest hunger pangs. He is the "living bread which came down from heaven." As we partake of what Christ offers, day by day we are ingesting the principles and precepts of heavenly Bread. When we devour this staple through the diligent study of God's Word, we are literally feasting on eternal sustenance. Our mornings should begin with the essential spiritual nutrients that are generously fortified in Christ.

In the same way that we need the Bread of Life, we also need Living Water for spiritual nourishment. When Jesus met the woman of Samaria at the well in John 4:7–10, He asked her to draw water for Him. Instead of extending Him a drink, she grew inquisitive and a bit sassy about a Jew seeking water from a Samaritan. Jesus spoke life-changing words to her that are still changing lives to this very day, "If you knew the gift of God, and who it is who says to you, 'Give Me a drink,' you would have asked Him, and He would have given you living water."

The sustenance of our lives is found in the properties that are contained in these two substances: bread and water. In both instances, Jesus was speaking about an eternal, abundant life, which begins right now! To "eat this bread" is to have faith in the person of Jesus Christ and in the purpose for which He left heaven and came to earth. The living water springs from Christ Himself, an ever-flowing source that is able to quench the deepest thirst of the human soul. All believers may ingest the life of Christ by feasting on the living Word!

Got Milk and Honey?

The Word of God is referred to in 1 Peter 2:2 as "pure milk." It contains the nutrients necessary to strengthen spiritual bones and stimulate growth. Listen to the nurturing language of the text: "As newborn babes, desire the pure milk of the word, that you may grow thereby, if indeed you have tasted that the Lord is gracious."

Peter is admonishing those "newborns" in the Christian faith to desire the pure, untainted substance of God's Word to begin nurturing their new nature. He makes the important connection between the purity of the Word and their healthy growth in God. The former sustains and supports the latter. Without the daily sustenance of the living Word, there is no thriving and stretching into the image and likeness of Christ—who is the Firstborn of many sons.

Since I finally surrendered my life to Christ nearly twenty years ago, I am grateful for the spiritual hunger that instantly filled my soul. Early in my journey, many of the older saints often referred to me as being "spiritually greedy." I spent hours in the Scriptures, searching life-sustaining morsels on which to feast and share with others. During Bible study, I asked tons of "novice" questions that often made the elders laugh and remember when. Many of the older mothers would quietly caution me to "slow down and take a breath." I wanted to know *everything* about this new life that was running warm in my veins. The Word of God seemed to jump off the pages of my Holy Bible, and I highlighted each Scripture as it leaped into my understanding. I had tasted the grace of the Lord, and I sought Him earnestly.

The gospel of John was my first book of study and meditation, and it is still my favorite! The close-up snapshots of Christ that John took and documented in his gospel were so appealing to me. I fell in love with John's very *first* photo of Christ: "In the beginning was the Word, and the Word was with God, and the Word was God" (1:1) Like a teen at a rock concert, I swooned and swayed in worship at His awesome profile. I had to get closer . . . and closer. . . . and closer. . . .

The season of new birth is one of the most exciting periods of Christian life. Babes are to suck voraciously from the breast of God to receive His tender nurture and intimate touching. Their sensitive new systems cannot handle heavy doctrine, religious tenets, and theological discourse. "For everyone who partakes only of milk is unskilled in the word of righteousness, for he is a babe" (Hebrews 5:13).

Here the writer shares a grave concern. We have seen too many young Christians ashamed of being "babes" in Christ. They are eager to jump headlong into religious activities and church work before establishing a firm foundation and a regimen of spiritual nurture in the Word of God. Sadly, church leaders and administrators often encourage their new members' zeal for service without nurturing their new faith.

In Psalm 19:7–11, David says that the Word of God is like honey. He testifies from personal experience that Jehovah's laws and statutes have a definite sweetness that makes obeying them a joy and a delight. I can just see David standing in the tabernacle, testifying this spiritual truth before all of Israel; his excitement filling the sanctuary, interspersed with shouts of exuberance—"Amen!" "Yes, sir!" Alrrrright, now!" and "Bless His holy name!" —coming from the congregation during testimony service.

> The law of the Lord is perfect, converting the soul;
> The testimony of the Lord is sure, making wise the simple;
> The statutes of the Lord are right, rejoicing the heart;
> The commandment of the Lord is pure, enlightening the eyes;
> The fear of the Lord is clean, enduring forever;
> The judgments of the Lord are true and righteous altogether.
> More to be desired are they than gold,
> Yea, than much fine gold;
> Sweeter also than honey and the honeycomb.
> Moreover by them Your servant is warned,
> And in keeping them there is great reward.

As David looked clearly at the required precepts of God, he did not regard them as burdensome or difficult, but sweeter than sweet! Here, he gives the analogy of the Word being sweeter even than honey and the honeycomb.

Since God's Word is so delightful, it ought to be a part of our daily intake. Even when we don't feel like there is an answer to a difficult situation, if we would just open the Psalms, the Old Testament prophets, the Gospels, or the Epistles—we would see just how alive God's Word is in every circumstance.

Ezekiel, the prophet of God, came to a similar conclusion following a direct and personal encounter with the word of God. Often referred to as "son of man," Ezekiel's life was to become a living parable to instruct the Hebrew captives in Babylon.

In the second and third chapters of his prophetic writings, Ezekiel describes a huge hand stretched out to him with the scroll of a book in it. The scroll was spread before him, and there was writing on both the inside and outside of the scroll. As I read this passage, the vision of a large piece of parchment written in a type of calligraphy came to mind. Written on the scroll were "lamentations and mourning and woe"(2:10), according to the prophet. Ezekiel had to internalize the message of God in preparation for speaking it to the people. And even though it was a *hard word*, the prophet still called the word of God *sweet*.

Solid Food for Meat Lovers

The writer of the epistle to the Hebrews (see 5:12) spent a lot of time comparing spiritual immaturity to spiritual maturity. He wanted the church (both then and now) to understand that the Word of God is layered on two distinct levels. The first layer is milk for the "babes in Christ" who have undeveloped spiritual systems that require nurturing. The second layer is "solid food" or strong meat for those of "full age" who have grown into a well-exercised life with God. His words are penetrating and important: "For everyone who partakes only of milk is unskilled in the word of righteousness, for he is a babe. But solid food [or strong meat] belongs to those who are of full age, that is, those who by reason of use have their senses exercised to discern both good and evil" (5:13–14).

To be of "full age," or spiritually mature, indicates that the Word of God is not a secondary thought or a last resort. For the spiritually mature, knowing and doing the "word of righteousness" has become a daily practice that has grown into an exercise of heart and habit. And those who make a habit of obeying the precepts and messages of God's Word are the only ones who will increase, grow, and mature in their faith toward God.

It is at this point of our walk with Christ that we can accurately identify "good works" versus "evil devices." Through the high priority of the Word, coupled with its active use in our lives, mature saints are able to discern all things. The practice and exercise produces the needed growth and maturity. So at the same time that the Word is helping a babe to grow up, it is simultaneously increasing the spiritual perception of a saint. The Word has wonder-working power for both milk drinkers and meat lovers.

Eating Flesh and Blood?

When Jesus first started talking about the Bread of Life in the public square, many of the Jews who had come to Capernaum seeking Him wanted to know how they could get a loaf. The encounter reminded me of my grandmother's old neighborhood in West Palm Beach, Florida. When Ms. Captola, Mr. Bently, or one of the neighbors started talking about a sale on turnip greens at Mr. Robinson's grocery store, it seemed as though everyone got a taste for greens that night.

But this was no normal neighborhood chitchat at Capernaum, because there was no bread truck coming around the corner giving loaves away. Jesus Himself was the Living Bread! He had already told them, "the bread that I shall give is My flesh, which I shall give for the life of the world" (John 6:51). But the more Jesus unveiled His identity, the more irritated they got! They wanted the goods without all of the spiritual mumbo jumbo. Huge quarrels broke out, and the Jews who just wanted some free bread were in conflict with those who wanted to understand the full self-disclosure of Jesus. Finally, in a moment of disgust, someone shouted, "How can this Man give us His flesh to eat?" (verse 52). Many felt unsettled and frustrated. Getting free food is supposed to be easier than this! I can almost see them spitting to the ground and declaring Him insane.

But Jesus didn't clear His voice in discomfort or bat an eye of uncertainty. He simply answered them with deeper revelation. The simple analogy about bread and water suddenly turned into a full-length drama about eating His flesh and drinking His blood. His descriptive monologue cut to the core:

> *"Unless you eat the flesh of the Son of Man and drink His blood, you have no life in you. Whoever eats My flesh and drinks My blood has eternal life, and I will raise him up at the last day. For My flesh is food indeed, and My blood is drink indeed. He who eats My flesh and drinks My blood abides in Me, and I in him. As the living Father sent Me, and I live because of the Father, so he who feeds on Me will live because of Me." (John 6:53–57)*

What a turnoff Jesus' words were to those in the crowd just looking for a handout! "This is a hard saying; who can understand it?" many of them surmised with downcast faces (verse 60). Suddenly, following the bread Man became too expensive. He asked too much from His followers. Perhaps He was trying to start some sort of strange cannibal sect or something! It was hard for the Jews to accept the idea of eating flesh and drinking blood in any context—natural or spiritual. Their kosher diet forbade them to even taste blood. Therefore, they could not receive Jesus' graphic depiction of a revolutionary faith that unlocks life everlasting by denouncing culture and religion!

And yet the real point was so simple: *To know Christ intimately on the inside would grant them an eternal life of the kind that religious works could never provide.* As Peter finally understood, Jesus is "the

Christ, the Son of the living God" (v. 69). But they could only hear and see in the present—the here and now.

Painfully, the Scriptures declare, "From that time many of His disciples went back and walked with Him no more" (v. 66). Jesus certainly has a way of weeding out the self-seeking from the sincere. It appears that He purposefully accelerated His teaching on eternal life to dissuade those who didn't want to feast on the bare truth!

Because of God's great love for humanity, God manifested Himself: "And the Word was made flesh, and dwelt among us, (and we beheld his glory, the glory as of the only begotten of the Father,) full of grace and truth" (John 1:14 KJV). When we receive our "daily bread" and chase it down with a glass of "living water," we are investing in our own vitality, development, and growth. It is through reading, studying, praying, and worshiping that we feast on the "flesh" of Christ and are changed from the inside out. His flesh and blood will be delicious to those who are His disciples. It's the only way we will be conformed to Him in every way.

Six Ways to Feast on the Living Word

Since Jesus is the living Word, every aspect of abundant and eternal life is in Him. As African-American Christians, we must find creative ways to feast more thoroughly on the person of Jesus Christ. This ingesting of His nature and character goes far beyond a weekly worship service or Wednesday night Bible study. We need our "daily bread," and the world's greatest chef is always present to serve up just what we require for that particular day. It's all in the seeking and the asking.

DAILY QUIET TIME. In light of the importance of Holy Scripture, time must be set aside every day for personal meals with the Master in His private dining room. A true child of God seeks the Father intimately for daily nourishment and "fresh springs."

This is the greatest indication that our nature and appetite have been changed.

As the deer pants for the water brooks,
So pants my soul for You, O God. (Ps. 42:1)

Our ancestors called this "stealing away." And they were absolutely right. It's time we must literally take away from other things, because the demands of life in a fallen world will not allow us to take time for the Creator. So we must be determined and steal time from our sleep by rising earlier than usual. We can also steal time from our lunch break by bringing along a Bible and books for a high noon refreshing. Or we can steal time from the telephone by refusing to answer during certain periods of the evening.

Quiet time with the Lord is personal and intimate. It cannot be shared with a group, a friend, or even a spouse. Family devotion is extremely important, but even it cannot take the place of personal time with the Lord. Our God is a jealous God, and He longs to spend time alone with every one of His offspring. So steal some time from daily activity and bring it as an offering to the One who loves you most!

JOURNAL WRITING AND NOTE TAKING. One of the greatest joys of my life is my twenty volumes of annual personal journals. In them are the God-given maps of my life. As we have "journeyed together" on this spiritual pilgrimage, I have literally "taken notes" on the multitude of things that Jesus has gently tried to teach me. He has illumined His Word, whispered sure promises, chastened me sore, encouraged me deeply, and given me visions of things to come. Every instruction is written down for me to revisit from time to time.

I have recorded prayers, Bible truths, dreams, lessons learned, agonizing defeats, conversations with comrades, and spiritual directives given by others on the pages of my journals. They are the place where I meet with God. As I open to a fresh page, I offer to the Lord a clean and empty heart. He can fill it as He desires. I always come to the proverbial "garden" alone to wait and listen for my Lord's voice. It is one of my most scrumptious feasting times, because He always shows up with something unforgettable, unfailing, and altogether lovely.

PERSONALIZING THE PSALMS AND OTHER PASSAGES. It is important that we learn to pray God's Word back to Him. Since heaven and earth are going to pass away and not one jot or tittle from the Word (Matthew 5:18), we should put all of our trust in the never-fading, never-changing revealed will of God. This should motivate us to exhaust both short and long passages of Scripture for use during our prayer time.

There are two ways to do this. First, read a passage and extract all of its essential elements for points of emphasis. Write out everything on paper, breaking each verse down to a simple understanding. I found a treasure in Psalm 144:12 (KJV) when I was teaching a women's Bible study on prayer for our children. The verse says: "That our sons may be as plants grown up in their youth; that our daughters may be as corner stones, polished after the similitude of a palace."

William and I made a list for sons and daughters that was developed something like this:

SONS	DAUGHTERS
Taking nourishment from the sun	Standing tall under pressure
Full of vibrant life	Strong and sturdy
Thriving in season and out	Defining proper boundaries
Rooted and grounded in wisdom	Upholding truth
Strong and healthy from inside out	Sustained in strength

Giving of themselves (oxygen)	Sculptured with honor
Balanced environment	Well-favored
Well-watered	Sculptured with grace
Properly fertilized	Noticeable dignity
Learn and apply truth	Beautified with holiness
Productive	Wholesome

When we have personalized the Word, we then are empowered to pray God's Word with clear thoughts and purpose. It is a dynamic way to feast on the Word!

The second way to pray the Psalms is to redefine them into several layers of understanding that can be voiced back to God in sincerity. I discovered this in Psalm 139 and have prayed it with power ever since. Take time to read this psalm on your own now. My elementary breakdown is below:

God knows me . . . even my thoughts.
He knows my direction, as well as my need to stop and rest.
God knows what I am going to say even before I speak it.
God's knowledge is past discovering. He knows everything!
God is everywhere.
No one can hide from God. He sees me even in the dark.
He is always present to help me in any situation.
God knew me in my mother's womb.
God formed me and made me Himself.
He watched me grow day by day. I am His design.
God saw me before I was born. He is the great sonogram.
I am always on God's mind.
His enemies are arrogant and foolish.
Because we are in relationship, His enemies are my enemies.

I must yield myself completely to such a great and awesome God.
Search me! Try me! Lead me! Forever!

The process of personalizing is very basic, but taking a psalm or any passage of Scripture and making it your own will bring the Word alive, front and center in your understanding. It's a great way to feast on the person of Christ.

THE WORD-A-WEEK WORKOUT. The former president of our ministry board, Phil LaSpino, was a pro at this feasting technique. He would take one word from the Scriptures and develop an entire research paper on it. He's done some powerful one-word studies on ordinary terms like: *Father, beginning, church, harlot, Christian, Adam, of, the Holy Spirit,* and *faith.* Each study is so penetrating that readers find themselves almost becoming experts on a single subject. Phil searches meanings, applications, Bible characters, wars, doctrines—anything associated with that one word. It takes him several days to compile everything and another couple of days to type it so others can benefit from his study. He was so good at it that he inspired me to add it to my feasting schedule. Although I don't do it every week, I'm always blessed when I do. Some of the words I have enjoyed studying in depth are: *flesh, believe, word, mammon, knowledge,* and *sonship.*

Spending this type of time in the Holy Scriptures takes you from Genesis to Revelation. Popular Bible teacher Kay Arthur of Precept Ministries says there is nothing like "personal discovery" when it comes to studying the Scriptures. The Bible is full of hidden treasures, and a committed and skilled "workman" will dig deep enough long enough to strike gold! True riches await! Start with *one word* today!

WEEKEND MEDITATION AND REFLECTION. This is a time at the end of a busy week to reflect on from whence you've recently come with regard to family relationships, church activities, work duties, personal discoveries, etc. The best way to begin is to start reading God's written revelation to humanity.

As a Christian, your greatest need is to know the Word of God—to allow His truths to strike fire deep within your heart and mind. During this weekend "downtime," you read a passage of your choosing until the sizzle of the match ignites in your heart. When the verse burns with personal relevance, you will feel it strongly. At that place of passion you stop and meditate. Based on the previous week, a lot of things may flow through the recesses of your mind, but keep pulling your thoughts to the flame of fire that is billowing in your spirit.

Meditation involves reviewing various thoughts by mulling them over in your mind and heart. It is the means by which spiritual food is digested. Meditation is where you take deliberate time to deeply consider a scriptural truth that vitally affects how you live, grow, and walk with God. Meditation unveils unlimited viewpoints and marvels from Scripture that otherwise would never be seen.

It is here that God wants to reveal some things to you, so be still. The fire of God will draw you close with a specific passage, but you must have the mental discipline to gaze earnestly upon the truths revealed from the midst of the flames. A weekend time of meditation can give you the momentum needed to allow God's power to make some extraordinary changes in your life. Let the fire burn!

A MONTHLY RETREAT OF SILENCE. Ecclesiastes 3:7 says that there is a time to keep silent. With all of the constant hustle and bustle in our world, African-American Christians need to plan time to shut out the world and listen to the presence of God with undisturbed ears. When William and I lived in Atlanta years ago, we went on a Retreat of Silence with a couple in our couples' fellowship. At that point, we were pure urbanites who knew nothing about being quiet and still. We lived on Ashby Street—one of the busiest streets in the city—where the noise of police sirens, truck horns, sidewalk conversations, drug deals gone bad, and wino fights were the norm. So a retreat to a local monastery on the outskirts of Atlanta was a welcomed opportunity for spiritual growth and some needed alone time with God. When we arrived, we each received keys to our private rooms and synchronized our watches for the four-hour retreat.

A retreat of silence is an extended period of time in which a person seeks seclusion away from the world, and where there is no man-made noise or other human being with whom to converse. The purpose of the retreat of silence is to meet with the Lord and meditate on His Word; to bring Him the pleasure of your full attention; to obey Scripture concerning stillness (Psalms 37:7; 46:10; 62:1; Zephaniah 1:7; and Zechariah 2:13); and to refresh your soul and spirit.

On this kind of retreat only a Bible, notebook, and hymnbook (if desired) are necessary. All other books and reading materials should be left for another time. Often included in a retreat of silence is a nature walk or hike in the woods. It's a time to clear your head and empty your heart so that you may hear from heaven. There is barrenness in busyness and numbness in noise that takes its toll on us as spiritual beings. This kind of monthly retreat will fortify your soul.

To this very day, I still take retreats of silence. When I get overloaded with people and projects, I can almost feel the wind stirring and the trees rustling as the Spirit of the Lord says tenderly, "Come aside and rest awhile."

Panting After God

It is during quiet times, more so than corporate settings, that we come to know God intimately. Church gatherings are necessary and empowering. Conventions are energizing and electrifying. But personal communion is essential and life changing!

During these intimate moments with the Creator of the universe, He bares His soul and reveals His heart to us as dear friends. By availing ourselves more and more, we can begin to tap into the deep, ever-flowing reservoir of a loving God.

The Word is our true connection to Christ. It is the substance that the Father uses to fashion and form us into the likeness of His firstborn Son. As we feast on the Word daily and pant after its living streams, we will be thoroughly furnished. Everything in God's Word is essential—from the Old Testament history books to the Wisdom Literature that includes the Psalms; from the prophecies of God's messengers to the four Gospel accounts; from the Acts of the Apostles to the Epistles written to the church. Heaven and earth will eventually pass away, but nothing from God's Word will! So treat your soul and spirit to a perpetual smorgasbord of living truth that will nourish you and your family daily.

4

The Sweet Taste of Personal Surrender

G irl! What are you doing now?" my college roommate screamed as she entered our tiny bedroom.

"I've got to pray and you all are too noisy and too distracting!" I said in haste, removing my heavy trunk and tossing all of my shoes out of the closet. "I've got to meet alone with God in a quiet place. I need a prayer closet!"

Gail threw up her hands in total frustration. "That's it, Yogi [her nickname for Yolanda]! You don't eat 'cause you're always fasting! Now you're throwing all your stuff out of the closet just to pray? Girl! You have lost your mind over all this saved stuff. I don't think it takes all that!"

But surrendering to God often takes all of that, and then some! Pulling away into quiet places with God is one of the greatest struggles of Christian life. Whether we are just starting out in prayer or have been praying for many years, we all need a fresh dose of intimate surrender.

It is important that we find new and radical ways of entering into closer fellowship with our Lord.

For me, it was emptying both my heart and dorm room closet. This was my first obstacle to personal surrender, and there have been many others since then. But as my Aunt Evelyn always preaches, "The things of God are free, but they ain't cheap!" It will always cost us something to meet privately with God in surrendered prayer. Yet this time of closet prayer, or personal intimacy with God, is the most satisfying of all aspects of our walk with Christ.

Early on, I learned to pray with spiritual might! My marching orders were taken from the red-letter edition of my first King James Version Bible: "But thou, when thou prayest, enter into thy closet, and when thou hast shut thy door, pray to thy Father which is in secret; and thy Father which seeth in secret shall reward thee openly" (Matthew 6:6). Undoubtedly, my roommates thought I was a religious fruitcake when I emptied my closet for daily intimacy with Jesus. Yet communion with Christ was more valuable to me than my social reputation. This private sanctuary was the only quiet place (in a dorm room with three other college women) that held no worldly distractions. I learned to close off the rest of the world, practice the presence of the Lord, and listen for His "still, small voice." Over time, I became more acquainted with my new Savior and Lord. In those intimate moments, He taught me two foundational techniques of surrender:

♦ To increase my gaze upon Him; and

♦ To decrease my attention upon myself

Where is your quiet place? How do you find solitude with the Lord? Have you carved out a specific time and space that defines your quest for personal surrender? If you haven't, you should start making such important decisions today.

Yielded to the Uttermost

Walking *closely* with God is an individual and daily exercise. It involves our personal conduct and the way in which we live our faith each moment. There are times, however, when the only way to access the soul food and living water of God is to empty our natural plates and find a nice-sized prayer closet! Only then can our spiritual hunger and thirst be thoroughly satisfied.

Personal surrender is born out of a continuous commitment to keep Christ central in our lives, despite the elements that try to hinder our focus and strangle our peace. Surrendering enables us to become faithful people who daily follow a faithful God—despite everything seen and unseen.

My yielded response and daily dependency upon the Lord in this season at college defined the way I eventually would learn to walk with Christ. I came to see myself the way that the Father wanted me to. It was His desire that I forsake all forms of religious zeal to pursue the real power that comes only from being close to the fire of God in surrendered worship. I now yearned to turn off the television, limit my phone calls (during varied periods), study more diligently, and fast regularly. In his classic devotional *My Utmost for His Highest*, Oswald Chambers vividly describes this process of surrender. His words spurred me on with greater determination to yield fully to Christ: "To reach that level of determination is a matter of will, not of debate or of reasoning. It is absolute and irrevocable surrender . . . [where you] shut out every other thought and keep yourself before God in this one thing only—my utmost for His highest."[1]

This pursuit is not fleshly works where we try to earn Brownie points or work our way into the grace and favor of God. Our salvation was sealed at Calvary. It is complete in Christ Jesus! Done! Surrender is a mere act of accepting all that God has done. It's our way of embracing the new life that Jesus has purchased for us—through acts of sincere appreciation. We die daily and pray in season and out of season, not to convince God of our goodness, but to be genuinely closer to the Father and to be transformed into the image of His dear Son. We fast, not to show our spiritual nobility, but to declare to the heavens that our meat and drink are to do the Father's will. We meditate on Scripture and devour God's Word because we are feasting on the sustenance that helps us understand the new creature we have become in Christ and to gain a picture of our Father. There is a method to our spiritual madness, and over time, it becomes an insatiable personal mission.

Preparing Your Prayer Closet

Prayer is acknowledging the sovereignty and power of God with thanksgiving. When we make up our minds to pray continually and fervently, everything in the universe will seem to stifle our plans. After the busy years of birthing babies and training toddlers, my spirit longed to revisit the passion for "closet" prayer that I had in college. At the onset, each day was difficult and rough to start. Without doubt, this was new, uncharted terrain. Though I remembered how to enter in, I seemed fuzzy on sustaining the joy of just being in God's presence. It appeared that my heart was "too grown up" and full of adult activity. I had forgotten how to access the miraculous wonder of childlike faith that had unlocked the Lord's chamber doors to me in years past.

The ground of my heart was hard. I felt like a pioneering Indiana Jones with a machete in hand, trying to forge an unbeaten trail through gigantic kudzu in a desperate search for the Holy Grail. Everything seemed to be against my advancement into the spiritual rain forest of the living God. When moments grew still and it was time to listen to the Lord and receive His impressions, I'd repeatedly enter a quiet lull, which sent me dozing off. Ashamedly, I'd jolt myself erect, straining to hear from a wise and loving Father. Each day I gained a little more "staying power," but I often ran out of words, songs, and fiery passion. I lamented in anguish and frustration.

How could I talk so effortlessly on the phone about Jesus and not be able to talk to Christ Himself for the same amount of time? Why was it easier for me to be more religious than relational when it came to spending time with Christ Jesus my Lord? What was the reason that intimacy with God seemed so bland and impersonal?

Clearly, the inner flame of my love and faith was not as robust as I had assumed. This time the emphasis was not so much a physical closet but the spiritual closet of my heart. Out of His great love for me, the Father led me on a daily inward journey to reacquaint myself with Him and rekindle my love for Him in the secret place!

Over time, my life of prayer was fortified with adoration, confession, thanksgiving, and supplication—the ACTS of prayer.

- **A IS FOR THE ACCLAIM OF PRECIOUS ADORATION.** The first words to part our lips are words of awe, appreciation, and applause: The Lord responds to our sincere and heartfelt words of adoration. You could even go through the names of God and exalt Him for different ones that you have experienced.

- **C IS FOR THE COMFORTING HUMILITY OF CONFESSION.** How can we approach God and stand in His presence with unconfessed sin in our hearts? During this time of prayer, we seek His mercy and forgiveness. Prayers of confession roll out the proverbial red carpet for the King of Glory to draw near with our sins removed and Jesus' blood applied.

- **T IS FOR THE TREMENDOUS RENEWAL OF THANKSGIVING.** Knowing that He has heard the ugly stuff in my life and still loves me makes me want to worship Him out of the depth of my born-again spirit. This is the aspect of prayer that says, "In spite of all I've done to displease Your grace, You still cover me with Your wings of mercy, and I thank You."

◆ S IS FOR THE SUSTAINING POWER OF *SUPPLICATION*. Our hearts fall into deep places of request as we ask God to restore our marriages, convert our children, preserve our jobs, or deliver us from our vices. To supplicate is to entreat and ask earnestly and fervently in prayer. Because God is our everything—Creator, deliverer, healer, Savior, Father, and Friend—there is nothing in us that He cannot change or correct to please Himself, if we will only yield.

Turning Ordinary Prayer into a Fiery Interlude

As I became more consistent in surrendering my life through prayer and fasting, fresh things began to explode on the inside, and I found myself in an entirely new place of surrendered prayer. In this new discovery, I found that certain elements ignited my time with the Father and sustained us in loving serenade:

SINGING NEW SONGS. Singing helped to remove the "sameness" from prayer and helped me to utter the thoughts of my heart without reservation or analysis. It's the fresh, sweet, and daily offering that we only minister unto our Savior in intimate worship. Even through song we may kiss the Son and enter into a covenant of fidelity that says no one and nothing is more important. A pastor has referred to it as "feeding Christ," because only God's people can give Him the "fat" of our lives—that is, a sweet-smelling sacrifice of total surrender (Psalms 96:1; 98:1; 144:9; 149:1).

PRAYING THE SCRIPTURES ALOUD. An opened Bible is a helpful resource for prayer. I have prayed with the Scriptures before me, using them like ammunition to deal with various situations in my life. For example, from Galatians 2:20, I spoke aloud, "Oh, God, I am crucified with Christ, dead to old appetites and ice cold to former habits. I have been nailed to that old rugged cross with my new Master and eternal Savior. That woman who was born of Thomas and Shirley White on October 16, 1961, ceases to live. Now Christ Himself lives fully in me—reviving me from the dead and pumping resurrected life into me. Yes, my new life still resides in this pecan-brown skin and behind these hazel eyes with these African-American roots, but the essence of my being is brand-spanking new" (Psalm 33:4–9; Isaiah 44:23; 55:11; Romans 10:17).

INCORPORATING FLEXIBLE MOVEMENT. As Christ opened up Himself in me, I no longer could stay in traditional prayer positions. I walked around the room, swinging my arms with joyful praise. I would clap, lift my hands, skip, leap, and jump up and down. I called it exulting over God! There is surely a time to kneel quietly. Yet I discovered that the opposite is also true. There is a time to move with flexibility and spontaneity in prayer. And doing so energized me from head to toe, bringing new life to familiar prayers (Psalms 66; 100).

LIFTING MY VOICE WITH A SHOUT. There were times when I could not be silent. At those times I was vocally explosive—declaring with power and might the glory of my King! With my mouth engaged in prayer, I exalted, magnified, and lifted the Father with all of my breath! Truly, I wanted heaven and hell to know that God reigns and rules over the nations. And, most importantly, that His lordship prevails in me (Psalms 47:1–4; 77:1–3; 98:4; Luke 17:15–16)!

FLOWING IN INTERCESSION FOR OTHERS. Often I found myself concentrating on missionaries whom I had not thought about in my everyday prayer life (even with a notebook and prayer requests before me). Children in foreign countries would come front and center—falling off my tongue like fountains of water. Couples that William and I had just met or those from our past would enter my heart with a specific burden. I felt used of God in ways that I'd never experienced before. I knew the Lord was entrusting me with secret situations that I was privy to utter just there—in His presence, never speaking of those secrets in ordinary conversations (Galatians 4:19; 1 Timothy 2:1; James 5:16–18).

DISPLAYING DEEP EMOTIONS WITHOUT WORDS. After singing songs and hymns, praying the Scriptures aloud, and interceding for others, I had entered another dimension of prayer, where words could not be uttered. In those times, I would fall on the floor crying and moaning in anguish and distress to the heavens, communicating in a language that only the Father could understand (Psalm 130:1–2; Romans 8:26–27; Hebrews 5:7).

LISTENING FOR THE FATHER'S CLOSING REMARKS. The ultimate joy of prayer was when everything grew completely silent in a holy hush. In these moments I have obtained clarity and illumination on matters that I knew came from the Lord only. At other times, only the sweetness of His pleasure enraptured me. But He always showed up to acknowledge our time together and to fill my heart with a renewed desire to return soon for more (Exodus 19:18–25; 1 Kings 19:12; Psalm 42:1–2).

Physical Signs of Needed Surrender

As children of God we should recognize when we are too alive to our own flesh and mind. When that happens, old ways, old thoughts, and old appetites begin to descend upon us like old friends stopping by to play catch-up. There is a disgusting familiarity about our daily decisions, choices, attitudes, and judgments. They are all skewed to the carnal column. Our only focus is on "me, myself and I," and a corpse-like figure (supposedly "dead in Christ") begins to rise from a graveyard plot within our own soul. Instead of the fragrance of Christ (1 Corinthians 2:14-16), the stench of the old man seeps into our nostrils.

This is a strong signal coming to alarm us to "turn down our plate" and "stay put in our prayer closet." It is a red flag of warning waving in the wind. And the disarray of our lives will confirm it! Life begins moving too fast. Situations spin out of control and no direction is clear. Everything is too urgent and everyone is too demanding. Or, nothing is critical or eventful. Important issues are overlooked or forgotten altogether. The demands of life are strained and strenuous. In the natural, proper meals are not prepared and laundry mounts profusely. Attitudes flair and misunderstandings flourish. It is apparent that the spirit is suffocating under the weight of constant movement and activity. A conscious and deliberate decision must be made to "come aside and rest awhile," as the Lord Jesus instructed His weary disciples at one critical point.

At times like these, each of us must go the "rock that is higher than I" to gain a sense of spiritual and social rest, and both are needed. Prayer and fasting will give us the spiritual hunger and thirst we need to seek more of God and surrender deeper areas of our lives to Him.

Fasting: An Offering of Great Proportions

Voluntarily refraining from food for a time, provides the opportunity to give our full attention to spiritual matters. The fast must be accompanied by sincere prayer in order to be effective in securing an answer from God. (Always consult a medical professional when considering a fast.) Fasting starves the physical body for a period of time in order to feed and regenerate the spirit. And as we fast, our physical appetite decreases as our hunger for God increases.

When fasting for spiritual reasons, the main objective is to minister to the Lord through worship and giving ourselves to Him totally. Fasting is an act of genuine sacrifice and personal surrender. There are three primary benefits to fasting:

- It disciplines the body, heightens the spiritual appetite, and brings deliverance.

- It purges our soul cravings, increases the force of our prayers, and intensifies our ability to discern the direction of God.

- It destroys unbelief, develops faith, and energizes our will to do "greater works" in Jesus name!

There are at least three kinds of food fasts: regular, partial, and absolute. During a *regular fast* we refrain from all food and drink, except water. Jesus fasted for forty days and nights and the Bible records that "he was afterward hungred" (Matthew 4:2 KJV). The Bible does not indicate that He was thirsty, however. In a *partial fast,* we abstain from a certain meal each day and restrict the quantity of food and drink we consume. The *absolute fast* means that no food or liquid of any kind enters the mouth. This kind of fast is never to exceed three days. The apostle Paul endured an absolute fast when he was struck down on the Damascus Road. "And he was three days without sight, and neither did eat nor drink" (Acts 9:9 KJV). Whether we are on a regular, partial, or absolute fast, our main objective is to minister to the Lord. The Lord God told the people in Zechariah 7:5 (KJV), "When ye fasted . . . did ye at all fast unto me, even to me?"

Sometimes the Spirit of God will expose areas of our lives that we need to "fast" or abandon for a season of time. This is necessary to help us refocus our time and energies on our first love, who is Christ. One of the greatest distractions to the surrendered life is the television. Turning away from "electronic entertainment" is a way of saying to the Lord, "I refuse to be preoccupied with my own personal pleasures. I want the satisfaction of being alone with You." Can you imagine how much this thrills the Lord? "Thou shalt have no other gods before me," God says emphatically (Exodus 20:3, KJV).

But often television and our entire world of news, technology, and entertainment become obsessions or addictions that must be resisted vehemently, lest we be overcome. This rendition of Psalm 23 clearly makes the point:

The TV is my shepherd;
My spiritual growth shall want.
It maketh me to sit down and do nothing for
His name's sake; because it requireth all my spare time.
It keepeth me from doing my duty as a Christian,
because it presenteth so many good shows that I must see.
It restoreth my knowledge of the things of this world
and keepeth me from the study of God's Word.
It leadeth me in the paths of apathy
and doing nothing in the kingdom of God.
It presenteth entertainment before me,
and keepeth me from doing important things with my family.
It filleth my head with ideas
that differ from those set forth in the Word of God.
Surely, no good thing will come of my life,
because my TV leaveth so little time to do the will of God.
Thus I will dwell in the house of idleness and sloth forever.

Learn to turn down your plate and turn off your television in order to spend precious and fruitful time in the chamber of God. This is the place where we grow in the wisdom and knowledge of Christ. It's time to enter in and get busy with God!

Hindrances to Surrendered Rest

What keeps us from absolute surrender and yielding fully to the lordship of Jesus Christ? Why are we unable to dwell in the quiet rest of God without thinking of our busy agendas? Are there deeper reasons why we fail to fully embrace Christ through a surrendered life? How does the surrendered saint receive the promised rest?

As an introduction to a series of articles on spiritual rest, the editors of *Discipleship Journal* wrote the following: "None of us will ever know true soul rest apart from regular surrendering of our wills to God. Yet the concept of surrender runs counter to our preoccupation with ordering our own lives. Instead of yielding to His hand like pliant clay, we can take an unbending stance that requires the trauma of breaking rather than the gentleness of molding."[2]

Sometimes we resist yielding openly. At other times it's unconscious. But our failure to yield shows that we must strive to resist the pull toward independence and seek surrendered rest. Any other way leads to spiritual exhaustion. This complete lack of rest and internal exhaustion is what theologian A. W. Tozer called the "unnatural condition [that] is part of our sad heritage of sin, but in our day it is aggravated by our whole way of life."[3] As a Christian, you may recognize signs of spiritual exhaustion in your own life. Spiritual exhaustion is defined by our inability to meet daily with God, to study His Word, spend intimate time with Him in prayer, and to just "be" in His presence without rush or regiment. There are so many demands on our time as we fill our schedules with more activities, programs, projects, and responsibilities. Even though we live in an age of increased knowledge and technology, there seems to be less time to slow down and smell the roses. We whisper through clenched teeth, "God, this is crazy! One of these old days I'm going to . . ." But that day zips past us in the rush of duties and deadlines.

We can go before the throne of grace daily to seek divine mercy and help in times of need (Hebrews 4:16). We can talk honestly and forthrightly in private with our Father and seek His counsel for the tough areas that define our home life, neighborhoods, nations, and world. Christ has announced our birthright, and we would be foolish to turn a deaf ear to His invitation, "Come to

Me . . . and I will give you rest" (Matthew 11:28).

All to Thee I Surrender

Yielding is our entrance into the throne of grace. Surrender is our personal key. Abiding is our spiritual decor, and sanctification our eternal lease. Over time, God's Holy Word does the work of sanctifying (exterminating, cleansing, painting, and decorating) us as He sees fit! All of this is quite clear in the book of Galatians: "I am crucified with Christ; nevertheless I live; yet not I, but Christ liveth in me" (2:20 KJV). The power of surrender is that we no longer live for ourselves; our lives belong wholly to the Lord.

Through personal surrender we learn to live in the secret place of the Most High, to draw refreshing water from the fresh springs of God, and to renew our dedication to the Spirit-led life. So decide today to give *everything* to Christ. Stamp it with your ultimate will and boldly proclaim, "Lord, I surrender all!"

A few elements to avoid during prayer:

USING VAIN AND LOFTY WORDS. Avoid saying prayers over and over again or approaching God in stiff and formal language. "And when you pray, do not use vain repetitions" (Matthew 6:7).

COMMANDING OUR WAY RATHER THAN SEEKING GOD'S WILL. Imposing our will above the will of God is dangerous. "Nevertheless, not as I will, but as thou wilt" (Matthew 26:39 KJV).

BARGAINING WITH OR THREATENING GOD. Telling the Lord, "If You will do this, I will do that," shows grave disrespect for God's sovereign wisdom. It is also unwise to tell God, "If You do this thing, I'll serve You more" or "I may not be able to do what You want." Remember, God's ways and thoughts are higher than ours.

Father knows best! "It is said, Thou shalt not tempt the Lord thy God" (Luke 4:12 KJV).

SEEKING REVENGE ON OTHERS. Petitioning God with mean-spirited vengeance reveals a wicked and ungodly heart. We should never ask God to hurt or harm anyone out of spite or personal pain. Vengeance belongs to the Lord; He has promised to repay others for their abuse in your life. Jesus told us, "Love your enemies, bless those who curse you do good to those who hate you, and pray for those who spitefully use you, and persecute you" (Matthew 5:44).

PART TWO

The Intimacy of Our Marriages

5

An Elegant Evening and Dinner for Three

W e closed the door on surrounding conversations by interlocking our fingers and squeezing our hands into oneness. After eighteen years of marriage, William and I were celebrating our anniversary with a romantic dinner on the Chesapeake Bay, tenderly engaged in a host of memories over flickering candlelight and warmly buttered lobster. The cozy restaurant was filled with a special ambience, and the chatter of many voices filled the background, but only our dialogue seemed important. Our gazing eyes mirrored one another's reflection as we joyfully graced another marriage milestone.

Smiling and nodding in occasional agreement, we reminisced on how far we'd come as we reviewed the awesome and mysterious ways that God had helped us survive the financial blues, the baby blues, the church blues, and the moving blues. There were a lot of blues running across the eighteen years of this union, but laced throughout our blues was an undeniable bright red cord. We both recognized the familiar roping, because it was the most cherished gift we had received on our wedding day. It had come unwrapped as a gift from above, and the Father Himself had draped it over both our heads, woven it around our waists, threaded it through four legs, and tied it around our ankles.

Over time, as hardship and difficulty, lack and leanness have invaded our dreams, the red cord has fastened itself tightly about us. This cord has bound us together when fierce marital storms raged. And it gently snuggles us close when we secretly desire to slip far away into selfish isolation. Our red cord is not a prison rope, but an indestructible strand of love. It is our daily reminder that our marriage is not two, not even one, but three!

The Threefold Cord and the Third Partner

The "threefold cord" promise was revealed to William and me nearly a week before our July wedding. We had been seeking the Father earnestly for a covenant verse of Scripture to seal our marriage for a lifetime. In the midst of the traditional hoopla of planning and preparations, the Lord whispered a love passage in my ear from Ecclesiastes 4:9–12. This passage has been our marital anthem from then until now.

> *Two are better than one, because they have a good reward for their labor. For if they fall, one will lift up his companion. But woe to him who is alone when he falls, for he has no one to help him up. Again, if two lie down together, they will keep warm; but how can one be warm alone? Though one may be overpowered by another, two can withstand him. And a threefold cord is not quickly broken.*

At a glance, marriage appears to be a *horizontal* union between a man and woman. But Solomon's poetic allegory in Ecclesiastes reveals a different viewpoint. He unveils a more dynamic *vertical* relationship and paints it in brilliant red!

British Bible teacher and author Derek Prince adds interesting insights about this "threefold cord" in his book *The Marriage Covenant*. "The 'threefold cord' illustrates marriage as it was conceived at creation, a binding together of three persons—a man, a woman and God!" writes Prince. "The relationship between the man and the woman is still on the human plane; but when God is added to the relationship, it introduces new, spiritual dimensions. He becomes an integral part of the marriage—the third partner!"[1]

William and I have learned to cherish the central position of Christ in our union. He settles arguments, corrects selfishness, enlarges our understanding, and challenges us to always reconcile around the common good or the "big picture." He counsels from a strategic third perspective that causes us both to decrease in order to seek His wisdom. When His ways are revealed (which are always "higher" than our own), we can't help but bow in humility and adoration. Instead of clawing and scratching to get our own way, we've grown more accustomed to and excited about getting "God's way" clear and straight before us. He is the undeniable third partner, and He always knows the "way to take" that leads to life!

In Al Janssen's wonderful book *The Marriage Masterpiece*, he also writes of the "third partner" who was given to the first couple. Janssen provides an important key to our understanding of God's purpose for marriage and what we have lost since the Garden of Eden. "Before the fall, Adam and Eve enjoyed a unique three-way relationship with God," Janssen writes. "[And] in some mysterious way, their union was a reflection of God Himself."[2] Janssen shares that when Adam and Eve ate of the Tree of Knowledge of Good and Evil, the magnificent reflection that God intended for marriage was marred. "Instead of a threesome, each giving to the others, marriage became a twosome, with each spouse primarily interested in having selfish needs met."[3] An understanding of the third partner, and especially "the threefold cord," will do much to restore the splendor and magnificence of holy matrimony.

This red cord of three strands is still a binding and vivid picture of God's pattern of marriage for believers today who are united through their faith in Christ. As a husband and wife, we wholeheartedly agree and commit to be interwoven forever "come hell or high water," as my grandma Gladys used to say. This strong cord is a central element to be reckoned with in marriage because it is "not quickly broken" nor "easily torn apart."

From the world of rope making, we learn that the largest number of strands a rope can have that all touch one another is three. If a fourth is added, no strength is gained because all the strands no longer touch. It is fascinating to understand that a rope of only three strands is strongest. One, or even two, of the strands may be under pressure and start to fray, but as long as the third strand holds, the rope will not break!

Christian marriages are under tremendous pressure—and African-American unions are no different. When the going gets tough—the pressured often get going! All because they lack this simplistic vision: *Marriage is three, not two!*

I'm convinced that the threefold cord is indestructible! The true strength, however, lies in the "touching" of each strand. Through daily and consistent touching, the marriage is kept strong and vibrant against all odds.

The Principle of Touching

This *principle of touching* has made a tremendous difference in our marriage. William and I have found it vitally important that all three strands constantly touch. When they do, every issue can either be worked out or talked through but inevitably made clear. Answers to difficult questions and solutions to tough dilemmas can be resolved and peace maintained.

This principle was put to the test early in our marriage. My maternal hormones were whizzing out of control after the birth of our first son. I'd taken the traditional six weeks off and returned to work on schedule. But every morning as I dropped Joseph at the baby-sitter's, a part of me seemed to die. The look in his eyes told me that he needed me, and I felt guilty for ignoring his unspoken request. Everything troubled me, about leaving my son all day. The arrangement was sorely unnatural to me, and I grieved inside to be home with our infant son. "Joseph did great today!" the sitter would say with a smile. "He's growing so fast!" Her good reports only served to sadden my already-aching heart. Finally, I made up my mind to be true to my convictions. We had discussed my work status on several occasions prior to Joseph's birth, but this time I decided to simply tell William that I was going to be a stay-at-home mom just like God intended! But he wouldn't budge on the issue.

"Sweetheart, we've been over this a dozen times," William cajoled. "If you can just work to the end of the year, I'll get an increase on my job and then we can bring you home."

"I'm sorry, but Joseph and I can't wait for another six months. He's growing every day and I'm missing everything!" I shouted in anguish. "And you just don't understand what I'm feeling inside!"

Tears began to stream down my face, and both our conversations melted into a strange silence. We were at an impasse—one of the biggest of our two-year union. *What was the use of talking anyway when we had to shout our opposing points of view from different planets?*

Deep inside, I was wondering why I had even married such a poverty-stricken and insensitive ogre. William later told me that he wished he had married a careerist who loved working and appreciated the halls of day care. Foreign feelings of regret suddenly invaded our young marriage like creeping vines of ivy.

The work-versus-stay-at-home issue created a hole in our hearts and home. We ceased to "touch one another" by communicating our concerns. William walked around on eggshells, immobilized by the fear of saying the wrong thing. Meanwhile, I dragged off to work each morning and returned to bed each night with flowing tears. As a young husband, William tried to do everything to relieve the marital strain—washing dishes, vacuuming, running my bathwater, changing the baby—but there was no relief or resolution in sight. From his perspective, I simply had to continue working at least until the end of the year. Yet from my own perspective, I had to be with our child now! There was no compromise.

After an unbearable week, depression began to set in, and William could sense my spiraling emotions. He called his mentor and our friend, Alex, a seasoned minister and an experienced husband and father. He had co-officiated our marriage ceremony and also led our monthly couples' fellowship. We trusted his counsel and knew he would help us rediscover the sustaining strength of the "threefold cord" that was somewhere about us—though we couldn't quite feel it.

As William and I both shared, we also heard each other for the very first time. I could see the reality of our household needs with greater clarity, and William voiced a sincere desire to have me home with Joseph—in the short run! After a lengthy time of honest sharing and biblical direction, we knelt in prayer. Alex encouraged us to bring our requests to the Lord as "one flesh," seeking only the perfect will of God. We were challenged not to pray for our separate desires, but for "the blended direction of the third partner." It was a life-changing breakthrough! As the three strands began to touch and intertwine, we could sense God's enabling power. The red cord was strengthening its grip around us.

The Love-and-Conquer Hug

Once off our knees, William and I embraced each other with confidence that God would meet us at our points of weakness.

And at that moment we discovered a "hugging technique" that would serve us for the rest of our married days. We learned to hold on to one another until the "third partner" eased the strain and tension between us. We affectionately call it the "Love-and-Conquer Hug." It's one of the practical ways that the threefold cord operates in our lives. This technique is not performed out of romantic feelings but holy desire. We simply latch on to each other in a "bear hug" in order to get at God's heart and to humble ourselves to hear Him speak. With our arms wrapped around one another in a tight embrace (with no words spoken aloud), we are saying in agreement, *You and I have the same Holy Spirit; now let's be made one in this matter according to His wisdom and not our own.*

Whenever we are at an impasse with no hope of resolution, we simply grab on to each other for dear life (as if our lives depended on it!) and we don't let go until a sigh of surrender arrests our separate wills and we are knit afresh to the will of Christ. Usually, one wise partner has to initiate it, because the other is so bent on the disagreement that the disharmony must be snatched away and enraptured in a bold and spiritual embrace!

The Love-and-Conquer Hug has been essential to slaying self-will and defeating the unseen spiritual adversaries that lurk around all marriages. The hug is an intentional act of decreasing and deferring in order for God to increase and implement His sovereign will. The answer doesn't fall out of the sky immediately, nor does a "eureka!" lightbulb come on. What does happen, however, is that we silently die to selfish whims and wants. This act of self-abandonment somehow crushes barriers and unlocks the perfect will of our living Lord. We have found the hug to be an effective way to shut our mouths and quiet our souls long enough to hear the still, small voice of our third partner!

The benefits of employing the Love-and-Conquer Hug are enormous! In the home-versus-work situation, Christ soothed our separate frustrations and brought clear direction. Within two weeks, I started a new job, managing a private computer business for William's employer, who also was a family friend. I worked six hours a day (in a one-man office), answering the phones, learning about computers, filling orders and . . . mothering my new baby! That experience and many others over the years have convinced us that as long as couples "touch," they can weather the inevitable storms that beat against contemporary marriages.

Talking in Technicolor

The power of an unspoken message can be penetrating, but there is another way to "touch" in a marriage and keep the red cord wrapped tightly. We call it "Talking in Technicolor." It involves creating vivid word pictures to communicate with meaning and power. Word pictures are drawn from everyday life and become like "touching strands" that create listening ears and an attentive heart for the speaker. These well-crafted words can empower us to capture the emotional attention of the other, impart memorable messages, heighten intimacy, and create lasting change. As I see it, meaningful communication helps others "see," through vivid illustration and example, what we are really "saying."

This is the second way that the threefold cord is positively reinforced in our marriage. This technique forces us to take the time to use language that is appropriate and meaningful in expressing our ideas, needs, joys, and disappointments to another without unnecessary conflict and strife.

This became more evident to me while I was ministering at a women's retreat. One woman began sharing how difficult it was for her to get her husband to help with the children in the evening. After working hard all day, she as a secretary and he as a mechanic, they both were exhausted. But at 5:30, her "second job" would begin as she picked up the kids from after-school care, cooked dinner, bathed younger children, and helped older ones with homework—all while her husband "chilled" in front of the television.

The more she ranted and raved about the situation and the need for his help, the more he flipped from ESPN to Showtime in an effort to unwind and be elusive. Finally, the Lord instructed her on how to get his attention and communicate in a language he would understand. "Honey, I'm running out of gas and nearly on 'E,'" she began in a loving but serious tone. "My spark plugs are clogged and my transmission is spewing dirty oil. If I don't get a skilled mechanic right away, I might throw a rod or break an axle, and I'll be good for nothing but spare parts at the junkyard. I definitely need a good mechanic right now. Is there any way you can help me?" Instantly, his face lit up and everything in him showed concern. "Sure, baby!" he said lovingly. "I didn't know it was going that bad for you. What can I do to help out?"

Just talking in simple "car language" created a clear enough "picture" for this wife to communicate her frustrations meaningfully and enlist the full support of her mechanic hubby. Naturally, we as wives were all committed to communicate in "sports language," "computer language," "movie language," and whatever language that our spouses understood best. Talk about radically transforming communications in a marriage! Just learn to speak in "another language," and always communicate in Technicolor! This goes both ways, for husbands and wives.

The Art of Creating Word Pictures

Employing our new "love language" became an exciting and personalized ministry for William and me to one another. It was liberating to learn that we didn't have to holler, argue, or manipulate in order to get our points across. Honestly, I was a trained debater and orator, so my poor husband had no recourse for winning an argument when we were in full throttle! Yet even though I'd officially "win" by leaving him speechless in the wind, we found no real satisfaction in not really communicating the point; nor did we find any gratification in failing to reach a resolution due to my "much speaking." Learning to craft simple word pictures to express our ideas, needs, concerns, or disappointments has become an enjoyable extension of the threefold cord. Through word pictures, we often are forced to stop ourselves midstream and seek the third partner for creative ways to effectively speak the truth in love.

This is the same admonition we receive from Philippians 2:3–4 (NASB): "Do nothing from selfishness or empty conceit, but with humility of mind let each of you regard one another as more important than himself; do not merely look out for your own personal interests, but also for the interest of others." As we learn to talk in the language our spouses understand best, we are investing valuable resources into our individual dreams and our entire marriage relationship.

Recently, after returning from a ministry time away, William shared his intimate love with me by talking in Technicolor! "I am so humbled and grateful that God chose you as my wife," he began with passionate eyes. "The day we were married, our Father opened up the great china cabinet of heaven where all of His finest china is stored. Once inside, He opened another compartment where a more unique and precious collection of china was placed. But then, He lifted a final door and from there pulled you—His most coveted and valuable china piece—so rare and delicate that it stood alone, incomparable to anything else He possessed." I swooned, of course, from the breathtaking heights to which William's word picture had elevated me. How truly special I felt to both the Father and my husband as these words filled my heart and mind. You see, only William is fully aware of my love for and connection with beautiful china—especially teapots. I collect them in all shapes and sizes, and having hot tea in my favorite cup is a cherished part of my day. With loving words of wisdom, William chose to embrace me with familiar language and to utilize a perfect "picture" that I will never forget.

I, too, have talked in Technicolor to get William to hear me more succinctly or to embrace an area of constructive criticism that I was trying to share. With my husband having such a logical and analytical mind, I have had a hard time getting him to embrace the enormous thing that I see by faith. Whether it's a new area of ministry or a new house, he always tends to reserve all emotional entanglements until more concrete evidence is brought forth.

One Saturday morning I awoke with a deep desire for change. We had outgrown our small house and I knew that the Lord was preparing to "lengthen our cords and enlarge our borders." Clearly, the Scriptures teach that without faith it is impossible to please God (Hebrews 11:6). I felt strongly that He had impressed my heart with the desire for a different dwelling for our family. So I wanted William and me to dream a bit about the future and to seek God for our new home—despite the lack of affordability.

As William pecked away at the computer across the room, I lay in bed organizing my Technicolor script. Suddenly the lines came crystal clear to me so I spoke them out confidently. "Honey, how would you like to come over here and make *love dreams* with me right now?" The sexual connotation got his attention immediately and his head jerked. With his face lit into a full grin, he jumped up from the keyboard and waltzed over to our bed.

"What *exactly* are love dreams?" he queried in a voluptuous tone, crawling up close to me.

"Well, it's when two *married* people share their most intimate thoughts and feelings by dreaming wildly of a mutual desire," I said carefully. "But, in order to make love dreams, you've got to strip off your T-shirt of reason, pull down your Fruit-of-the-Looms of logic, and get fully naked with me in the bed of faith. I so desperately want to make love dreams with you about our new house right now. Will you indulge me?"

This word picture was irresistible! I penetrated his natural mind-set and led him to a spiritual garden. My public finance statistician and budget analyst hubby was enthralled. Together, we began dreaming about a house three times our income and were having a ball designing our future home! I'm convinced that talking in Technicolor will gain a spouse's full attention every time!

Through the power of the spoken word and the language of love, strong marriages can enter new realms of communication, and struggling marriages can be fortified! Let's face it; God used words to frame the universe, so surely they are powerful enough to re-create a couple's marital atmosphere and redesign the interior of their home life. If your marriage is struggling, don't despair; just learn to draw your spouse closer to you by creating words in Technicolor! Your marriage will never be the same. In fact, the threefold cord is lengthened by our desperate hugging and creative talking and becomes the binding extension of the marriage covenant. Let's take a look at how all these strands of love are woven together.

The Marriage Covenant

In the New Testament, the Greek word for covenant is *diatheke* (which means to set something out, straight, or in order). The Hebrew word for covenant used in the Old Testament is *b'riyth* (meaning to bind). According to our two words, covenant has to do with the setting forth of specific terms and conditions that are binding.

We have all seen TV relationships established on a human plane where two friends twist their pinky fingers together and promise to never tell their shared secrets; or two young lovers who cut their palms to interchange flowing blood in a declaration of eternal love. There also have been agreements established between kings to merge their hearts and resources to become one in battle. This, however, more closely resembles a contract than a covenant. The Christian marriage is not erected out of emotional expressions of fantasy, nor is it relegated to a legal contract of mutual benefit to two parties. It is a lifelong and binding covenant.

The covenant described in Scripture transcends a mere contract between two human beings (a horizontal connection) and is a relationship initiated by God Himself between the divine and the human (a vertical hookup). Marriage is the process where a man and woman are supernaturally sewn together with spiritual thread. Separate limbs, divided hearts, and individual goals are masterfully woven together and cosmetically blended to create an entirely new being forever known as one flesh. It is a surgical procedure performed with skillful design and intricate care by a loving Creator. This blending of lives is a wondrous and splendid re-creation in every way.

Every intimate and permanent relationship of God with humanity is based on a covenant—God's heartstring binding Him to humankind and humankind to Him. God is the superior power; human beings must agree to God's established rules in order to walk with Him in a covenant relationship. The big deal about covenant is that it's not just "me and you, babe," as Cher sang to Sonny in the 1970s. Covenant is that relational longevity that God orchestrates, calls, ordains, chooses, and then steps in the middle of to turn a twofold attraction into a threefold love affair that is forever.

When the Strands Simply Unravel

The threefold cord is essential in every Christian union. But what happens if the strands cease to touch or couples finally choose to disconnect from their marriage covenant? If we are not enjoying the level of life that God has promised us in our Christian marriage, there's been a breach (or forsaking) of the initial covenant somewhere. You know, those loving words we vowed at the altar before many witnesses . . . and before God. It seems easier these days to make a vow at a wedding altar than to back those vows up with consistent "strand-touching" on a daily basis.

Even though Christian couples have the cord of covenant wrapped around them, sometimes their strands may come unraveled or are prematurely cut. Issues that range from general bitterness, unforgiveness, and adultery to child-rearing differences, financial woes, and selfish immaturity are knives that may sever the rope of love in ways that the couples believe are too difficult to mend. We need to look at marriages with faulty strands, shaky vows, and forgotten promises in order to understand much of "the fallout" among couples.

Perhaps we can gain some insight from the interaction God had with Israel during the prophet Malachi's day. During this time, God wanted to take stock of Israel since their entrance into the land of Canaan and review their handling of His promised inheritance. After a quick assessment, it was obvious that the Israelites had failed to obey God's command and meet His requirements—especially those concerning marriage. A liberal and nonchalant attitude had permeated Israelite society, and little was done to keep the home fires burning. In Malachi 2:13–14, the prophet speaks as the mouthpiece of God:

> *You cover the altar of the Lord with your tears,*
> *With weeping and crying;*
> *So He does not regard the offering anymore,*
> *Nor receive it with goodwill from your hands.*
> *Yet you say, "For what reason?"*
> *Because the Lord has been witness*
> *Between you and the wife of your youth,*
> *With whom you have dealt treacherously;*
> *Yet she is your companion*
> *And your wife by covenant.*

It's clear that Israel's marital failures had nothing to do with their religious works. They were "covering the altar of the Lord with their tears." They were in the sanctuary sustaining an outward show of contrition before God. Yet, with all of this ceremonial drama, their marriages were in havoc! You can imagine them in today's church . . . the deacons moaning in prayer on the altar, the trustees shouting, "Say it, Doc! Preach it!" And God, who sees everything, is not pleased!

We are experiencing the same realities today in the Christian church and family. And it is no different in the African-American community. We know tons of brothers and sisters who are busy with religious activities, yet they are unable to make their marriages shine to the glory of God. Church work and religious fervor do not seem to empower couples to succeed in marriage. It almost seems that a preoccupation with ministry (by one or both spouses) sometimes has a negative influence on the healthiness of a marriage.

William and I have learned to balance our call to ministry with the responsibilities of marriage and family simply by folding one into the other with delicate care and keeping all things in perspective. God is first, followed by our marriage relationship, then the training of our children, and finally our ministry vocation and career assignments. With God at the helm, He directs the activities and priorities of our lives and helps us maintain equilibrium. There are times when we must focus more keenly on ministry, but never to the detriment of our marriage relationship. There are seasons when our marriage and home life dominate, but not to the point of disobeying our call to advance the kingdom of God. Daily following the still, small voice of the Lord becomes similar to the new technology known as GPS, or global positioning systems. He directs our paths, balances our energies, and gives purpose to our lives. We always want to be found on the Father's GPS screen, at the right place, in the right time, and with the right motive.

William and I avoided a lot of these pitfalls by listening to a popular pastor share, years ago, about his failing marriage—because in it a lot of these critical issues were out of balance. His preaching ministry was flourishing and his church was growing by leaps and bounds. His schedule was full and his itinerary set far in advance. With all of this activity going on, this preacher man certainly felt that he was pleasing to the Lord because he was doing the work of the kingdom!

Yet one night while he was working feverishly in his church study—poring over more program ideas—he heard the Lord chasten him with a strong command: *"Why don't you go home to your wife and leave Mine alone!"*

Today, this pastor and his wife perform weekend marriage seminars for couples that are life changing. During these engagements, he testifies about how he arrived home in the wee hours of the morning following his divine chastisement only to find his wife in tears and at the end of her rope about their lifeless marriage. True repentance and godly sorrow followed. This broken pastor took an extended sabbatical from his church and his appointment book to restore his floundering marriage and minister directly to his hurting wife. He talked with great contentment about his new schedule: cutting the grass, going shopping with his wife, and spending "quality" time with the children. Together this couple has a beautiful ministry to hurting couples. They have a tried-and-true testimony on how to revive the fire of a covenant marriage in the wake of many faulty strands, shaky vows, and forgotten promises. From them we learned that there is true barrenness in busyness. Christian husbands and wives cannot replace doing work for God with being faithful to His ordained institution of marriage. He is never pleased when we do.

Faulty Strands, Shaky Vows

Our pastor friend became "a winner" in marriage only because he accepted God's wisdom and recognized the value of his covenant companion. Israel, on the other hand, continued on their failure track and did not acknowledge or honor their "wives by covenant." They wanted the prettier woman working quietly in an adjoining field or the foreign beauty queen who dressed seductively down in the town square.

Israel had come to view marriage as a relationship thrown together by their own fleshly standards. In a great sense, they felt free to initiate or terminate marriage based on their own terms. They had no revelation of a threefold cord or a third partner! Yet God informs them (and us) that He views marriage quite differently.

Let's return to Malachi for a moment. When Israel came into the Promised Land, God was angry because they had defiled His holy institution. The men had taken foreign wives and had forsaken "[their] companion and . . . wife by covenant." They had lost all fear and reverence for the laws that govern the marriage relationship. By the time Malachi speaks as God's prophetic oracle, they had "committed abominations" and lowered themselves into the sin of infidelity. Malachi's words in 2:11 are stinging:

> *Judah has dealt treacherously,*
> *And an abomination has been committed in Israel*
> *and in Jerusalem,*
> *For Judah has profaned the Lord's holy institution*
> *which He loves:*
> *He has married the daughter of a foreign god.*

The prophet is lambasting the Israelites for handling God's holy institution like it was a man-made entity of human origin. Here we see that the Lord adores and loves the institution of marriage and regards it as "holy." God created marriage out of His personal character and expects it to remain pure and undefiled. Marriage is one of God's greatest ideals. He designed it and created it to reflect something of Himself and His relationship with humankind.

Despite a couple's best efforts, the marriage relationship can grow cold and callous if both spouses fail to keep the home fires burning through constant touching and interchange. I am reminded of this reality by the following anonymous poem, a look inside a marriage:

THE WALL

Their wedding picture mocked them from the table,
these two whose minds no longer touched each other.

They lived with such a heavy barricade between them that
neither battering ram of words
nor artilleries of touch could break down.

Somewhere, between the oldest child's first tooth and the
youngest daughter's graduation, they lost each other.

Throughout the years each slowly unraveled that tangled ball of
string called self, and as they tugged at stubborn knots, each hid
his searching from the other.

Sometimes she cried at night
and begged the whispering darkness to tell her who she was.

He lay beside her, snoring like a hibernating bear,
unaware of her winter.

Once, after they had made love, he wanted to tell her how afraid
he was of dying, but, fearing to show his naked soul, he spoke
instead about the beauty of her breasts.

She took a course in modern art, trying to find herself in colors
splashed upon a canvas, complaining to other women about men
who are insensitive.

He climbed into a tomb called "The Office," wrapped his mind in a shroud of paper figures, and buried himself in customers.

Slowly, the wall between them rose,
cemented by the mortar of indifference.

One day, reaching out to touch each other, they found a barrier
they could not penetrate, and recoiling from the coldness of stone,
each retreated from the stranger on the other side.

For when love dies, it is not in a moment of angry battle,
nor when fiery bodies lose their heat.
It lies panting, exhausted, expiring at the bottom of a wall it
could not scale.

This poem unveils some important points about troubled marriages. Marital strands often unravel when three basic elements are lacking:

◆ Honest sharing and creative communication

◆ Unconditional love and spontaneous romance

◆ Spiritual endurance to overcome huge hurdles and difficult barriers

To get them back, we need a few things:

HONEST SHARING AND CREATIVE COMMUNICATION. Never remain silent for too long. There is a subtle danger in not drawing close with creative words that can reveal deep feelings. Prolonged isolation and a lack of touching through daily communication are dangerous for any couple. Call each other on the phone from home or work. Send e-mails. Write occasional love notes or send surprise cards in the mail, but keep talking!

Refuse to argue and manipulate. Turn complaints into constructive communication. Learn to express yourself with word pictures that will capture your spouse's attention and feed his or her imagination. Keep talking in Technicolor!

UNCONDITIONAL LOVE AND SPONTANEOUS ROMANCE. Avoid getting lost and separated from one another in the daily demands of life. Maintain a constant gaze upon one another. Stay connected. Take long walks, get away alone periodically, or participate in a favorite sport, activity, or ministry. Schedule a brief touching time with your spouse on a daily basis and set a weekly date.

Remain tender and transparent, vocal and vulnerable at all times—be willing to humble yourself, forgive, apologize, and/or consider the needs of one another with deliberate care. Set your heart to always go the extra mile, turn the other cheek, and give your spouse your sacrificial best. This kind of investment has far-reaching dividends.

Use the setting of physical intimacy to create special times of spiritual (and emotional) exchange. This is the best time to unveil and share your deepest feelings, fears, and desires.

SPIRITUAL ENDURANCE TO OVERCOME BARRIERS. Stay committed to reconstructing and rearranging areas of the marriage as new changes and improvements are needed. The key is to remember the original covenant (or blueprint) and to revisit the initial plan often. Though remodeling is essential, the well-laid foundation will support it! Don't be afraid of demolition and reconstruction. Change is good and necessary, because it produces growth and maturity. Focus on the "big picture," and the results will be deeply satisfying.

Build your marital endurance by "considering the other person higher than yourself" (see Philippians 2:3). Find expanding ways to become "mutually submitted to one another in the fear of

God" (see Ephesians 5:21). Invest sacrificial sweat and equity into the marriage so that—together—you can finish the course and win the race.

Hitched Together, Hooked Tight, and Holy Tied

The wedding is magnificent! The honeymoon is a dream. The marriage is to be a lifelong love affair. If we can understand the inherent power of the red cord, over time we will become hitched together, hooked tight, and holy tied. From the Creator's perspective, holy matrimony is serious business, a sacred covenant signed with human ink. It is not for the frail or timid. The uncertain and uncommitted cannot successfully partake of its fruit.

The process of time and tenacity will produce a successful marriage. Christ is the single element that causes a couple to stay the course and commit for the long haul—despite every temptation, test, and trial. The Lord Jesus Christ alone is the interlocking power of the Christian marriage! Both the threefold cord and the third partner stand ready to assist you in your marriage relationship and to fortify every area of your spiritual union.

Now let's see how the husband can best lead and serve his family while modeling the principles of Christ.

6

Power Lunch for Christ-Led Husbands

What does it mean to be Christ-led? A good place to begin answering this question is with the words of David, "The Lord is my shepherd . . . surely goodness and mercy shall follow me all the days of my life" (Psalm 23:1, 6 KJV). The Lord is captured in the Scriptures as the Shepherd of Israel (Psalm 80:1 and Isaiah 40:11). He cared for them as He led them. As the Shepherd led His people, they followed (for the most part). If we accept that Christ is Shepherd to those He leads, then it stands to reason that if we are to be like Christ, we are to be a shepherd to those whom we lead (John 12:26).

In the life of a lowly shepherd, we find a wealth of understanding about how to be led by Christ and how to lead others as we follow Christ. In Psalm 23 (KJV) we read:

The Lord is my shepherd; I shall not want.
He maketh me to lie down in green pastures: he leadeth me beside
the still waters.
He restoreth my soul: he leadeth me in the paths of righteousness
for his name's sake.
Yea, though I walk through the valley of the shadow of death, I
will fear no evil: for thou art with me; thy rod and thy staff they
comfort me.
Thou preparest a table before me in the presence of mine enemies:
thou anointest my head with oil; my cup runneth over.
Surely goodness and mercy shall follow me all the days of my
life: and I will dwell in the house of the Lord for ever.

David probably found it very easy to pen this psalm because of his boyhood experience as a shepherd. Through the metaphor of the Good Shepherd, we learn not only how to love those we lead but how we should respond when our sheep sometimes go astray. I can imagine that as David sat watching his sheep, thinking about the constant care and attention they needed, he considered their helplessness and defenselessness. He recalled the times they strayed from paths and their constant need for guidance. He thought of the time it took for them to trust him before they would follow. He remembered the times when he had led them through danger, and they gathered close at his heels. He pondered the fact that he must defend them, guard them, instruct them, and find them green pastures beside still waters. He recalled the bruises and scratches he had dressed, and he marveled at how frequently he had to rescue them from imminent danger. Amazingly, none of his sheep were even remotely aware of how well he watched over them. With a smile, he mused how God is very much like a good shepherd. There are countless illustrations about the life of a shepherd that provide examples of how a Christ-led husband should love and tend to the needs of his wife. Shepherds don't drive their sheep; they lead them.

Christ led His people by example when He was on earth. Likewise, husbands are to lead their wives in the same way. I often chuckle when I think about the commercial where a father is standing in front of the bathroom mirror shaving as his toddler son observes with amazement while perched atop the toilet seat. The father glances over his shoulder and sees the utter fascination on his son's face. Next, you see the son sitting in the sink with a face full of shaving cream using the back side of a comb to mimic the father's shaving technique. As children of God, we are called to be followers or imitators of God by following His example (Ephesians 5:1–2).

Husbands, our wives will be so inspired to follow our lead when we seek after Christ. Remember, a shepherd does not drive his sheep; he gently leads them. Christ, the perfect Shepherd, knows our pace. When we lag behind or we just don't respond readily, He doesn't scold us. Rather, because He knows our limitations, He encircles us, gathers us up, and carries us close to Himself.

The shepherd was constantly on the lookout for predators seeking his sheep as prey. Sheep didn't have to go looking for the shepherd—it was the other way around. He was out looking for them as they often wandered off. After a day of grazing the countryside, the shepherd herded the sheep into a rough stone pen, but one without a gate—the shepherd himself was the gate. He would lie down in the gateway. If anything or anyone was going to get to the sheep, then it was quite literally going to have to go through him first. This is why Jesus says in John 10:7–10:

"Most assuredly, I say to you, I am the door of the sheep. All who ever came before Me are thieves and robbers, but the sheep did not hear them. I am the door. If anyone enters by Me, he will be saved, and will go in and out and find pasture. The thief does not come except to steal, and to kill, and to destroy. I have come that they may have life, and that they may have it more abundantly."

My brothers, the Lord Jesus Christ is the true Shepherd. When we are Christ-led, we are His apprentice shepherds watching over our flock, our family. Do you demonstrate the kind of care for your family that Jesus has for His sheep? Are you willing to sacrifice all for the needs and desires of your wife? To answer in the affirmative is only possible when we submit to the true Shepherd and become Christ-led husbands.

Mesmerizing Love and Magnetic Cleaving

The Lord admonishes the husband to *leave his parents and cleave* to his wife. This is an important first step to becoming a man not easily led astray into foreign paths. The process of *cleaving* becomes the spiritual glue that keeps the husband centered on his new responsibilities to family development and personal maturity. Old affections and attachments are brought under this new union and rearranged in honorable ways. As men, we are to be enraptured with our new bride and satisfied with *her breasts* always! (see Proverbs 5:19.)

The word *cleave* as defined in Webster's Dictionary has two distinct definitions. They are as opposite as light and darkness, and both of them reflect marriage! The first is "to adhere to or to cling to." The second meaning is "to divide by force or to separate." God created the institution of marriage to give man someone to work with, a partner suitable for him. His wife was someone to talk with, work with, laugh and love with. God created woman because He saw that it was not good for a man to be alone. When Adam saw his new wife, he fell in love with her and clung to her—his helper and friend.

The separation began the moment our adversary, the devil, convinced the woman that it was okay for Eve to do *her own thing*. In that moment, she decided that *her will*—not God's—was the best way. When Adam followed, strife and division entered the world, and the word *cleave* took on two distinct meanings —adherence and separation. God's intention was for a man and woman to live according to the first meaning. When two people, brought together by God, live according to the second meaning, they forget they are working for the same goal and start pulling toward their own ideas, their own ways.

When Yolanda and I got married, we started out with our own thoughts and ideas about how to establish and manage a household. We were willing to listen to each other's ideas and opinions and to defer to one another because we were in love. Over time, as we began looking out for our own interests, we each slowly began clinging to our own ideas and ways of doing things at the expense of the other. Soon, instead of cleaving to each other the way that God designed, the cleaving became a separation of ideas and values that led to strife and discord in our home. This realization became painfully apparent after the birth of our first child.

I was brought up in a household where both my mother and father worked full-time outside of the home. In the late 1960s and early 1970s, the fulfillment of the American Dream required two-earner families. Yolanda, on the other hand, was brought up in a household where her father worked and her mother was a full-time homemaker. We were two individuals brought up during the same era, embracing the same cultural values, but reared in different family systems. God in His infinite wisdom decided that the firstborns of two radically different upbringings would be united as one in matrimony.

Prior to the birth of our first child, Yolanda and I both worked and pooled our resources toward the same goals. I had determined that it was time for Joseph to be weaned following the customary six weeks of maternity leave and Yolanda could hitch her wagon and head back into the workplace. Well, that's what I expected; and besides, that's what our friends similarly were doing. We talked about it, and Yolanda convinced me that our son Joseph needed more time at his mother's breast. Soon, six weeks turned into three months. Our bills, accustomed to the fortification of two paychecks, did battle with only one. Soon, our one paycheck found itself warring not only with familiar adversaries (house note, car note, and school loan), but also with new ones, like medical bills, baby food bills, and diapers. The paycheck fought the good fight but recognized that it was losing ground. Yolanda eventually went back to work and eased the burden of the paycheck considerably, but her heart was far from the need to work outside the home. We constantly argued about whether or not Joseph was getting the kind of quality attention that Yolanda could give him if she were home.

"Ah, honey, he'll be okay," I sighed, hoping she would agree. "No, you don't understand what goes on at those places," she barked. "Why, just the other day I read how this daycare in California was abusing the children, and in Texas two kids were left unattended in a van in ninety-degree weather," she continued. Every day, new stories of day care mania dominated the discussion during our evening meal. "Okay, okay," I finally relented. Although my heart was not in it, I agreed that Yolanda should become a full-time mom. However, I was gripped by fear, wondering how we were going to pay the new car note and other bills that would accumulate.

With the subsequent births of Jeremy and Jordan two and then four years later, we found ourselves wrestling with the same eight hundred pound gorilla: Should Yolanda stay home to nurture and raise our children or return to the workplace? More often than not, *cleaving* took on the second meaning in our marriage; that is, to separate. We constantly fled to the safety of our own values, our personal needs, and our own ideas about raising a family. After exhausting our efforts and finding no peace, finally we turned to our Lord, who lightens burdens and offers rest from our labor. The Lord reminded us of the threefold cord. He also stressed to us the importance of embracing Him by laying our individual wants and desires at the altar. During a quiet time with the Lord,

He spoke to me from the Scriptures and said: *"I am the way, the truth, and the life; no man finds peace and comfort except through Me. Cease from your strivings, give up your way of doing things, and embrace Me with your whole heart, mind, and body."*

And in doing so, I was able more readily to embrace the words of Peter, "Likewise, ye husbands, dwell with them according to knowledge, giving honour unto the wife, as unto the weaker vessel, and as being heirs together of the grace of life; that your prayers be not hindered" (1 Peter 3:7 KJV).

The Lord was telling me through these two passages that I had to accept, by faith, that He would meet our needs. My paycheck was not my source: He is. This revelation freed me from my mental struggles with the concerns of this world. He also made it clear to me that I needed to be sensitive to my wife's needs and vulnerabilities. I finally realized that I am required to live with Yolanda according to what I know about her and not the other way around.

God in His awesome wisdom was not just concerned about companionship for man when He instituted marriage; through it He also wants to reveal His glory in the earth. In the book of Ephesians, Paul compares the relationship between husband and wife to that of Jesus Christ and the church. As Christ is to the church, His bride, the husband is to be toward his wife. When the world witnesses a Christ-centered marriage, He is lifted up and truly glorified.

The Servant-Leader

It almost seems a contradiction of terms: servant-leader. Servants are thought of as lowly and meek. Their place is to serve those of greater esteem and stature. On the other hand, a leader is thought of as always being first, receiving the greatest portion and the highest honor. Jesus taught His disciples that whoever among them would be chief must be the servant (Matthew 20:27).

Despite all normal human assumptions, leadership is not determined by how much a man is exalted, but by how much he serves. In fact, the greatest display of leadership is one's ability to directly serve those for whom he has responsibility and jurisdiction. A husband must put love into action if he expects his wife to be willing to follow his lead. He must understand the power principle behind serving his wife, even as Christ serves the church, and garner the ideal characteristics of true leadership through service.

What kind of leader are we talking about? In his pamphlet "What Does God Expect of a Man?" Kurt DeHann describes biblical leadership as "responsible, compassionate, understanding, accountable, competent, respectable, authoritative, pioneering, exemplary, and God-fearing."[1] Being a leader does not mean making all the decisions. Nor does it refer to being the boss in marriage, in the church, or in society at large. Leadership implies taking the initiative, accepting responsibility, and shouldering the weight of accountability before God.

DeHann defines a servant as "responsive, respectful, willing, loving, self-sacrificing, and submissive." Servanthood does not mean unthinking obedience. What it does mean is willingness to lower one's self, to humbly serve another person, and to put the best interests of someone else above your own enjoyment. Christ, the perfect servant-leader excelled to the fullest in demonstrating all the attributes of both servant and leader as described above.

In our society, a leader who is not characterized by giving orders and commanding respect is often labeled weak and ineffective. Stuart Scott in *The Exemplary Husband* also writes of leaders who serve. He states:

> *Serving does not lessen one's authority or leadership. Instead, it enhances it—especially the leading-by-example aspect. One who leads as Christ leads is always thinking of others, not self. He is willing to sacrifice his own comfort and even his own well-being for those he leads. He is willing to put himself last, prefer others,*

and even serve those he leads. Christ gave us an amazing example of serving when He humbled himself by washing the disciples' feet.[2]

The message to His disciples rings loud and clear. If Christ was willing to be a servant, we should be too. Our wives are called to be a helpmeet (suitable) for us, but we must be willing to be a servant to her. As we demonstrate service through leadership, she is free to reverence and complement us.

Sometimes Leadership Is a Lonely Place

A leader is sometimes called on to make unpopular decisions. Commanders on a battlefield are faced with decisions that put the soldiers they lead in harm's way. Nonetheless, they must lead. Yes, leadership can be a lonely place. I watched a movie recently that depicted the events leading up to the Bay of Pigs situation in Cuba. As you may recall, in 1963 the Russian government was secretly building offensive missile sites on the Communist-led island of Cuba, which is located a mere ninety miles off the coast of Florida. President John Kennedy had to act decisively and was prepared to arm his words with action in response to this aggressive military threat. Similarly, the terrorist actions of September 11, 2001, demanded a swift and decisive response from President Bush.

I recently found myself in a situation where, relatively speaking, the burden to lead was just as heavy, albeit certainly not as critical as the ones described above. Unbeknownst to me, God was going to use the unexpected death of my father-in-law to assess my leadership potential. Yolanda was on a flight the day we learned of her dad's death. The boys and I were to follow as soon as the arrangements were in place. We rented a car and drove from Washington, D.C., to Atlanta. Because three family members had vouchers for one-way air travel, we decided a one-way car rental would be best. This meant we had to purchase two additional one-way airplane tickets once we got to Atlanta. After a couple of days in this southern city, I found time to call the airline about travel arrangements for my other two sons. Our flights were scheduled to leave the following Tuesday, about a week later, so the challenge was trying to find seats on the same flight for my younger sons, Jeremy and Jordan. We were successful in making reservations for the boys on the same flight. The night before we were to board the plane back to Washington, I pulled out all of the tickets to check the departure time and seating arrangements.

I was shocked and felt numb beyond belief when I looked at the tickets! Joseph, Yolanda, and I were scheduled to leave at 5:30 P.M. on Tuesday, November 13. However, Jeremy and Jordan were scheduled to leave on a flight departing Wednesday, November 14, at 5:50 P.M. In hindsight, when I made the reservations a week earlier, I knew we were scheduled to leave on the following Tuesday, but I thought the date was November 14, not November 13. The tickets were nonrefundable and there were no exchanges without monetary penalties. *How am I going to tell Yolanda?* I asked myself. Immediately, I wanted to grab the fig leaves and somehow try to cover up this blunder . My mind began to flood with instances when Yolanda had made far smaller mishaps, and my response had begun with either finger-pointing or nose flaring, and after a few "I told you so's," I would conclude with, "You shoulda listened to me." I felt so guilty and longed for the understanding and forgiveness I denied her on those occasions. I finally gathered enough courage to tell her what happened, and her only reply was "What are we going to do?"

Our plan was to take the boys to the airport with us and try to work out an arrangement that would permit the boys to travel with us with no or little penalty in light of the circumstances. If that didn't work out, we would call Yolanda's mom and have her come back to the airport, pick the boys up, and return them the next day to catch their flight. I was not too warm to the idea of them leaving the next day by themselves, not to mention the stress it would have put on my mother-in-law. But a man's got to do what a man's got to do, right?

Well, we all arrived at the airport two hours before our scheduled departure time. The airport was so crowded and the lines so long, you would have thought it was the weekend before Christmas. After what seemed like hours of negotiating back and forth with the reservations attendant, it was clear I had only three choices: (1) Have the boys take the flight back the next day; (2) pay $200 and have them catch a flight one hour later; (3) pay $500 and have them fly back on the same flight with us. I rapidly weighed the pros and cons of each alternative over and over in my head. It was obvious that the attendant, as well as those waiting in line, were reaching their patience threshold. I had to make a decision. I cried out in my mind, *Lord, what should I do?* Hearing nothing, I decided to pay $200 and have them leave together an hour after Joseph, Yolanda, and I departed.

Leadership can be a lonely place. I got the tickets and walked toward my family. Their eyes begged for information on what had transpired. I cut right to the chase. "Jeremy and Jordan will be leaving an hour behind us and it cost an additional $200," I said. Yolanda retorted, "Two hundred dollars and they don't get to go back with us. Why didn't you just have them come back tomorrow? We don't have $200 to spend on additional plane fare." What I heard was, "What a dumb decision! First, you screwed up the kids' flight arrangements, and now this!"

I did not respond. Instead I began walking in the direction of the gates. We had to clear several security checkpoints and then ride an underground train to reach our departure gate. We proceeded in silence. The boys knew something had happened between Yolanda and me but were not sure what. When we finally arrived at our departure waiting area, we dropped our bags and plopped down into the chairs. I prayed, *Lord, help me with this.* I began to explain to Yolanda and the boys what had occurred with the reservationist. I shared with them the choices I had and why I chose the one I did. I then told Yolanda that I was not looking for her to agree with me, but I expected her to respect and support my decision. She replied that she respected my decision and that her initial reaction was purely emotional anxiety and the need for some assurance that everything was going to work out. My boys also assured me they would be okay. God honored my standing tall and not wavering in leading my family.

Afterward, I went to the departure desk to see if I could get adjacent seat assignments for Jeremy and Jordan. When I gave the attendant their tickets and requested they be seated together, she began to punch in some data on her terminal screen, and in a matter of minutes she informed me that they had seats together and that their flight was leaving in fifteen minutes. "Fifteen minutes!" I exclaimed. "Their flight is not scheduled to leave until 6:30 P.M. and it is only 3:15," I continued. The attendant said she misunderstood and thought I wanted to get them on the next available flight. She then asked if we wanted to change our departure time from 5:30 P.M. and get on the 3:30 P.M. flight with them. I asked, "Is that possible?" She said, "Sure, and that flight is only half full." We all ended up on the same flight and sitting together, leaving two hours earlier than expected! Husbands, when we seek God first and are willing to walk down the lonely path of leadership, He promises never to leave or forsake us. To God be the glory!

Have the Right Passion in Marriage

What does it mean to be passionate about something? According to Webster's dictionary, it means "to be influenced or dominated by intense emotion or feeling; having or revealing intense enthusiasm." When we are passionate about anything other than Christ, we will produce wrong desires and expectations. Conversely, when we are passionate about Christ alone, we will have right desires and expectations. In *The Exemplary Husband*, Stuart Scott identifies several wrong and right desires husbands formulate about their wives based on the focus of their passions.[3]

SOME WRONG DESIRES AND EXPECTATIONS IN OUR MARRIAGES

- My wife will please me with her physical looks and dress, her talents, abilities, and accomplishments outside the home.

- I can do what I really like to do with my time.

- My wife won't be late or keep me waiting.

- My wife will be the sexual initiator, or be ready sexually when I desire her. She will be the perfect sexual partner, no matter what is asked of her.

- She will treat me with respect.

- I will have plenty of money to be able to live as I please, or live the "good" life.

- I will know/find total love on a human level.

- There will be peace and harmony around me always.

SOME RIGHT DESIRES AND EXPECTATIONS:

- I will know Christ and delight to walk with Him (Philippians 3:10–14).

- I may know God's Word and obey it (Psalm 119:18, 101, 112, 131).

- I may seek Christ with my whole heart and become more

like Him (Psalm 119:2).

♦ I will be used of God to witness for Him (Matthew 28:19-20).

♦ I may be pleasing to Christ regardless of my circumstances (2 Corinthians 5:9).

♦ I may cultivate an attitude of joy and gratitude in what God is doing in my life (1 Thessalonians 5:16–18).

♦ I may have confidence and joy in how God has decided (place and circumstances) He can use me best for His glory (Romans 8:28–29; James 1:2–4).

♦ I may serve others rather than be served (Galatians 5:13).

♦ I may look forward to heaven as the place of bliss with Jesus (John 14:1–3).

When we make Christ the center of our passion in marriage, we will have a biblical focus and healthy expectation that is positive and friutful.

Examples of Loving Our Wives

As Christian husbands, we must come to realize that life comes from God and nowhere else. For me, this means that you must love your Yolanda when she is unlovable. Scripture admonishes us to. "Husbands, love your wives, just as Christ also loved the church and gave Himself for her" (Ephesians 5:25).

There are times when I come home from a hard day and expect Lon (my shortened version) to be considerate of my needs, but she isn't. God is concerned with my response. If at that moment my satisfaction comes from being treated as I should be, I may fly off the handle when she responds contrary to my expectations.

The issue isn't whether or not I am right. Perhaps she really is treating me badly, and it is okay for me to feel hurt and disappointed. But if I fly off the handle, then I'm saying that my happiness or satisfaction comes not from God, but from being treated as I desire.

Paul admonishes us to love our wives; that is, to put her needs first. Why? Is it because she deserves it? No. It's because of our reverence for and desire to please Christ. We are called to love unselfishly because of who Jesus is, not because of who our wives are. We are to love our wives because Christ loved us and died for us.

Doesn't that make it easier to love our wives? We don't love them because they deserve it, but because we desire to please God. And He certainly loves us in spite of—not because of—who we are. That's great! That means we can love our wives even if we don't like their behavior. But you may say, "Man, you don't know my wife. All she does is put me down, nag me, and disrespect me." Again, remember that Christlike love is not based on the response of the one being loved; our unconditional love must prevail despite the circumstances. This is what makes us Christ-led in our love relationships.

Spiritual Grooming for Him

As we loaded into our van for church one Sunday morning, I was stunned by the impeccable manner in which my oldest son had prepared himself. I sighed warmly. After all these years of instruction, he had finally learned how to groom and dress himself appropriately. His clothes matched and were neatly pressed. His shoes outshone the sun that morning, and the air was filled with the fragrance of the cologne (mine, of course) that he was wearing. But before I could pat myself on the back for teaching the boy, he raised his arm to climb into the van, and the stench of his coming into manhood accosted me from underneath the covering of cologne. In an uncontrolled tone, I barked, "When was the last time you took a bath, man?" He stuttered sheepishly, "Ah, when Grandma came to visit last weekend!" I was dumbfounded and bewildered. My mother-in-law calls this "nice-nasty." It's a pitiful term to have to bear around our house.

Although stunned and disappointed at my son, the Lord used this situation to teach me a life-changing lesson about living for Him. You see, when it comes to spiritual grooming, the outward appearance is not enough to be pleasing to the Father. He wants us bathed and cleansed from the inside out! In the Old Testament we read, "Man looks at the outward appearance, but the Lord looks at the heart" (1 Samual 16:7). Or recall the words of King David in Psalm 19: 12–13 (KJV), "Cleanse thou me from secret faults. Keep back thy servant also from presumptuous sins; let them not have dominion over me: then shall I be upright, and I shall be innocent from the great transgression."

Spiritual grooming is about dressing for success in the inward places that only God sees. In the New Testament, Jesus warns, "Woe unto you, scribes and Pharisees, hypocrites! for ye make clean the outside of the cup and of the platter, but within they are full of extortion and excess. . . . Cleanse first that which is within the cup and platter, that the outside of them may be clean also" (Matthew. 23:25–26 KJV). As husbands, let us desire to be clean from the inside out—loving our wives, serving our families, and leading our homes as Christ leads us.

7

Flowers and Brunch for God-Fearing Wives

The temptation was unbearable as the woman's eyes locked onto the forbidden tree in the midst of the garden. Adam stood close, but he was agonizingly silent as the words of the tempter kept ringing in her ears, "In the day you eat of it your eyes will be opened, and you will be like God, knowing good and evil" (Genesis 3:5). Suddenly, a gnawing sensation began to rise deep within Eve. All five of her senses were burning with an intense and uncontrollable desire to disobey the clear command of God: "Of the tree of the knowledge of good and evil you shall not eat, for in the day that you eat of it you shall surely die" (2:17). Yet the more Eve gazed upon the tree, the more she ached to behold its subtle intrigue and inherent power. The glistening fruit seemed to beg for her taste, and she was overwhelmingly enticed.

As her desire grew and ripened, what was once forbidden now appeared good, pleasant, and even desirable. *Perhaps it will make me more wise, savvy, and attractive,* she must have reasoned within. *How can I deny myself this ultimate indulgence? Just think of the new knowledge and insight I'll gain. I'm so confident that this tree will satisfy me and elevate my husband. Why shouldn't we partake? We won't really die.* With one swift bite, Eve flung the fear of God aside and entreated Adam to do likewise. Sadly, she had been deceived without realizing that the fear of the Lord is the only thing that makes us truly wise.

Defining Godly Fear

Theologian Charles Bridges (circa 1846) supplies us with a clear definition of what it means to fear God: "It is that affectionate reverence by which the child of God bends himself humbly and carefully to his Father's law. His wrath is so bitter, and His love so sweet, that hence springs an earnest desire to please Him," he writes passionately.

Let's see if we can define what it *really* means to fear God. Here's my working definition: "Godly fear is the demonstrative reverence that a child of God offers the Father by bowing humbly and carefully to His laws and commands without the slightest reservation or compromise." When we fully recognize and acknowledge the severity of the Father's wrath and the sweetness of His love, an earnest desire will spring from our aching hearts to always please Him! This burning drive to please God becomes the single most important element of one's life.

In *A Woman That Feareth the Lord,* Emalyn Spencer writes, "This fear of God that we speak of is not synonymous with terror, horror or alarm. Rather, it is a reverential awe born of the realization of who God is and what He is: The absolute and eternal creator, owner and ruler of the Universe; infinite in holiness and power and knowledge; perfect in love and mercy and justice."[1] We will learn to appropriately fear and love God in this way when we are acquainted with the character of God and understand what He wants from us as His children.

The Woman Who Fears God

The Scriptures declare that "a woman who fears the Lord, she shall be praised." In Proverbs 31 *godly fear* is recorded as the Christian woman's highest achievement. This crowning phrase follows a detailed profile and striking portrayal of a wife of excellence and virtue. Our commitment to love our husbands, mother our children, care for our communities, and govern our business affairs with Christian integrity flows directly out of reverential fear for the Lord.

When a woman is God-fearing, she abandons all personal choices that conflict with the character of God. We live our entire lives with a holy dread of displeasing the One who loves us so. For this reason, the Scriptures declare that such a woman is worthy of praise. She upholds His holy standards above her own natural tendencies.

One of these natural tendencies is selfish desire. Resident within our feminine nature is the temptation to manipulate the commands of God to gain our own way. It all began in the Garden of Eden when Eve made a life-altering decision without proper fear for her Lord. Genesis 3 tells us that the serpent was able to deceive the first woman because her needs and wants superseded the Lord's. Even Paul in 1 Timothy 2:14 (KJV) reminds us that "Adam was not deceived, but the woman being deceived was in the transgression." Although Eve knew the command of God concerning the forbidden tree, she was unable to resist consuming its fruit when she saw that it might be beneficial to her personal success and spiritual promotion. We can know to do "good," but when we compromise, we do what the Bible calls *sin* (James 4:17).

When Godly Fear Wanes

This "Eve trait" and the propensity to sin rises wildly out of nowhere when my God-fearing standards are lowered and my reverence for William is minimized. I end up "moving out ahead" of them both to seek my own way. This is a dangerous place for a child of God.

My own "garden experience" was fully unleashed when I opened a tempting piece of mail a couple of years ago. William and I were struggling to "make ends meet" and were barely making it from paycheck to paycheck. I didn't have a job or a car to find one—and felt trapped on the "back side of the mountain" here in rural Maryland. Periodically, I battled sweeping feelings of pity and woe, despite unceasing prayer to maintain my faith in the promises of God.

Tons of "get-rich-quick" mail had passed through my fingers before—only to end up tossed into file 13, unopened. But the yellow-colored packaging of a particular envelope appealed to me somehow on this spring morning. Despite the smooth schemes of "treasure traps" and "prosperity pits" that run rampant through the U.S. mail promising overnight wealth and seeking to hoodwink the gullible, I opened the envelope.

As I did, I found myself reasoning tearfully with the Father, "I don't want to be rich. I just need some kind of relief from these mounting bills of debt and unceasing phone calls from creditors! What's so wrong with that?" My words were screaming with rebellious intent. Before I knew it, I was at the dining room table eating the juicy fruit that fell enticingly from the letter tree. . . . "Build a Brighter Financial Future for Your Family"; "Earn Wealth That Will Make All Your Dreams Come True"; "Live the Kind of Life the Rich and Famous Enjoy Every Day!"

In an instant, I was catapulted back to the Garden of Eden, and the serpent was whispering. "Perhaps this is the way God is opening up for you," he reasoned to my mind. "The Lord has promised that you would inherit a blessing and 'eat the good of the land.' If you do this business, you'll have some *real* financial earnings to decorate your house and build your ministry. Surely this is it, girlfriend! Go for it! What an opportunity to finally realize your dreams!" In a flash, I'd agreed with the devilish rationale of the serpent and picked up the telephone. And boom—my "Starter Kit to the Newest Kind of Wealth" was on its way!

There was no prayer or communication with the Lord nor a sincere seeking of His will or wisdom. Neither did I call my husband-companion to discern this sudden burst of inspiration. I ate alone from the Tree of Knowledge of Good and Evil that morning; and it seemed "good," "pleasant," and "desirable" to my eyes. A vision of personal promotion and spiritual success dangled before me. Instantly, I believed that money *really* did grow on trees!

Understanding the Safeguards of Godly Fear

The fear of God is an impenetrable safeguard around the Christian woman's emotional whims and fleshly desires. We've already learned that reverential fear is God's direct link to maintaining our obedience. The more we become acquainted with His awesome character, the more we will wisely choose to keep His commands—uncompromisingly.

Therefore, godly fear is an invincible force that keeps us moving to greater heights with our Father. It makes our footing sure and unmovable along steep pathways. Being God-fearing wives fortifies our spiritual humility and sharpens our natural sensibilities. It protects us from erroneous decision making, worldly temptations, and devilish propaganda. As we honor and revere God in this way, we are properly aligning ourselves under His protection. The Christian woman who has become a God-fearing wife lives in this special place of wide prosperity and peace. She is doubly blessed and twice honored by her Father and her husband. Only a wife who fears the Lord can rightfully receive such blessing and praise.

Needless to say, when I received my wealth-building kit in the mail a few days later, I was convicted at the core of my being. Everything in the introductory video was appealing to the "lust of the eyes" (palatial mansions, fancy cars, luxurious boats); "the lust of the flesh" (tropical vacations, lavish parties, tailored clothing); and "the pride of life" (worldly fame and financial fortune). With fear and trepidation, I pulled out my well-worn Bible and it flipped to 1 John 2:15–17 (KJV):

> *Love not the world, neither the things that are in the world. If any man love the world, the love of the Father is not in him. For all that is in the world, the lust of the flesh, and the lust of the eyes, and the pride of life, is not of the Father, but is of the world. And the world passeth away, and the lust thereof: but he that doeth the will of God abideth for ever.*

I had attempted to abort the "waiting process" of a loving God and forge my own way to provision and prosperity. My lust had become glaring and painfully apparent to me. I asked true repentance to escort me into the presence of the Father as I bowed humbly in godly sorrow.

I wept sincerely before the Lord and asked Him to purge my inner sanctuary of all defiling elements associated with mammon (the love of money and the personification of wealth). It was a moment of spiritual decision making: *Will I serve the true and living God who loves me with an everlasting love and who always has my best in view? Or will I bow to the master of mammon and spend all my waking moments worshiping and pursuing wealth?*

Having experienced my own "Eve encounter," I don't believe I've ever been as critical or judgmental of the woman in the garden since. Have we not all sinned and come short of God's glory in one way or another? How I bless the Lord God for His overflowing pardon! Perhaps you are standing in the blinding yet glittering light of deception offered by the god of this world. Maybe it's not money, but some other enticement like adultery, unforgiveness, pride, or selfish ambition. If so, simply fall to your knees right now and bow before Jesus Christ the Lord, who is the Way, the Truth, and the Life. Nothing and no one else can truly satisfy but Him alone!

Being a God-fearing woman is essential to becoming a Spirit-led, godly wife. A woman needs this foundation laid before the Lord in order to build a successful relationship with her husband. Godly fear produces the life-giving substances that will fashion you into the virtuous wife you aspire to be. So let's revisit the age-old issues of submission, adorning, and reverence. When used properly, these three elements can become powerful tools in your hand and make you a valuable helpmeet to the man you love.

The Power of Christlike Submission

I always cringed when a woman asked about submission at a church retreat or Bible study. The term has been so abused that I always prayed a silent prayer before answering—in hopes that the discussion would not start World War III! That was until I read the text thoroughly and watched as four refreshing words leaped off the page with renewed simplicity.

"Wives, in the same way be submissive to your husbands" (1 Peter 3:1 NIV).

For the life of me, I'd never seen "in the same way" before! But, on that particular day, the Holy Spirit chided me softly, *"You skipped something."* So I read it again. This time, the light of illumination was brilliant. It was clear that we were to submit "in the same way" as someone or something. But who? What? Those questions demanded that I go back to chapter 2 in search of the answer. And was I blessed! It was abundantly clear that Christ has been given as the Christian wife's best example of biblical submission. We are to follow Christ and walk as He walked into submission. How liberating this revelation was to me!

In this epistle, Peter provides a poignant example for wives to follow. He heralds Christ's submission to the will of the Father through His suffering and sacrifice on the cross. Christ yields and humbles Himself to death, so that we "might die to sins and live for righteousness." This is heart wrenching! The Bible records that "when they hurled their insults at [Jesus], he did not retaliate; when he suffered, he made no threats. Instead, he entrusted himself to him who judges justly" (1 Peter 2:23 NIV). Ladies, Christ is our example of the victorious power of submission. It is not a derogatory term, but a call to greatness! By submitting ourselves to our husbands (who truly come in all shapes and sizes, makes and models), we are empowered "in the same way" as our Lord to walk through difficult days and emerge with the victory!

In modern times, sisters have battled the social pressure to not submit to a man (be he saved or unsaved) because we are not second-class citizens of the kingdom of God! Such teachings are erroneous and devoid of the life-giving properties that accompany Christlike submission. When a woman is conscious of almighty God and assured of His loving-kindness, she must be willing to "begin at Jerusalem" and become a witness for Christ in her own home! As we walk in this way and follow Christ, we will eventually become "uttermost women" who glorify God in all that we say and do.

Christlike submission affords us the privilege of releasing spiritual influence. When we submit to our husbands as Christ did to the Father, we are in a powerful position to bring radical change and restoration to our home and marriage. Even without reading a Bible or hearing any ongoing conversation, our husbands can be "won by the conduct of their wives" and be brought closer into the realm of the Spirit and will of God for their lives.

A wife who lives in the reverential fear of God draws her husband—not by testifying or debating—by her spiritual chastity, moral character, and profound respect for the things of God. This silent influence is administered without her preaching, leaving Bible tracts on the toilet seat, or writing a verse of Scripture atop Sunday's meat loaf! Such influence flows out of the beauty of a quiet spirit that is inwardly adorned for the Lord.

Adorning Ourselves for Christ

The African-American woman in Christ fully understands the ceremonial ritual of dressing for a Sunday worship service. First, we put on our important undergarments like the girdle, slip, and stockings. Then we "put on our face," which includes a dozen routine steps—from facial cleansing and foundation to blush and lipstick application. Next, our hairdos must be curled and styled; braids fixed and arranged, or wigs combed and teased. From there, we move swiftly into our outfit (usually a dress or tailored suit) that must be zipped, tucked, and buttoned. Finally, we accessorize with jewelry, scarf, shoes, handbag, and, on special occasions, a flamboyant, "knock 'em dead" hat or headpiece.

Dressing for Sunday worship is a lot of work for the average sister. However, when it comes to His married daughters, the Lord places us before a *different dressing room mirror* with steeper standards that reflect the "hidden heart." As Christian wives, we must learn to adorn ourselves from the inside out. The apostle Peter portrays God's requirements with these words:

Let not your adornment be merely external—braiding the hair, and wearing gold jewelry, or putting on dresses; but let it be the hidden person of the heart, with the imperishable quality of a gentle and quiet spirit, which is precious in the sight of God. For in this way in former times the holy women also, who hoped in God, used to adorn themselves. (1 Peter 3:3–5 NASB)

The word *adorn* implies an outer appearance, but God's Word exhorts the Christian wife to put stronger emphasis on developing an inner character and personality of the heart that is pleasing to her Lord. This quality is referred to as a "gentle and quiet spirit" and is considered to be an imperishable trait that will not fade away. This inward demeanor is considered precious in the sight of God.

The internal private mirror that the Holy Spirit has installed in a woman's heart is the place where we dress for God. Each morning we can look squarely into "the perfect law of liberty" (which is God's Word) and joyfully adorn ourselves in true beauty and holiness. Secular women have been screaming and yelling for decades about women's rights and feminine liberties, but for the Christian woman, Christ is the great emancipator! He openly proclaimed our liberty from the shackles of sin and the chains of self-destruction. He paid the penalty of our transgression with His own blood. We are free and liberated to be holy women of God!

In Proverbs 31:25, a woman of virtue is described as being clothed with "strength and honor." She dresses in the power and influence of God, and the internal beauty of her heart is all that others really see! She is a true ambassador for the Lord, not overly concerned with her outer appearance or her costly attire. As daughters of the King, we must become like-minded, adorning ourselves inwardly and arraying ourselves with the character of our Savior.

The RH Factor

Once we are walking in godly fear; have learned the purpose of submission, the power of influence, and the prerequisite of spiritual adorning; and have worked out our "hidden heart issues," it becomes much easier to offer our men the special kind of reverence they need to become better servants of Christ. This reverence is a strong admonition that our heavenly Father instructed the apostle Paul to deliver to His married daughters. It is clearly outlined in the letter to the Ephesians (5:33 KJV): "And the wife see that she reverence her husband."

During many years of counseling with wives in strained marriages, the proverbial question was always, "Me? Reverence him? I'm sorry, Yolanda, but I can do b-a-a-d all by myself!" Even though these women were Christian wives, the RH factor, or reverencing him, was a huge hurdle to tackle . . . until they were able to grasp that true reverence is a matter of love and encouragement, not a blind ego trip! Such esteem is a powerful outpouring of love for the person each of these woman vowed to be married to for life.

Quite honestly, many of these husbands had serious character flaws that were difficult to esteem. Some were stubborn, mean-spirited, and self-centered. Others weren't bad men—just ordinary, blue-collar workers who would go to work, come home, eat dinner, and watch TV without giving any emotional input to the marriage. These women felt belittled and offended by the Lord's staunch command to "reverence" someone so undeserving. Reverence is such an enormous word that is easy to grant to a divine and holy God but difficult to offer to a fallible and faulty husband. So, I began to pray diligently, "Father, please show me how we can unlock biblical reverence for our men—whether they are saved or unsaved, gentle or brutish, loving or unlovely. Your married daughters are in desperate situations! We need a set of keys to maintain this critical area of our lives."

Over time, the Lord gave me seven keys that would easily produce reverence in a wife's heart and cause it to spill all over her husband! I discovered that the power of "reverence" is hidden in its applicable meaning. It centers more on esteem and encouragement as we consider our husband's basic needs, seek his continual counsel, and cheerlead for him in the game of life—regardless of his present score! Reverence also has a way of producing extraordinary "tallness" (or stature) in an ordinary man and making him the kind of leader and gentleman that a woman dreams of. Overall, I quickly saw "reverence" as the Christian wife's strongest ally! It could be employed to bring amazing results. By analyzing the larger (and more practical) definition of this biblical mandate, wives are empowered to understand that:

◆ Reverence is a useful cheerleading tool for esteem and encouragement.

◆ Reverence turns complaints and criticisms into constructive concerns.

◆ Reverence chooses to defer, not demand.

◆ Reverence avoids the superwoman trap!

◆ Reverence gets rid of old wives' tales about money.

◆ Reverence helps to maintain unconditional love.

◆ Reverence inspires intercession and brings life-changing results.

Esteem Is a Cheerleading Tool

No matter what your husband does for a living or how much money he makes, he does something for which you can esteem and encourage him. If wives do not believe in their own husbands, who will? When a husband is out working and actively competing in the *game of life,* he needs his wife to be his personal cheerleader. William and I were very fond of the television show *Roc* when it came on in the early nineties. Roc's wife, Eleanor, really modeled this principle of cheerleading. Her husband was a trash collector, yet she would snuggle close to him at the end of the day, rub his big, bald head, and tell him enthusiastically that he was the best garbage man in the city of Baltimore. Esteeming and encouraging your husband becomes easier when you identify his strengths and admire his unique way of doing "little things." Yet many women say, "But my husband doesn't do anything!" Come on. Think hard. Observe him for a week and make a bona fide praise list. Then have some fun esteeming and encouraging the man you love! Really, it will mean a lot to him to have you on the sidelines every day shouting, "You can do it, honey!" "I believe in you!" "You're the greatest!" Your cheerleading days are not over! It's time to pull out the schoolgirl pom-poms and rev up the old, "Leroy, Leroy, he's *my* man; if he can't do it, no one can!"

Turn Complaints and Criticisms into Constructive Concerns

King Solomon knew a lot about wives; he had seven hundred of them! In Proverbs 25:24 he says, "Better to live on a corner of the roof than to share a house with a quarrelsome wife" (NIV). The harsh words of a woman can be stinging! A woman in a Bible study I taught confessed her dealings with her husband. "With my mouth, I used to cut him up one side and down the other," she shared with little remorse. "He wouldn't know what hit him!" Today, this same woman has learned to share her concerns in a way that does not tear her husband down or demonstrate a lack of reverence. And she testifies to the peace that this change has brought into their home. Women who want to esteem and encourage their mates will have to learn to communicate their desires and concerns constructively. In order to be heard, we must change our tough approach and create a non-threatening atmosphere. This will mean lowering our voice, softening our tone, and choosing an appropriate time to talk that is agreeable to both parties (not during Super Bowl Sunday or NCAA March Madness).

Learn to Defer and Not Demand

Marriage is not a win, lose, or draw swords relationship. When spouses defer, we submit to the opinions and decisions of the other. Each partner must resist the temptation to demand his or her way within the marital relationship. It is important that both spouses protect the marriage union from becoming an "I win, you lose" battlefield. Compromise, consider each other, and put aside power plays in order to achieve family unity. I have strong feelings on many issues, and discussions with William often reveal his differing opinions. When important situations arise that affect our marriage and family life, we both outline our point of view. After we listen carefully to one another, a "best way" is decided upon. Many times, I defer to William as the decision maker, based on his keen understanding, professional expertise, or spiritual insight. At other times, he defers to me, given similar considerations. We choose to support the final decision (even if it later proves not to have been the best) and resist the temptation to say, "I told you so!" Learning to defer will curb a spouse's tendency to dominate or manipulate in marriage. It empowers men and women—together—and helps them to walk in a refreshing partnership with the Lord.

A Godly Wife Is Not Superwoman

A Christian wife must learn not to do everything. Women have become pretty adept at working eight hours, coming home to cook dinner, helping with homework, feeding the family, bathing the kids, sorting the laundry, and sweeping the kitchen—all before collapsing across the bed! This is not to mention the 2 A.M. wake-up call from lover boy. African-American wives have a right to be exhausted because we simply do too much! We complain about the enormity of our tasks, yet we never transfer the organizational skills that work so well for us at the office to our homes. Techniques like delegating authority, prioritizing work activities, and outlining team projects are crossover abilities that will work for both employees and family members. (See chapter 11, Household Operations.) We could list twenty or more routine duties that must be performed and maintained in a household on a daily basis from washing dishes and cleaning bathrooms to dusting furniture and packing lunches. Here is where project delegation and teamwork comes in! Many men are willing to help more, but women must yield areas of responsibility to them.

I struggled with this for years. William would offer to wash the clothes if I would fold them and put them away. I didn't really want him to do the laundry because he did not sort properly nor dry them to perfection. So I would end up washing a load, drying it the next day, and folding several days later. It was a disorganized mess! Now I have learned to ignore the "I'll just do it myself" voice and accept my husband's generous offers of help. Things are not always done just the way I would do them, but they're done! Being a superwoman deprives our men of the opportunity to lead through serving. In order for our husbands to become great leaders, they must shoulder more of the responsibility of serving their families. Husbands can lead their homes by being involved in and responsible for daily aspects of family life. Perhaps then we'll have enough energy to wake *them* up at 2:00 A.M.!

Get Rid of Harmful Myths About Money

One of the most harmful pieces of marital advice that many African-American women receive from well-meaning female kin is, "Never let your right hand know what your left hand is doing." In other words, don't tell your husband everything—especially about your money! Unfortunately, heeding this advice had bred an atmosphere of distrust between men and women. Today it has become fashionable for a woman to be financially independent from her husband—filing income taxes separately, banking separately, paying separate bills, and fulfilling separate spending desires. This leaves some men to feel only partially responsible for the family they are supposed to be fully responsible for. A combined checking account rids the marriage of these separate and secret compartments and fosters much-needed trust. This does not mean that a woman cannot establish a savings account or that husbands and wives cannot divvy up the family income in ways that are beneficial to their particular union. What must be avoided, however, are the secrets, distrusts, and insecurities that keep the marriage operating in the dark about its resources.

Maintain Unconditional Love—Regardless

The Bible's love message in 1 Corinthians 13 (NIV) is timeless: "Love is patient, love is kind. It does not envy, it does not boast, it is not proud. It is not rude, it is not self-seeking, it is not easily angered, it keeps no record of wrongs" (verses 4–5). We all need to meditate on these truths and act on them. Unconditional love separates flaws, behaviors, and shortcomings from the actual man. Without this God-inspired love, many husbands are bound by the expectations of their wives. And when they don't *act right*, we withhold our love and affection until they *straighten up their act*.

I must confess to having held this selfish attitude in the early years of my marriage. I had expectations of what William was to do and be like. When he performed according to my expectations, he was lovingly rewarded. When he didn't, he got the cold shoulder. Conditions like these stunt the growth of a marriage and choke the health from it. If we want to encourage strong leadership in our men, let's learn to love them unconditionally.

Interceding on Your Man's Behalf

Admittedly, there are husbands who either are not interested in leading their family or who lack what it takes to be better leaders. As a loving wife, you may have tried everything, and still no change occurs. Wives who find themselves at this point must seek God's greater influence and turn their brokenhearted cries into prayers of intercession. To intercede is to stand in the place of another and plead on his behalf. It's the difference between praying, "Lord, he ain't right and don't want to do right," and "Lord, give him a mind to lead this family. I thank You, Lord, for a husband who leads." As a personal intercessor, we must plead our husband's case and voice our heart's desire for him.

When I met Gwen, she was a struggling single mother with three children. She was hurting but also proud of her independence. After a time, I introduced Gwen to Jesus, and she began living a Christian life. She confessed her faults, and her entire countenance changed for the better. Gwen talked a lot about her children's father, Jeff. They had lived together for a period, but could not seem to get along. Jeff moved out and began hanging out in the street, selling drugs and seeing other women. Furthermore, he was contributing nothing to the care of their children.

Over time, God softened Gwen's heart. She forgave Jeff and wanted a change for him. She also desired that they marry and become a family. So she and I began to pray and intercede for Jeff. But it was Gwen whom God changed first. She grew into a virtuous woman with a heart to serve. She stood strong on her Christian values. Whenever Jeff would stop by to visit, he noticed that certain things about Gwen and her home were not the same. Despite his ways, Gwen showed love and was tender toward Jeff. Most of all, she became his personal intercessor!

After a long while, Jeff became a Christian and asked Gwen to be his wife. He changed his priorities, got a steady job, and found a house for Gwen and their children. "Only God could have done this!" Gwen shared with tears of joy. Women have tremendous influence. Through our actions, we can help our men want to assume a greater leadership role in the family. Even more, through our reverence we can inspire them to become husbands that are led by the Spirit of God.

Doing Him Good Always

Before you are left with the impression that I've always had this "wife thing" down, let me tell you how I arrived here over much time and training. I was a selfish twenty-three-year-old when I married my mature, twenty-nine-year-old husband. He was so giving of everything. What was his automatically became mine. On the other hand, what was mine was up for a lengthy discussion. I secretly picked the better (although smaller) portions of food, took more closet and dresser space (because he didn't need it), and was generally stingy about sharing my last piece of coveted pie or cake after meals. It took years for the thread of God to sew my will to the tender needs of my husband. Old habits and the selfish nature really do die hard. At least mine did!

Slowly, over time and with the help of the Holy Scriptures, much consecrated prayer, and a few godly teachers, I learned how to revere William as Christ would have me to. The issues of submission, adorning, and reverence were thoroughly worked out in my life as I studied and prayed to become a God-fearing wife. I've faltered and failed a lot, but God is truly my helper!

Every Christian wife (across all races, denominations, and creeds) has looked at the virtuous woman in Proverbs 31 with a silent sneer of inward guilt. We can never quite measure up to her impeccable dress, her well-managed home, her positive community influence, and her spiritual devotion with God. As a young wife, I was particularly haunted by verse 12: "She does him good and not evil all the days of her life."

This man trusts his wife unwaveringly and is confident that she's "got his back." He never double-checks her figures or makes an extra call of inquiry on a matter. He knows unequivocally that she's taken care of all the details according to his best interests. He's got ironed shirts and clean underwear for work each day. His life savings have not been squandered nor his certificates of deposits cashed in for the newest sale item. Her man is convinced of her godly character and spiritual maturity—because he is the direct beneficiary of her loving care!

This model of wifeliness was an awesome challenge to me as a twenty-first-century African-American woman. Over and over again, I diligently sought God for more grace and less "me" when it comes to being an excellent wife. I peered into Proverbs 31 and asked questions like, "Have I earned William's heart of trust? Can he be assured that I will take care of him and his business well? Is there any room for his doubt or mistrust in physical, emotional, or financial areas?" This kind of personal inventory kept me on my knees for years as I prayerfully pressed toward excellence and virtue by asking the hard questions. Consider your own role as a God-fearing wife as we ask these questions together:

HOUSEHOLD MANAGEMENT. Does the heart of my husband safely trust in me? Is he confident that I am a suitable helper, assistant, and aid to him? Can he relax, knowing that I will swiftly handle the areas he has given me to manage? Am I wise, frugal, and thrifty with the household budget?

HEALTH MANAGEMENT. Do I encourage him to exercise regularly and eat healthily? When was the last time I cooked his favorite meal and served it with special care? How can I promote good grooming and personal hygiene and encourage him to take better care of his temple?

PERSONAL GROWTH. Am I committed to do him good and not evil all the days of my life? Do I support his times alone with God and away with friends? Do I take an interest in the things that he considers important no matter what it is (i.e., sports, car racing, bowling, computers, etc.)? Do I buy him birthday and Father's Day gifts that I like or ones that he would love? (There is a difference!)

MARRIAGE AND FAMILY ENRICHMENT. Have I shown him sensual warmth on a consistent basis? Am I always a complement in dress and demeanor to him when we are in public together? Do people know that I am *his* wife? Do I plan sufficient times of relaxation and recreation into his schedule? When was the last time we had a romantic getaway? Do I support his leadership in the family, or do I undermine him in subtle ways? How can I applaud the time he takes to discipline and instruct the children in righteousness? What extra help can I provide him today (i.e., manicuring the yard, paying the bills, keeping a peaceful home, etc.)?

PROFESSIONAL DEVELOPMENT. Am I praying for my husband's success in his present job and future career? Have I employed my wit and industriousness to advance my husband's cause and agenda? Do I encourage him to work hard and be his best by cheering for him daily? When was the last time I told him how wise and talented he was in his chosen field? Do I make sure that he has everything that he needs to be successful in his area of expertise (i.e., clothing, tools, technical equipment, membership in professional associations, best-selling books, trade newspapers, industry journals, etc.)?

SOCIAL INVOLVEMENT. Have I encouraged his involvement in the neighborhood and reminded him lately that he is a gatekeeper and a pillar in his community?

SPIRITUAL SUCCESS. Have I really become his personal intercessor by standing in the gap for him on a regular basis? When was the last time I applauded the use of his gifts in the church? Does my quiet influence cause him to realize and achieve his vision for the kingdom? Am I helping him walk in his purpose and destiny?

Overall, loving and esteeming our husbands is a worthy and attainable goal. I'm a witness! By being honest with the Lord on these kinds of questions, you can assess your current status and activities as a wife and rate yourself in light of God's Word. The Holy Scriptures are your road map for becoming a God-fearing wife. God will add Spirit-led energy to your willing feet and get you stepping in the right direction. Believe me, once you begin infusing healthy doses of love and esteem, your marriage and family will not be the same!

PART THREE

Our Parenting
and Home Life

8

The Parents' Prayer Breakfast

A s William and I came running into the family room, we saw arms and tears flinging about wildly, along with some furniture. Our two youngest sons had gotten into a knock-down-drag-out fistfight over the remote control! Meanwhile, our oldest son was giggling from a nearby recliner, casually saying, "Y'all stop it," as he flipped TV channels—with the remote.

As we pulled the boys apart, Jeremy taunted his younger brother, "You can't whoop nobody! You fight like a girl *anyway!*"

"Shut up, Jeremy!" Jordan tearfully retaliated. "I ain't scared of you with your ugly self! That's why I can't stand you!"

"Boys!" I shouted. "This strife has to stop, now!" After getting the boys calmed down a bit, we began with our usual strategy for addressing sibling wars by rehashing the specific offense point by point in courtlike fashion.

Calling our first witness, William asked sternly, "Okay, Joseph, how did all this get started?"

"*Well,* Jordan had the remote first," he began slowly. "But I think Mommy called him and he left the control on the chair. But it's really Jeremy's time to hold it because he washed dishes today." (The explanation outlined two cardinal rules at the Powell house about preferential seating and controlling the remote. Rule #1: If someone has a particular seat and they get called away to perform a duty, they automatically get their seat back. Rule #2: The week that a person has duties washing dishes, they also have first rights to the remote control as a reward for their labor.) With that understanding, we proceeded with our inquiry.

"Jordan, if it's Jeremy's time to hold the control, why did you have it?" William asked pensively.

"Daddy, Jeremy wasn't even thinking about the control," Jordan began with tears of anger still in his eyes. "I had it before he even came in the living room!"

"Yeah! I let you hold it too—crybaby!" Jeremy chimed in, disrupting the order. "Then when I got it you tried to jack me!"

"Liar!" Jordan retorted.

"You're a liar!"

"Boys! We are not having this bickering back and forth!" William spoke firmly, attempting to regain control. "And, Jeremy, you keep your mouth closed until I speak directly to you! Do you understand?" I prayed silently as Jeremy rolled his eyes and muttered an unintelligible, "Yes, sir," under his breath.

The situation seemed to take hours to defuse, as rivalry festered amidst intermittent put-downs.

As parental referees, we nearly got "coldcocked" in the fierce interchange by verbal refrains like, "Y'all only care about *him!* He always gets away with everything!" or "I can't stand this family cause y'all are soooo unfair!"

When War Breaks Out

Sometimes parents contemplate whether they should intervene in sibling squabbles when intermittent yells and whining reach a fever pitch. This is a judgment call. But every now and again, World War III breaks out, and disagreements explode into a full-blown war, crossing the line into physical violence or verbal humiliation. This is clearly a time for intervention.

As prayer goes to work in invisible realms, there are a few "military strategies" parents can employ to help keep their sanity in the heat of the battle.

Separate the children, and in a commanding voice tell them clearly, "The fighting stops now!" Don't become emotional or assign blame too quickly. It doesn't matter who started the fight. Focus on diffusing the tension so negotiations can begin.

Avoid jumping to conclusions. Begin with a quick investigation. Don't assume that the older or "louder" child is always the aggressor and the younger or "quieter" child is always the victim. Host a mini-courtroom drama to get all the facts and emotions clear before you pass judgment and sentence. It's never advisable to come charging in like Zorro and the 41st Cavalry. Play Sherlock Holmes and Perry Mason instead.

Don't overreact to threats and put-downs. Phrases like "I'll kill you," "I hate you," or "You big sissy," will sometimes flow back and forth during sibling wars. Try not to take your children literally. They are just caught up in a web of intense emotion and are momentarily unable to use better judgment. Inform them simply, "We will not threaten one another or call names!" and center the conversation on peaceful resolution.

Encourage compromise and reconciliation. When there are no rules to guide and correct sibling rivalry, it's always good to offer your children several options. If two older siblings are fighting over food, for example, they can always share the remaining piece, make more (if it's available), or eat something else that's plentiful and available to both. Offer them similar options and choices that can lead to sharing.

If all else fails, remove the object of conflict, and have each child spend time contemplating his actions. Often, just the threat of denied pleasure and enforced isolation will be enough to get your troops onto peaceful ground.

Though sibling arguments can be loud, frequent, and exhausting for parents, much of it is all bark and no bite! So, even when battle lines are drawn, don't fear that the Cain and Abel scenario lingers near. Your calm assistance and powerful prayers will help to make a tremendous difference. And, in the end, remember these rivals will probably end up being best buddies one day.

Calling Godly Parents

When it comes to parenting, the Father desires that we mirror Him. So we should always have the "spiritual Windex" handy to keep the reflection clear. Our kids should see the true and living God *directly* through us! Only God can mold human beings into godly parents. He alone will make us wise stewards of prayer and living epistles in the lives of our children. As parents, we can sing that old gospel song that goes, "Please, be patient with me. God is not through with me yet!" If you're anything like William and I, you're a work in progress when it comes to Christian parenting!

As the Lord continues His renovations on us, we can confidently show our children the importance of obeying God and living a godly life. This is a tall order for all of us who are parenting in a new millennium—with all of its cultural stimuli and entertaining distractions. However, with the indwelling Holy Spirit we are able to perform in astounding ways.

"For the children ought not to lay up for the parents, but the parents for the children. And I will very gladly spend and be spent for your souls; though the more abundantly I love you, the less I am loved" (2 Corinthians 12:14–15).

These words by the apostle Paul should grip the heart of any parent attempting to raise their God-given offspring. The "more abundantly I love," he says, "the less I am loved." Even though Paul was talking honestly about the struggles of leading and loving the church folks at Corinth, the same heart cry could come from any parent on the planet. When children are young, our parental work clothes seem to stay on 24/7/365. And it doesn't always change once they're older! It's a constant chore to get each child on a daily routine, properly focused, and moving in the right direction. How do we accomplish it? William and I ask for more grace and the whole loaf of our daily bread early in the day.

This process of "laying up for the children" is a call to personal sacrifice. God literally employs parents *full-time* to do the work of effectively turning a sinful generation into a godly seed He can use. Don't feel qualified for the assignment? No one does. I look at Joseph, Jeremy, and Jordan every day and remind God of all the stuff I've failed to accomplish, teach, or model. With two tall teens and one preteen staring down at me, I feel like I'm running to beat their eventual ship-out date!

It took us a while, but William and I finally got a foundational understanding about parenting. And here it is: Our three sons belong to the Lord. They are on loan to us for a brief season of rigorous spiritual, personal, and academic training. The Hebrew writer confirms this in Psalm 127:3 (KJV), "Lo, children are an heritage of the Lord: and the fruit of the womb is his reward." Even though they have been given as gifts to us, they are not solely ours, but His.

My husband shared liberating insight that further freed me on this "godly parenting call." With a touch of relief in his voice he wisely explained, "We are not responsible for producing godly children. We're responsible for being a godly father and mother! The Father God is the only One who can make them *godly!*"

Naturally, parents are responsible for developing the potential of their young and grooming their gifts until they come to maturity. Spiritually, it is the call of parents to labor in prayer and instruction until Christ is formed in their children's lives. But the weight of their choices should not burden or condemn us. There will be many prodigals to leave and return to the homestead. We can only do our part in humble service to God. Godly parents don't always produce godly children because God gave each person free will. Each generation is responsible for developing a personal relationship with God Almighty. We can point the way and live godly lives before our children, but we cannot walk the way for them. God alone begins the work of restoration in us, and He alone completes it. Though challenges arise and choices vary, *don't abandon the process.*

As a young lady-in-waiting, my mother admonished me to "study" my young sons and to learn them well. "Only by constant study and observation will you know them well enough to discipline and direct them as they grow up," she cautioned. "Each child is different—and you can never forget that!"

Mom's advice has served us well over the last sixteen years. We are still learning to master Joseph's "party-over-here" personality and unfocused disposition, Jeremy's independence and stubborn will, and Jordan's drive to lead and "fire-starter" antics.

Godly parenting requires more than the provision of food, clothes, and a roof over their heads—it demands daily sacrifice. Yet we are determined to wisely manage this *living heritage* that resides in our home and to trust God for the outcome.

Understanding Mother Wit and Father Power

Years ago, I came to the realization that William and I possessed unique, God-given abilities for dealing with our three sons. He was driven by impenetrable *father power,* and I was compelled by intuitive *mother wit.* This revelation came while I was writing an article for *Urban Family Magazine.* My enlightening episode went something like this:

It was a pillow war of enormous proportions. I was exhausted and almost volatile as my young sons squawked over whose pillow was whose. With their unceasing screams and high-pitched whines, I was near the breaking point. "Just keep the pillow you have and go to bed!" I yelled wearily. "O-k-a-y, what's going on in here?" His tone of voice brought instant relief. As I eased away with a sigh, my husband stepped into "combat duty." Within seconds, attitudes were adjusted, pillows reorganized, and peace filled our home again. He strolled out of the "zone" unscathed by the grenades of sibling rivalry. "This is exactly what I'm talking about," I began ranting. "The ability of fathers to bring control and order! As a mother, I definitely have the nurturing appeal. But, as a father, you've got the power!"[1]

Mothers provide the vital element of nurture and esteem to their children. Personally, I see myself like the mother puma with her cubs. I know when they're hungry and can sense approaching danger. I groom them from head to toe and understand their individual strengths and weaknesses. I never hesitate to put maternal "spit" on their faces to make sure they are presentable to the world. It's not a mental effort; it's almost instinctive. The Mother's Hall of Fame has bestowed upon me life's biggest award: the eyes in the back of my head. With the help of the Holy Spirit, I've come to see, hear, and know almost everything about my male offspring.

But William is the ruling lion marking out the "safety zone" and establishing protective territories for his "pride." Like Mufasa in Disney's *The Lion King*, he provides the rigor and toughness to rally the young troops and move them into action. He trains them for battle and refreshes them with roughhousing and play. The sound of his roar and the stealth of his presence work wonders. With an effortless demeanor, he moves mountains, rearranges playing fields, and negotiates peace treaties. Since the world can be a real jungle, this combo pack of mother wit and father power makes us an impenetrable force in the lives of our growing sons. Nevertheless, how do these two distinct traits operate in a practical way? Let's review each one for a moment.

The Mother's *Intuitive* Wit

To understand mother wit, we have to begin with a definition. *Wit* provides us with the power of knowing or "keen" perception. It taps intellectual (and spiritual) ingenuity and quickly sizes up a situation with accurate observation. The good Lord has truly blessed mothers with this heavenly trait. When a woman incubates a child for nine months, she maintains a certain knowing or wit about her offspring. Having lived with this other person in close proximity for an extended period, there is an abiding insight that remains constant—despite separation or distance.

The *true* character and description of a mother is similar to that of the Holy Spirit. On one hand, she is full of care and comfort, warmth and wisdom, help and harmony. On the other, she exercises enormous strength and knowledge and judgment. As the elder women counseled, "When children are young, they're on your lap; but when they're older, they are on your heart." Mother wit is an awesome parenting tool, given and granted by the living Lord.

The Father's *Impenetrable* Power

Things operate on a totally different plane when it comes to men and their children. Whereas mother wit is Spirit-led and intuitive, father power is physically engaging and impenetrable. All fathers possess the power! It is God-given and life enhancing. I strongly believe that utilizing father power can restore order in the fierce "wars" raging among children *everywhere*—particularly in our urban centers.

When used properly, this power can create confidence and develop potential. If neglected or abused, it can stifle possibilities and destroy dreams. In practical ways, father power is critical to affirming heritage, establishing discipline, and encouraging achievement in our children. What an awesome power the Lord has given to dads!

The Holy Scripture confirms this important relationship between fathers and their children. King Solomon wrote in Proverbs 17:6 (KJV): "Children's children are the crown of old men, and the glory of children are their fathers." Glory is defined as "something that brings honor, secures praise, and imparts a good reputation." This glory is an invisible tapestry or covering that surrounds a child—like a royal robe. Only a father can drape "glory" upon his children—and seal them with purpose and significance.

This patriarchal glory or covering is a child's most brilliant asset. This is a bold statement to make in the African-American community where a large percentage of children grow up with absent fathers. If a child doesn't have a father, does that child not have purpose and significance? Absolutely not! Real life has proven otherwise. Individuals of great accomplishment, like world-renowned brain surgeon Ben Carson and countless others, have been reared by single mothers and have excelled in ways of which the world must take note.[2] The key is providing a father figure. Grandfathers, older brothers, uncles, and surrogates must step in to fulfill the biblical mandate to provide "spiritual covering." I've talked with countless single mothers, and every one of them has shared how she prayed for a fathering mentor to be raised up for her children. And God sent pastors, friends, church members, and relatives to father their sons. "A mother cannot be a father too," says one friend, a single mother of three. "God's Word is true, and He has to provide and make up the hedge."

As the everlasting Father, He makes up for the lack in the homes where dads have abandoned their posts. We're not perfect in any parenting state (whether it's a single parent or a pair). But God's will is perfect and so is His Word! "The Lord sent some good Christian brothers to help me with my children," one single mother of two passionately shared. "But the Lord Himself really became a Father to my girls. I even told them that the Lord God was now their Father and they had the best Daddy in the whole, wide world!" The Holy Scripture confirms this so beautifully, as the Lord is described as a faithful Father to this special set of children:

Psalm 68:5 (NIV): "A father to the fatherless . . ." God sets Himself in the place of a man who, for whatever reason, is unable to fulfill his responsibilities. Knowing the importance of a father's position, the Lord avails Himself to cover and provide what is lacking.

Psalm 10:14 (KJV): "The helper of the fatherless . . ." The Lord always comes to the aid and assistance of His "special" children, just the way a natural father would.

Psalm 146:9: "He relieves the fatherless . . ." Our God provides comfort and encouragement to the fatherless. In wondrous ways, He bears their burdens and removes any weight that might keep them from advancing forth and being made whole.

Even though William's father was not present in the teen and later years of his life, he received the Father's comfort and instruction and powerfully demonstrates father power with our three sons.

Over the years, he has maintained special mealtimes with the boys by establishing an annual "Birthday Breakfast." It has been a coveted tradition of the Powell family since our sons were very young. Early on the morning of his son's birthday, William and his young protégé leave before the rest of the family awakens to share some one-on-one time together. It's a patriarchal celebration on the dawn of a new milestone in a son's maturation.

As a man keenly aware of his father power, William uses this occasion to discuss the new responsibilities that will come with turning one year older. He also shares his increased expectations in a specific area and imparts a verse of wisdom from the Holy Bible that our son will personalize in the coming year and learn to apply to his life.

With each birthday dawn and throughout the year, William models how our growing sons should one day walk in father power with their own children. And I pray to be an eyewitness to the glory this power can produce in each generation.

Our Timeless Home-front Assignment

"Hear, O Israel: The Lord is our God, the Lord is one!
You shall love the Lord your God with all of your heart,
and with all your soul, and with all your strength.
And these words which I command you today shall be in your heart.
You shall teach them diligently to your children,
and shall talk of them when you sit in your house,
when you walk by the way, when you lie down,
and when you rise up.
You shall bind them as a sign on your hand,
and they shall be as frontlets between your eyes.
You shall write them on the doorposts of your house
and on your gates" (Deuteronomy 6:4–9).

Is the Lord not saying the same things to you and me today? He wants us to be assured that He is on our side! As Christian parents, we are not to rely on Canaanite or worldly wisdom to strengthen our marriages, understand our children, or deal with our family problems. God would not be pleased if I called the psychic hot line, anxiously read my horoscope, or played the lottery in order to make ends meet. The Lord is our God. *Jehovah Jireh* will provide everything we need. He even told the prophet Isaiah to remind us of how real and relational He still is: "Before they call, I will answer; and while they are yet speaking, I will hear" (Isaiah 65:24 KJV).

Early on, the Lord taught Israel about the necessity of maintaining a strong bond with Him in order to have the tools necessary for parenting. In addressing Israelite parents, He made it clear that if they were going to have the stamina and wherewithal to defeat the godless culture of the Canaanites, they would have to possess ironclad loyalty and deep affection for the Lord God. Their initial actions would be vital to preserving strong marriages, well-adjusted children, thriving communities, prosperous businesses, and a healthy society. God does not mince His words; He simply lays it on the line: "You shall love the Lord your God with all your heart, with all your soul, and with all your strength" (Deuteronomy 6:5).

Once the Lord informed Israel's parents that they should have faith in Him alone and maintain an undying allegiance to Him, He pinpointed exactly where these two pillars were to be erected—in *"your heart."* Parents are to possess "heart knowledge"—not "head knowledge"—of the Lord. He wasn't seeking a personal relationship with religious folks, but trusted fellowship with true worshipers. And He's still seeking.

After dealing with the parents' relationship with Him first, God then instructs them how to lead and guide their children. He points specifically to the home as the place of spiritual training and discipleship. This Deuteronomy passage is a timeless, God-given assignment that parents cannot afford to ignore.

Moses exhorts Israelite parents to effectively instruct and train their offspring with God's law. We are instructed to:

- teach God's commands with diligence

- talk of them consistently and continuously

- use God's commands as a curriculum for life

- uphold them as a sign and witness to the world

Let's review our home-front assignments:

TEACH DILIGENTLY

"You shall teach them diligently to your children."
(Deuteronomy 6:7)

The Hebrew translation for this admonition is the word *shanan,* meaning "to sharpen like an arrow."[3] Our objective is to make the Word penetrating. As parents, our teaching efforts begin with a dedicated commitment that is steady and decisive. Even when my children don't quite "get it" or are seemingly unaffected by my efforts, William and I press on, looking for relevant and meaningful ways to give them the Word of Life. It is vital that we impart God's laws with passion and conviction in a lively and energetic manner. The Bible should never be boring or lifeless. Our personal love and reverence for the Word will pique our children's interest and ignite their desire to learn more about God and follow His ways.

Parents, we are our children's first and primary teachers. None of us can afford to leave teaching to the Sunday morning experts. No matter what is said in these formal settings, children tend to mirror the habits and practices of their parents—both good and bad. Their value systems are being developed by our active or inactive participation in their lives—especially at home. It's exciting to know that we can teach and apply some mighty principles that will remain with them all the days of their lives.

Creative ways to teach diligently:
First, *use your areas of strength and ability.* Because I am a minister, writer, and dramatic orator, we do a lot with the spoken word (i.e., dramatic readings, skits, mini-musicals, and sing-alongs). A carpenter might use analogies from furniture design or home construction to expand on Scripture. A gardener could develop nature lessons and do a lot of outdoor activities, like explaining what locusts are like or describing Christ as the Lily of the Valley or

Rose of Sharon. Our vocations and professions are chock-full of teaching aids that can be creatively used to instill important Bible lessons.

Don't be afraid to mix secular games with sacred text. Pull out board and card games like Monopoly, Uno, or Sorry to enhance Scripture lessons that emphasize not giving up when times get hard and you've seemingly lost everything! Games teach us visible ways of competing, concentrating, winning, and losing. These are vital, real-life lessons, so be creative!

Enjoy crafts and hands-on projects to provide visible reinforcement. Kids love working with glue, scissors, and construction paper, so this is an effective way to merge the spiritual and the natural to reinforce scriptural truths. When our boys were in prekindergarten and first grade, we taught them the Ten Commandments by making a Scripture Memory Picture. A piece of 8-inch-by-14-inch paper was divided into ten separate blocks with a fine marker. After we studied the commands, each of them drew a "thou shalt not" picture in each block to remember and obey God's Word.

TALK CONSISTENTLY AND CONTINUOUSLY

"And [you] shall talk of them when you sit in your house, when you walk by the way, when you lie down, and when you rise up."
(Deuteronomy 6:7)

As believers, we have a God-given responsibility to communicate with our children about God. We should share significant and relevant Bible stories with our children, answer their unceasing questions, use teachable moments to highlight God's goodness, and influence their lives with His astounding holiness. But in order to keep God's truth from coming off to them as sanctimonious and ceremonial, this kind of intimate sharing should flow from our hearts daily.

Furthermore, we can't afford to relegate God to one day in

the week, like Sunday, or to restrict Him to one place, like church. God is everywhere! Our children need to know this, especially as they mature and spend more time in the world and less time in our safekeeping. We can engage in biblical instruction in the living room, while riding in the car, beside a child's bed, on the front porch, and so forth.

Here are some insightful ways to talk consistently and continuously about God's Word:

Take the Bible along on a lengthy car ride. Whenever the family will be in the car for an extended period (say, more than thirty minutes), pull the Bible off the coffee table and bring it along! Or better yet, keep a Bible in your car at all times. The last time our family rode a distance together, I invited the boys to play a Who Am I? game of Bible intrigue. I'd give them a brief description of the person, place, or thing and say, "I begin with the letter . . ." and say the first letter of the name. For example, "I'm very old now and a new dad. I can hardly believe that God has finally given me a son and even promised me a countless number of descendants. My name begins with the letter A." To keep the "blurt outs" from disrupting the peace, the children answered in rounds. The first person to answer correctly earned the point. The first person might say, "Aaron," the second child, "Adam," and finally the third, "Abraham" for the point. It's fun and keeps the family Bible-centered even on a short excursion.

Don't let the teachable moments pass you by. Unexpected moments often provide the best opportunities for planting a seed of the Word. This became clear to me when our son Jordan then age ten, came into my room and slouched down in the chair.

"Do you know when God is gonna do the stuff I've asked Him about?" he asked, looking defeated with a tear welling up in his eye.

"Well, what have you been asking Him about?" I questioned, anticipating his response.

"Our new house and my trampoline," he said wearily. "I've

been praying for them a long time and nothing's happening."

My heart was broken. I knew that Jordan had been diligent in prayer, but the money had not yet materialized for either of his requests. "Jordan, I don't know when we'll have a bigger house or you'll get your trampoline, honey," I said tenderly. "But I do want to give you a Word gift to encourage you right now."

"What Word gift?" he asked halfheartedly.

"It's from Isaiah 40:30–31: "'Even the youths shall faint and be weary' (that's talking about your feeling right now). 'And the young men shall utterly fall' (because our strength is not in ourselves). 'But those who wait' (which means to patiently trust) 'on the Lord shall renew their strength; they shall mount up with wings as eagles', (you know how high eagles fly). They shall run and not be weary, (or tired). 'They shall walk and not faint' (nor give up hope)." Then I read Jordan a poem from my personal encouragement file (they come in very handy). I also encouraged him to write a poem about what he was feeling and what God's Word was saying to him. In five minutes flat, he had come out of the doldrums and lifted me to new heights! Here's what he penned:

Stay in the Race
by Jordan Powell

Jesus is your closest Friend,
Though you may be filled with sin.
He loves you till the day you die,
And is glad to see you in heaven's eye.
He will never forsake you or throw you down,
I'm sure it says that on His crown.
You shall see Him in that wonderful place,
As long as you just stay in the race.

Even our *follow-up on local and national news stories* provides our family with sources of prayer and scriptural focus. Whether local crimes or national disasters loom across the pages of news headlines or the nightly news screen, "real-life events" are an important way to show children the importance of prayer and dependency upon God. When the September 11, 2001, tragedy shook our nation, William and I opened the Scriptures to relieve our children's fears. "You will hear of wars and rumors of wars. See that you are not troubled; for all these things must come to pass, but the end is not yet. For nation will rise against nation, and kingdom against kingdom. . . . All these are the beginning of sorrows" (Matthew 24:6–8). They asked lots of questions. We showed them that God is in complete control and knowledgeable of all the sorrows that will take place, but He does not want us to be troubled. He wants us to watch and pray.

A CURRICULUM OF PREPARATION FOR LIFE AND WORK

"You shall bind them as a sign on your hand, and they
shall be as frontlets between your eyes." (Deuteronomy 6:8)

As we apply the laws and commands of God, our children are receiving an informal education in every arena of life—from economics and physics to science and the arts. As a family, we can learn to do many things well, simply by following the precepts of Scripture.

The Bible is an excellent *curriculum for developing both life skills and work ethics.* Here are a few teaching tips to show you how:

Read biographies of famous Christians. Reflecting on the enormous faith of African-American believers like Dr. George Washington Carver, Booker T. Washington, Sojourner Truth, and Mary McLeod Bethune can stimulate children to excel in school and life and model their unwavering faith in God. Their obstacles were so horrendous that our children will be motivated to learn of their victorious successes.

Quietly discuss the character of the waitress during restaurant service. This will strike up lots of conversation as you wait on your meal. Take a verse like Colossians 3:23 (NIV) as your teaching instrument: "Whatever you do, work at it with all your heart, as working for the Lord, not men." Agree to observe the waitress to see what kind of worker she is. Ask the children to study her movements and listen carefully to her words. What kind of attitude does she have? Does she seem eager to serve or uninterested? Is she working with all her heart or hardly working? Of course, the waitress should not know she has been scripturally scrutinized, but her work will provide a real-life model for a few future workers. Whether the waitress's service is excellent or poor, this talk time will stimulate lots of sharing about how we are to serve others and perform our work, no matter what the task is.

Dramatize the parables. "That's not fair!" We've heard those words a thousand times at our house and have had more discussions on fairness than any other subject. One day I got tired of saying, "Well, the whole world isn't fair," and decided to show the boys God's thoughts on this matter. We read the verses in Matthew 20:1–16 and I gave out parts. I played the landowner and the boys were the farm crew. In birth order they went out to the "farm pool" to stand on the corner and wait to be hired—first Joseph, then Jeremy, and finally Jordan. I revved it up with lots of drama, inspecting their clothes and hands and even asking a few interview questions about their work skills and previous performance. We had a pretend truck to drive us to the field, where I'd drop off one worker and return to find others—because the harvest was great. At the end of the "day," I pulled out lots of change from my pocket and paid each worker the same shiny quarter. And they began ranting, "That's not fair. . . ." Only to hear me reply, "Don't I have the right to do what I want with my own money? Or are you envious that I am generous?"

We followed up the dramatization with discussion questions:

Did the first workers have a legitimate gripe? Did the landowner keep her word or not? Why did they have such a fit about the money? Does God have a right to be "too generous" if He feels like it? Does Dad? Does Mom? Do you have that right with your own friends? How do we respond when others are included and given a break or a seemingly undeserved reward? Do we rejoice or do we envy? How would you run your business and treat your workers in a similar situation?

Jesus' clever ending to this parable states a larger insight: "So the last will be first, and the first will be last" (verse 16, NIV). Upon hearing this, the boys began to exclaim, "First is worst and second is best!" Which produced another set of disagreements!

A PROGRESSIVE SIGN AND WITNESS TO THE WORLD

"You shall write them on the doorposts of your house and on your gates." (Deuteronomy 6:9)

Our households should be a city of refuge for the poor and a Christian center for the needy. Our children need to see us live as Christians. Even our difficulties, hardships, and disappointments should reflect our faith, allegiance, and heart-knowledge of God and His Word—so that others will take note and love Him more.

A few ways to be a witness and uphold a sign and drawing card for the world are offered below. It takes some sacrifice, but the rewards are tremendous:

Sacrificial service to the widows. When the boys were young, we lived on a cul-de-sac. Most of our neighbors knew each other but were not close. The oldest member of the community was an elderly widow who had huge feet resulting from a rare disease. She often was unable to move about without great distress. William, the boys, and I visited her frequently for prayer and encouragement or just to find out if she needed anything. From time to time, we would do her grocery shopping and make sure that her medicines were taken properly. Even though she had a son nearby and other neighbors had lived there longer, we felt it was our Christian duty to serve this needy widow. At first the boys were somewhat afraid of her, until we shared with them the important work we were doing. "Religion that God our Father accepts as pure and faultless is this: to look after orphans and widows in their distress and to keep oneself from being polluted by the world" (James 1:27 NIV). The boys soon grew eager to deliver small packages and perform small chores on her behalf. In this way, our whole family was blessing the Lord our God and announcing our faith to the entire community.

Reaching out to community kids and their parents. Several summers ago, we turned our small house in the country into a ministry retreat for boys who didn't get to spend much time in a rural setting and a Christian atmosphere. Some of them were family and others were friends and neighbors' kids who needed an extra measure of biblical training and admonition. We called it Boys' Camp 2000, and our theme was entitled "Brother Love!" from Psalm 133:1. For six long months our boys prayed, planned, and prepared to receive our summer guests. The boys made clearings for tents, set up private stalls for showers (almost everything had to take place outside), identified camp games, and organized camp menus. It was the greatest outpouring of our faith that we had ever experienced. The boys grew by leaps and bounds as they served as junior counselors and shared their love for God with others. By the end of eight days and seven nights, William and I were worn to a frazzle, but we had lifted strong witnesses for Jesus to these young men and their families.

These spontaneous ways of "walking through the Bible" are exciting. It keeps kids excited about spiritual things and the importance of a Christ-centered life. Parents, we can make a big difference in the lives of our children by teaching them at home and keeping the illuminated Word of God ever before their feet.

Nutritional Meals from the Kids' Menu

D on't do that! You know better!" How often I've heard parents in church, on the playground, or at the mall yell these familiar words. I've even said them myself from time to time. But, what do we really mean by these words? How much do we assume is *know-how* that has never been *taught-how?* I once heard a secular child psychologist say, "As a society, we do a better job training our pets to obey certain tasks than teaching our children right from wrong!" His words were deeply convicting. As parents, we often make too many assumptions about what our children should know and are disappointed when their lack of understanding is openly revealed.

Lessons from a Neighbor's Vine

I was confronted with this reality some years ago when

my children were young but old enough to play outside without constant supervision. We had recently moved to an inner-city neighborhood. Living close to neighbors' homes and playing with youngsters from varied backgrounds meant new opportunities for creative as well as destructive play.

One afternoon a group of kids (including my own) were playing in the nearby yard of an elderly couple. A full green vine that beautifully decorated an ugly light pole was torn, tattered, and trampled to the ground by the children. After realizing their folly, they each fled in haste. Only my three were left to tell the story.

The damaged vine was a terrible eyesore. With disappointment, I reminded my children of our previous talks about respecting other people's property. Somehow, I had assumed they would make the connection at the proper time, but that little Sunday school lesson had not found its way into their hearts. Even though we'd discussed this issue on various occasions, they had never had an opportunity to apply it outside of our home.

"Boys! You know better!" I snapped angrily. "We don't disrespect people and destroy their property! I can't believe you've done this!" I said in exasperation. Honestly, I just wanted to fuss and wallow in disappointment, but the lesson demanded a full dose of hands-on teaching. *Did they understand this to be an act of destruction rather than innocent play? Did they know this was property that belonged to our neighbor? Could I give them room to learn and grow as they played and made mistakes?* It was apparent that the real teaching had just begun!

So I marched Joseph, Jeremy, and Jordan—all under seven years old at the time—to the elderly couple's home. They were trembling in their Osh Kosh sneakers and whispering promises to be good next time as we stood at our neighbor's doorstep. Each of them was trying to persuade me not to tell while anxiously tugging on my jean skirt. At that moment they were too scared to be sorrowful.

My boys had chosen to participate in the destruction of our

neighbor's property and they had to face it. To their dismay, I rang the bell! After offering a brief explanation and sincere apology, our elderly neighbor joined us in cleaning up the mess and rewrapping the vine. She told the boys how her mother had originally planted the vine many years ago and shared stories of the vine's long history in their family.

As my neighbor talked, the boys' eyes lowered. Tears welled up in my eyes as I saw each of my sons experience remorse for what they did. Surely, the Holy Spirit was working this valuable lesson into the crevices of their tender hearts. One by one they each wrapped tiny arms around our neighbor, offering her a reassuring hug of apology letting her know that they now respected her important vine.[1]

As we walked away, Joseph announced in a boisterous manner, "Mommy, we're not gonna let nobody tear up that vine again!"

"Nope! They better not!" Jeremy agreed valiantly.

"We'll protect it, Mommy!" Little Jordan added with a squeaky voice.

"That sounds good to me, brave soldiers!" I said happily as they raced off to another adventure. "Now they truly know better!" I sighed confidently.

After this incident, I found a great book entitled *Together at Home* by Dean and Grace Merrill that offers super hands-on activities to help children and adults apply Bible lessons. Throughout this chapter, I'll be providing a few of their practical activities that we've used at our house over the last ten years.

ACTIVITY: Let's start with an exercise to help children make wise choices. The entire family sits down to the dinner table with a blank sheet of paper. Everyone is challenged to draw a life situation where he has to choose between right and wrong. Everyone holds up the picture and explains the choice. One child might draw a picture about choosing friends. Another child might describe cheating on a test at school. A mom or dad might describe choosing between a Bible study group and shopping at the mall or watching sports. The point of the exercise is that everyone shows how vulnerable we all are to the temptation of a wrong choice. Once all pictures are displayed, each person writes one guideline on his or her picture for making a wise choice. The list for a particular family will vary greatly, but here are a few guidelines for making the right decision:

- Think about what Jesus would do.

- Think about the consequences of your decision.

- Stop and pray for help in making the right choice.

- Know what the Bible says about this (or quickly find out).

- Talk it over with parents, pastors, or other leaders.[2]

Teaching Young Children Truth or Consequences

Watching your child do wrong despite constant reminders to do right is frustrating. But choosing right over wrong is a life-long process of decision making. Children need our help in developing the right decisions *today* that will build into wise choices tomorrow. But many parents are of the erroneous assumption that when they *tell* youngsters what is right, their children will just do it. The "Do as I say and not as I do" practice may suffice for the short-term, but it is not beneficial to building a lifetime of successful Christian living. Our social surroundings are simply too sinful for this approach. As a culture, we underestimate the impact of repeated negative influences on our children in critical areas like profanity, dishonesty, and deception. These influences flow in from such ordinary places as cartoon and sitcom programming, radio airwaves, shoppers at the mall, neighborhood children on the playground, or telephone conversations by unregenerate relatives or older siblings.

Christian parents often limit their instruction to only issues of *good behavior,* like being polite, sharing playthings, or reciting favorite Bible verses. But we must learn to address both right and wrong choices with young children, especially those who are elementary school age, when there are so many outside influences.

Conversations about appropriate dress, violence on television, and sexual identity are equally as important as saying grace over meals, being tidy, and observing safety rules. These discussions are not always comfortable, but they are relevant and necessary. I want my sons trained to choose right over wrong and not to do right simply out of form and expectation. In my absence, I want the truths of God's Word to bring both conviction and direction to their choices.

Young children can genuinely weigh matters of choice when the terms are well defined. Explaining consequences in simple *if-then* statements helps young children better understand their actions. "Jordan, *if* you take your shoes off again, *then* you will have to come inside to play. It's too cold to be outside without shoes."

On the other hand, consequences can be positive and helpful incentives for right choices. "If we turn the Saturday morning cartoons off and get the house and yard cleaned, then we can rent a video and have popcorn later on."

Often we think first of material goods to reward our children for positive choices and achievements. However, verbal praise can motivate any child. Although the world often rewards self-interest and even wrongdoing, parents can model a different value system by showering children with compliments when they make the right choices. For example, "Keisha, you were so obedient to take only one cookie from Miss Sheila. I thank God for your wise choice before dinner!" Parents should make every attempt to extend the privilege of choice and consequence to younger children appropriately so that they can become better decision makers as they grow older.

ACTIVITY: It's easy to assume that children know things that they simply don't—especially when it comes to traditional Scripture verses. For example, many adults know the Lord's Prayer and can recite it from memory. But do most third graders know what "hallowed" means? An amusing story highlights this truth. A father asked his son, "What is God's name?" The boy answered, "God's name is Harold." Curious, the father then asked, "How do you know that, Son?" The son answered, "'Cause I learned it in the prayer, Daddy. You know, 'Harold be thy name!'"

In this exercise, take a piece of bright construction paper and draw a line down the middle. Write the classic King James Version of Matthew 6:9–13 on the left, and let the kids take turns playing secretary or scribe on the right. Recite and recast the prayer phrase by phrase. Use a dictionary or thesaurus to provide insights and stimulate deeper understanding. The goal is to make this prayer kid-sized, manageable, and understandable; however, a lot of uncertainties will surface before that. Simply do a lot of clarifying and tinkering with words until the final version is drafted. One of our versions went like this:

> Dear Big Daddy God, who lives in heaven,
> Your name is very special to me.
> I want to do what You ask me to here on earth
> Just like Your angels already do in heaven.
> Thank You for all the good food You give us every day.
> I've got a lot of sins, so please forgive me a lot,
> And I'll forgive all the people who do wrong.
> When I think "bad" and want to do wrong things,
> Help me to do what's right.
> I know You can help me because
> You are the most powerful King

Anywhere—that ever will be.
Amen. It's done![3]

Instructing Older Children About Humanity's Sinful Nature

For adolescents and preteens (ages ten to twelve), instruction in righteousness needs to be more direct. They must be introduced to the ABCs of the "sin nature" and understand that we are all born "in sin and shaped in iniquity," with a strong tendency to choose wrong over right. Our basic strategy is to instruct our growing children on how to receive the great help of God and His Holy Word in order to resist evil. Our children must learn to depend on the help of the Lord in all areas of life.

Take, for example, James 4:6–8, 10. Here's a passage of "life-saving" Scripture that can be understood by adolescents and preteens: "'God resists the proud, but gives grace to the humble.' Therefore submit to God. Resist the devil and he will flee from you. Draw near to God and He will draw near to you. . . . Humble yourself in the sight of the Lord, and He will lift you up."

We learned this lesson the hard way with our oldest son. He was on the threshold of turning thirteen and had begun to enjoy the music and acting of Will Smith. While doing a profile on the young entertainer for a school research paper, Joseph acquired tons of magazine articles, movie posters, and color photos of Smith. He also had received the popular CD sound track from *Men in Black* for Christmas and faithfully watched *The Fresh Prince* on television. It all seemed innocent at first, but William and I began to notice that our son was showing signs of excessive adoration for Smith and possible tendencies toward preteen idol worship. This became glaringly apparent when we saw his "shrine" of Will Smith paraphernalia all housed in a coveted Nike shoe box!

"What is this, Son?" William asked sternly, peering into the open box. Will Smith's name had been written on the flap with a large black marker, and many of his pictures had been cut out and pasted onto various parts of the box's interior. Inside was the *Independence Day* movie video, the *Men in Black* sound track, and lots of other paraphernalia bearing Will's name and image.

"It's nothing, Daddy," Joseph said anxiously. "I just got this box from Jeremy to keep all of my stuff in."

"Joseph, it looks like you took Jeremy's shoe box in order to make a shrine of Will Smith," William said in a serious tone.

"Yes, I took his box; but it's not a shrine, Daddy."

"Then what is it? Because it looks like a shrine," William said in a calm and even voice. "Do you know what a shrine is?" Joseph shrugged his shoulders nonchalantly, like he was anticipating the paternal speech that was sure to follow.

"A shrine is what religious groups or individuals build to show affection to deities or gods," William spoke clearly. "They set relics in a particular place and put them all together in a central place for the purpose of worship. Sometimes they have candles all around, or pictures on a wall or items in a chest," he went on, carefully ordering his words. "Now, this box may not be an actual shrine in your mind, but everything about it—the writing, the pictures, the items you've gathered together—all make it look just like a shrine."

Joseph only spoke a few words in his own defense. "But it's not a shrine!" He seemed to be trying to convince himself of this now in light of the truth that was pouring forth.

"You can deny it, my son; but God knows the truth," William chimed on, his words even-keeled yet potent. "We are a Christian family, and you have personally asked Jesus into your heart as Savior and Lord. God's Word is clearly against having idols and worshiping other gods." William grabbed his Bible and proceeded, "In Leviticus 26:1, God says, 'You shall not make idols for yourselves; neither a carved image nor a sacred pillar shall you rear up [or erect] for yourselves; nor shall you set up an engraved stone [or image] in your land, to bow down to it; for I am the Lord your God.'"

"Daddy, why are reading all of that to me?" Joseph asked with irritation. "I told you I wasn't worshiping nobody!" he pressed on with denial.

"Well, like I said, God knows your heart," William faithfully reminded Joseph. "It may not have been your intention, but it's gone too far, and your mother and I are not comfortable with this box in our home." Joseph rolled his eyes in silent disgust and peered around the room, as if looking for unseen help.

"If it's not a shrine," William spoke with a tender smile, "then you'll have no problem doing what I'm going to ask of you."

"What are you going to ask me?" Joseph queried, his arms now crossed and his eyes racing with hesitant curiosity.

"I'm giving you *one hour* to take all of your items out of this box. The videos and CDs should be put with the others in the family room. The pictures that have been glued to the box should be pulled off and tossed in the trash. Then you can decide on three items that you'd like to keep in your scrapbook, but everything else is to be thrown away. After you've cleaned out the box, you need to put Jeremy's sneakers back in it and apologize to him for taking his property without asking. You have one hour to take care of business."

By the time William finished speaking, Joseph's tears were streaming down in silent protest.

Later that evening, after everything was seemingly resolved, I returned to Joseph's room for some closing thoughts on the day. Nighttime is a good time to get a preteen to disclose their deepest feelings. So I sat on the bed, peered lovingly into Joseph's eyes, and affirmed my love for him. That's when I got the rest of the story!

"Mommy, I was so mad at Daddy today," he began.

"Yeah, I could tell, and I was praying too," I said quietly.

"Well, did you know that the devil was telling me to fight Daddy about taking my box? But I didn't listen to him," he said with the most pleasant look on his face. "A-a-n-d, the devil told me something else." He smiled, his eyes lowered while twiddling his thumbs.

"What else did he say, Joseph?" I asked, my heart racing furiously.

"He told me to get some matches, go outside, and burn the Nike box so Jeremy wouldn't be able to get it back," he explained candidly. "I knew I'd get a spanking for it, but he kept telling me to do it anyways!"

After Joseph shared this with me, I was able to help him understand the demonic fight that he had just come through by describing the three voices that are always swirling around us. Those voices represent: Self, Satan, and the Savior.

The voice of Self is concerned exclusively with what feels good or is beneficial to "me, myself, and I!" No one else is ever considered. It's all about generating self-gratifying feelings and fleshly desires. This voice says, *You should take that shoe box, 'cause Jeremy don't need it anyhow.* Our own voice is selfish, pleasure-seeking, and materialistic.

The voice of Satan is concerned with destruction. He always comes to "kill, steal, and destroy." He does not care about human life, personal property, or spiritual truth. He speaks to the mind, plants lies in the heart, and pushes people to believe him with blind urgency. He pushes against the will by saying, *"Take that shoe box outside and burn it up! If you do get a spanking, so what? You'll have the satisfaction of making Jeremy suffer for telling on you!"* His voice is harmful, urgent, and boastful!

The voice of the Savior is always concerned with truth and character. He comes to challenge you with His Word and to mold you into His own Christlikeness. He always wants you to consider others and seek a greater good for a nobler purpose than you can possibly see. He speaks forthrightly, *"Where is the brotherly love in destroying Jeremy's box? Hatred and unforgiveness are chains that bind. But unconditional love will set you free!"* The Savior's voice is always still, small, and gentle.

Joseph was successful in this battle because he overcame pride and chose to humble himself to God Almighty. By submitting to the Savior's voice, he was empowered to resist the vocal temptations of the Evil One and gain an important spiritual victory for himself. As our sharing time came to a close, we celebrated with a high-five praise and prayed together in triumph. Joseph was able to put Will Smith in his proper place and welcome the Lord Jesus back to the throne of his heart. How desperately our children need to understand the power of God's Word in order to live effectively for Christ!

ACTIVITY: A good old-fashioned game of tug-of-war in the yard or the park might be just the thing to get an older kid to cooperate with God concerning his attitude and actions. Establish a center line (using a sidewalk, jacket, or elongated tree limb) and divide the family into teams on the opposite ends of a strong rope, an old garden hose, or even an old sheet or blanket (twisted and knotted for strength). Be creative and balance the teams. Go through as many rounds as you can take, and then collapse on the ground together. While resting and looking upward to the sky, recite verses for your children. Ask them to find the connection between tug-of-war and what the Scriptures say. Begin with our selected passages from James 4:7–8, 10, and add Psalm 32:8–9 and Proverbs 29:1. Ask your kids to imagine God at one end of the rope and ask, "Who would win?" Then add, "Does God always use His power to make us obey?" Help your children understand that God does not want to push and pull against our resistance. He is strong enough to overpower us but seeks our obedience and fellowship.[4]

Blockbusters and Bibles

One of the practical ways that we have confronted the sin nature in our children is by combining Bible teaching with their favorite pastime—watching videos. Everybody likes a good movie, so we often enlarge our spiritual lessons and biblical worldview on the back of a good black-and-white flick or Blockbuster movie.

A well-developed story is powerful. Whoever tells the best story influences a culture and wins the heart of a generation. Even though Hollywood is sorely lacking in values, morals, and an accurate understanding of spiritual things, it has mastered the art of good storytelling (from character development to visual effects). It's the reason box offices gross millions of dollars each week on a new release. We are mesmerized by the imaginary and make-believe. But wise parents can use Hollywood's skill to instruct a generation in holiness and righteousness.

Once when we were studying the works of the flesh from Galatians 5, we allowed the boys to watch a significant portion of the R-rated movie *Rosewood*. The true-life story was set in an all-black, postslavery town. The movie was full of glaring depictions of hatred, racism, avarice, wrath, strife, envy, murder, and the like. We were able to stop the movie, talk through emotional scenarios, and teach them the lessons we wanted them to learn. This Bible-Blockbuster combo was effective in showing them the drastic outcome of a life led by the dictates of the flesh.

When we wanted them to really understand the profile of an overcomer (persevering against all odds) and how God works in the lives of ordinary people (using angelic beings), we watched the all-time classic *It's a Wonderful Life*. The movie's central character, George Bailey, struggles with disappointment, unrealized dreams, money problems, and, eventually, attempted suicide. When he hits rock bottom, the Lord is there to bear him up (with the help of Clarence, his guardian angel). In the end, George learns what a wonderful life is *really* all about.

We've combined Bible verses and movie footage for nearly a decade to impart major lessons to our sons. Through these mediums, they have confronted a host of lessons—from trusting God and standing for righteousness to avoiding pride and the deceptions of the devil. It's always a joy to see sacred text jump off the page, do "the bump" with the pictures from the big screen, and explode with understanding inside of them.

Transforming Bebe's Kids into God's Property

Nearly everyone is familiar with Bebe's Kids, created by the late comedian Robin Harris, then popularized by a popular movie of the same title. These untrained children, lacking appropriate adult guidance, tend to wreak havoc and destruction wherever they go. But, deep down, you know that with the proper guidance they could be really great kids. The truth is that we are all born "Bebe's Kids." No one is perfect, not even one! *We all have sinned and come short of God's glory.* Human beings severely lack understanding of who we are, how we are to behave, and what we are really born to be. It is the proverbial sin nature that mars us all. We can be outwardly tamed to a certain degree, but only the transforming power of Jesus Christ can effect the inward change that is eternal!

This biblical understanding is paramount to Christian child-raising. Even when our children are born and raised in good Christian homes, they can bear a frustrating resemblance to Bebe's Kids despite our best efforts. Because of the sin nature, our children are inherently born to be wild! This reality must be reckoned with in the light of God's Word, the Holy Spirit's work, and constant parental discipline. Over time, and in cooperation with the Lord of the universe, we can transform our Bebe's Kids into God's Property.

Training Each Child for Spiritual Success

While preparing for a Wednesday night Bible study, I received great understanding on Proverbs 22:6. "Train up a child in the way he should go, and when he is old he will not depart from it."

I had just finished reviewing some interesting communication principles for reading aloud to an audience. In them I discovered that readers can stress one or more words a little more in a sentence to make them stand out and give the sentence meaning. Such stress laid on words in the sentence is called *emphasis*. This is used when orally interpreting a passage of poetry and literature. More than 150 years ago, a communications scholar wrote that emphasis points out the precise meaning of a sentence, showing how one idea is connected with and rises out of another.[5]

For example, take the sentence, "This is the house that Jack built," and note how the meaning changes as you read it, stressing successively the separate words:

This (not another) is the house that Jack built.
This *is* (believe it or not) the house that Jack built.
This is *the* (it's the only one) house that Jack built.
This is the *house* (not a garage or barn) that Jack built.
This is the house *that* (not some other Jack) Jack built.
This is the house that *Jack* (not Tom or Henry) built.
This is the house that Jack *built* (he didn't buy it; he built it).[6]

It is clear from this example that emphasizing different words in succession not only adds force for reading aloud but also changes the entire meaning of the sentence as a whole. All of this background was penetrating my understanding when I opened my Bible to reread Proverbs 22:6, based on two distinct meanings given the use of emphasis:

Train up a child in the WAY (God's clearly defined pathway and precepts for living righteously unto the Lord) *he should go, and when he is old he will not depart from it.*

Train up a child in the way HE (one's personal pathway based on individual persuasions, prescribed characteristics, and developing personality traits) *should go, and when he is old he will not depart from it.*

Training up a child is one of the most important investments we can make in the kingdom of God and in the lives of our children. To *train* is "to dedicate," and the compound meaning of *train up* is "to dedicate through diligent and continuous teaching and instruction." Even though most popular Bible teachers instruct that this verse in essence means to "train up a child in keeping with his *individual* characteristics," I was thrilled to see the larger picture that we should also train him or her according to God's character and commandments. If we are creative enough to merge individual considerations with God's holy will, we will assist our children in achieving great spiritual success.

I find this to be so true in training our three fellas! Joseph has rhythmic intelligence and is a kinesthetic (hands-on) learner. He requires an in-your-face, continual training that is full of relevant, in-the-moment graphics and examples. He shuts down with a lot of talking and lecturing and is not open to long passages of Scripture reading and one-on-one discussions. I usually put the point before him in a "one-two punch" and leave him to work with it alone. With this sixteen-year-old, we use a lot of instructive media influences:

- Musicians who have a Christ-centered message, like Fred Hammond and Kurt Carr.

- Movies with a subtle theme or a good story line, like *The Matrix* and *October Sky.*

- Magazines that provide a deeper insight on Christian principles or social trends, like *Gospel Today, Newsweek, or Ebony.*

These mediums, used in tandem with the Bible, have helped us to train Joseph in righteousness, because for him the more traditional "Sunday school" mode is basically ineffective. He is a twenty-first-century teen, and orthodoxy just doesn't seem to bring him closer to the Master. So we improvise.

In a similar way, Jeremy is nontraditional. He is spatial and scientific in his personality and design. So we try to use high-tech associations and hard-hitting facts for training him in righteousness. We've spent years undoing public school evolution theories and other absurdities to get him to walk with God in the "science of faith." He doesn't do well with Christian fluff but wants it straight. It has been my greatest desire to see Jeremy develop a critical mind with a Christian worldview that asks the right questions about the universe. He does well with documentaries or lessons that coincide with the Discovery channel.

Our youngest son, Jordan, has linguistic intelligence and is an auditory learner. So, we can use traditional Bible studies and lengthy discussions around Scripture without boring him easily. He is stimulated by conversation and enjoys exploring different aspects of Scripture in relationship to his life and world. Our techniques are very direct and traditional with this son. Jordan is very engaging and talkative, so we can cover a lot of training ground with the Bible open wide and see the results bloom very swiftly.

Each generation is responsible for and accountable to God for their own relationship with Him. Yet the biblical and personalized training lessons driven home in these critical years will not vanish easily. Parents, grandparents, and guardians are the central instruments through which God educates and introduces His will to each young heart. So get your "curriculum" together, and begin training today with new dedication to see each child succeed spiritually. This training should spill over into larger realms as you work diligently to understand teen culture and address the various and changing needs of your teenagers.

Healthy Snacks and Thirst Quenchers for Teens

When it comes to teenagers' overall diet, we find that they do not always feast on the things that nourish the whole person: spirit, mind, and body. Whether natural or spiritual, they just don't always practice good dietary habits.

The average teen often refuses three balanced meals a day that are chock-full of all the proper food groups. They'd rather consume fast foods like burgers, pizza, and fries or grab quick snacks like chips and douse it all down with a soft drink. They simply have to be reminded to eat right, drink plenty of water, and even take their daily vitamins! These practices simply are not at the forefront of their young minds. Parents have to keep a watchful eye that their children don't overload their systems with empty calories.

Well, the same is true when it comes to spiritual nourishment. Even though teenagers look all grown-up and happy as larks, they often are deficient in their daily allowance of spiritual nutrients. Many still need some sideline assistance and health-conscious pampering when it comes to discerning the truth from a lie, the essential over the superficial, and the eternal from the fleeting.

There are several areas of which parents must be leery as they raise teenagers in the twenty-first century. For the African-American parent, however, the billboard concern is music. Our teens are inundated with the driving philosophy of hip-hop culture—a definitive lifestyle that covers a broad spectrum, from language and art to money and fashion. Without a doubt, music defines how young people view themselves and their world. So, in this chapter, we'll focus on the history and influence of hip-hop on a teen's values and choices. We'll also review the ongoing "bulletin board" area of fostering strong relationships with our teens through effective communication.

As parents, we must be mindful of how to articulate our love, care, and concern to our offspring. Teenagers are special young people—not kids anymore and not quite adults either. It's a challenging season indeed. Yet parents can develop a communication style that will endear teens and make a tremendous difference in their lives. For effective communications, remember to:

+ be consistent (about your own beliefs)

+ be decisive (about your response)

+ be respectful (in your style and tone)

When we follow these "three be's," our teenagers may feel more comfortable sharing their deepest thoughts with us and may even seek our wise counsel from time to time. This fact became more and more real to me while communicating with my own son about music.

Confronting the Unhealthy Influence of Gangsta Rap

"Joseph," I yelled down the hall with a voice of concern. "Come here, please!" I stood pacing back and forth as my lanky fifteen-year-old came bobbing down the hallway with the familiar telephone receiver attached to his ear. "Yes, ma'am?"

"Whose CD is this?" I asked, trying to keep the strain from rising in my voice.

"It's mine." Joseph spoke in a nonchalant tone. "One of my friends at school gave it to me for my birthday."

"There is a warning here about 'explicit content,' young man, and that disturbs me," I said while heading swiftly to private quarters. "Please get off the phone and come in my room. I'd like to hear the lyrics."

Within moments, Joseph and I joined his dad at the CD player. As William piped up the sound and the words filled the room, I grew nauseous. Every filthy curse word, derogatory term for women, and reprehensible phrase hit my spirit like bullets. Yet I didn't open my mouth. William looked at me in obvious disgust, but we silently agreed to let the music play on.

The three of us sat lifeless, listening to elongated messages about sex, money, murder, hatred, envy, self-worship, and rebellion against God and authority. As the bump and sway of secular hip-hop invaded our Christian home, I consciously sat stoic and mute, determined that Joseph would be the first to speak to this madness. The suggestive power of the music was intoxicating. As it reared its stealth in song, I grew angry at its forceful entry upon my family. *How dare Satan slip his filthy, seductive trash in on my son?*

As the music continued, Joseph grew more and more uncomfortable, twitching and shifting on the sofa. By the end of the second song, he blurted out like one holding a long breath, "Can we turn it off now?"

"Oh, no," I finally spoke with a sarcastic smile on my face. "It's just getting started!" But William interjected with puzzled concern, "Why do you want us to cut it off now, Joseph? If it's uncomfortable to listen to with your parents, then you shouldn't be listening at all."

Joseph talked wearily, trying to justify the musical genius of the artist, attempting to justify his new fascination with the "individual expression" of hip-hop. "I don't really pay attention to the curse words," he tried to explain, as if we were born yesterday!

After collecting my frazzled emotions and packing away most of my negative energy, I entered the discussion. "Joseph Kahlil Powell," I said slowly in a Clair Huxtable "let me help you understand" tone. "Do you know that we just attended a mini worship service?"

"What are you talking about now, Mom?" Joseph asked, slightly rolling his eyes.

"This rapper is preaching, honey!" I began in a controlled voice. "He's at the mike, (*instead of a pulpit*) and his mission is to get the followers (*i.e., the congregation*) to believe what he is saying and to follow him wholeheartedly. He's appealing to their hurt and pain or their desire for power and gain—whatever it takes— to get them to say 'Amen! I'm down with that!'" I said, increasing my vocal momentum.

"But this messenger is using deadly lies (*instead of the truths of Scripture*) and working his lyrics (*or sermon*) into a nice, thumping tempo to coax the crowd (*of sold-out followers*) to do just one thing: worship his god!"

"What god is that?" Joseph asked.

"Money, sex, greed, violence—any number of things! Because Satan's diversified, just like the rest of the world! He's upped the ante—twenty-first-century style—and made worship different based on where you live and what you like!"

William chimed in and explained to Joseph how Satan once led music in heaven. "Man, God created Lucifer, who led praise and worship in heaven with timbrels and pipes in his very being," speaking in an effort to endear Joseph to the truth. "He was a walking orchestra, a masterful instrument of music himself [Ezekiel 28:13–18]. But, iniquity was found in his heart. You know the story! He wanted to be worshiped like the Most High God!" William said passionately. "Don't you understand, Son, that Satan is crafty in this arena? He manipulates secular music from the dark side and laughs at the world's stupidity as he draws new worshipers unto himself."

It is clear that Satan will never cease his maneuvers against the family—especially teenagers, whether they are in a Christian home or not! Our adversary is hell-bent and determined to infiltrate the message of Christ right under our noses. But as parents we are a first line of defense for our children. And we must be on the alert and willing to confront Satan head-on with a scriptural sword and shield when he crosses the line! The souls of our children are at stake, and that should always keep us sober and vigilant.

On a Highway to Understanding Hip-Hop

After William and I shared our insights with Joseph about the ministry of music, Joseph dropped his fascination with gansta rap, but he continued to listen to other hip-hop artists, including Tupac Shakur. "Mom, you need to understand what 'Pac was rapping about—especially before he died," Joseph reasoned passionately on a long car trip from Atlanta to Washington. "He wasn't always talking about 'thug life' but about overcoming difficulty in an unjust world. Once you start to flow with the words, you'd really like what he was saying—because it's about real-life principles." I looked at my eldest son (who is so much like me) through a different set of lenses at that moment. Now he was appealing to my conscience with a sense of reasonableness and largeness that surpassed his sixteen years.

Since it was just the two of us, Joseph was able to share the fullness of his heart, and I quietly yielded to him my undivided attention. "Hip-hop is not just about 'gansta rap,'" Joseph explained. "It's a musical art form and a viewpoint that helps people communicate about the world around them and all the various stuff that's going on." He seemed likened to an explorer who'd just discovered a new route to a long-pursued territory. "Hip-hop is a vocal expression—set to music—that helps me process who I am and where I want to go in life." Joseph reasoned on in heartfelt emotion. "You just can't make all hip-hop out to be bad and of the devil, Ma." For hours, Joseph introduced me to the intricacies of hip-hop—emphasizing mostly the positive side. Terms like "playa hater" and various lingoes of this musical genre were broken down to help me understand this brave new world of my teen son.

By gracefully inhaling his words, I started "feeling" Joseph as he spoke so confidently about his musical interests. He sounded so mature and focused that I talked less, listened more, and asked only pertinent questions. As we traveled, Joseph shared his enormous passion for hip-hop music. He wanted to write rhyming lyrics and communicate his growing commitment to peace, justice, and equality through song.

Much later, I learned that Joseph had even chosen the pen name "Charm" and was one of the best freestyle rappers in his high school. Words seemed to flow out of his being with rhyming lucidity and exacting precision. As a wordsmith, I grew proud of his lyrical language and creative ability to communicate his deepest thoughts. One of his songs really touched my heart.

Going Straight
by Joseph "Charm" Powell

Charm got his mind right / he's in the limelight
Folks trying to blind sight / grip your nine tight
On a path to success / strive to be the best / nothing less

Only if you all knew / what I go thru
Didn't know I would make it this far / don't believe I'll show scars
Sleeping in cars / behind bars
Don't know where your life's going / pulling you by the neck
Never knowing where you're going to be next
'Member looking out my window / thinking 'bout why I'm here
Going outside in the rain / and crying tears / 'cause I'm living my
fears to the point.

When I was 'bout to give up / I slipped up
But Moms wouldn't let me stay down
She said, "You gon' turn around."
I'm not going to let you fail / they already think /
All young males belong in jail.
I didn't think it was possible / locked up / dead / or in a hospital
Sat down and thought about / Charm ain't going out like that
Start writing rhymes on paper / How about a career in rap?
A new person / soul searching
Do a lot for you / when you need it
Like food / it'll fill you up / when you eat it!

Chorus:
On a path with no direction
No compass, no map
Trying to do right,
But your life is off track
By a miracle you get control,
Ask God to save your soul
Help you out
Clean your slate
And from now on we're going straight.

Verse 2:
I felt what it's like when someone you love is taken away /
Something you built is breaking away
Then I tried to make it on my own / but it's harder when you're
alone.
Then you start to lose respect for life / and don't care to be alive
Getting attitudes with God 'cause He let you survive
Putting on a front / pretending everything's cool /
Family starting to wonder why I'm doing bad in school /
Then we start going to a new church / where the pastor saw
through my hurt
Then I felt God's hand / said He had new plans
I know you failed all four quarters / but you're gonna pass that
final exam.
Then I'm gonna get your music dreams off the ground
You put Me out of your life / and that's why you got turned
around
I'm going to point you in the right direction
And you walk in a straight line / and don't take no other roads
If you know it ain't Mine
Then I knew I heard God's voice for the first time / I'm going to
do what He says
'Cause that's what I believe is right / I know it's dark in my heart
/ That's why I receive His light.
I'm glad I heard Him 'cause if I didn't / destruction would be my
fate
So from this day on, Lord / the Charm's going straight!

That long ride with Joseph changed forever the way I would view this musical art form. As I devoured books and magazines, read commentaries, viewed BET videos, and conducted interviews, I was hit with the stark reality that hip-hop is multidimensional in its scope and presentation. There is the fun side, the dark side, and the upside, with "new sides" still unfolding. Hip-hop is a cultural phenomenon that affects everything from the 'hood to Hollywood and the street corner to Madison Avenue.

In the beginning, many considered hip-hop an urban fad, seeking its fleeting moment in the musical spotlight. But its economic stealth and increasing momentum have proven the critics and pundits wrong. Without a doubt, hip-hop is one of the most pervasive influences to sweep over the African-American community—and, indeed, the globe—in many decades. It has become a culture within many cultures with endless possibilities—both positive and negative. As parents, we must become intimately acquainted with hip-hop's origin and educated on its multifaceted, ever-evolving mission.

Age of Innocence: The Fun-Loving Genesis of Hip-Hop

The year I graduated from high school, an explosive cultural revolution began that would ultimately transform urban communities and global centers—but no one really noticed. It all happened in October of 1979. A new record label called Sugar Hill Records released a single titled "Rapper's Delight," credited to a trio known as the Sugarhill Gang.[1] It wasn't the first hip-hop recording, but it marked the first time that a national, even international, audience stood and took notice of this genre. This single lit up the *Billboard* charts, peaking at Number 36. And hip-hop has been dominating the industry ever since, rivaling the musical achievements of historic rock 'n roll and rhythm and blues. The revolutionary new sound style developed by African-American and Latino kids in the parks, clubs, and parties around New York City (particularly South Bronx) in the 1970s had been successfully packaged with commercial results. But its enormous influence was yet to unfold.

The beginning days of hip-hop were fresh and fun-loving as young DJs unleashed creative energies spinning records to keep the party going. They started using two turntables for their records, while replaying the instrumentals on a record to maintain a consistent beat. Over time, these musical masterminds blended various sounds to create the popular musical art form known as "scratching." This technique is similar to improvisational jazz where rhythm and sounds, words and beats are syncopated to enlarge the effect of the jazz singer or musician. This jazz technique is called "scatting," and was popular with such musical greats as Duke Ellington, Louis Armstrong, and Ella Fitzgerald. So in a great sense, hip-hop was a baby born out of the stylistic creativity of our most revered musicians.

Hip-hop continued to build on a wide musical foundation of jazz, as well as rhythm and blues (R & B). By the late 1980s, millions of young people were grooving to a new influential cultural dynamic. They started carrying small radio/tape decks that grew into enormous "boom boxes" through which to amplify their new music—taking its sound everywhere they went. As one urban pastor noted, "Young people began skating to the solitary music of their headphones and cruising to the blaring accompaniment of their car stereos. And what they heard shaped their lives and ours."[2]

Over the years, the message of hip-hop exploded into an enormous youth culture. It defined their way of dress, speech, and behavior, all with an "in-your-face" attitude. Hip-hop became widely known as "rap music" when MCs took center stage and a DJ provided essential background sound characterized by dynamic lyrics belted out to syncopated beats. Millions of kids soon swooned to rap artists everywhere as they were pumped to "Throw your hands in the air. Wave 'em like you just don't care!"

Despite its various messages, hip-hop thrived and communicated widely to a diverse spectrum of American youth, from the urban core to the suburban sprawl. Eventually, the genre penetrated the color barrier, scaled economic walls, and crossed into international territories. Like an unstoppable stream, hip-hop flowed into every area of life, from television advertising to fashion trend-setting.

Age of Ignorance: The Dark Side of Hip-Hop

By the early nineties, the fun flavor and party innocence of hip-hop turned dark. In many cases the music portrayed the negative side of urban life, glorifying violence, materialism, crime, drugs, and misogyny. Younger rap artists emerging on the scene showcased their "thug life" and "bad boy" images with a bold flair of social indecency.[3] The element of "conscience" rapping about the pain and struggle of urban life was out, and the destructive message of gangsta rap was in. Enter popular rap artists like Tupac Amaru Shakur, Christopher "Biggie Smalls" Wallace, and NWA, ushering in with them labels like Bad Boy Entertainment and Death Row Records.

Throughout the nineties large numbers of inner-city youth maintained a consistent diet of gansta rap. These songs railed against the establishment, which included parents and the police, and cast a negative light on education and honest employment. Children during this period were "weaned" on rap artists caught up in a vicious cycle of "mo' money, mo' murder, and mo' mayhem." A prevailing preoccupation with death and dying loomed over our gifted and talented children—driving them to inevitable destruction. And we all mourned deeply, feeling helpless against its surge.

Age of Influence: The Sweeping Tide of Hip-Hop's Economy

Over time, hip-hop underwent a metamorphosis that looked and sounded similar to "old school" rap, but was, in essence, drastically different. The destructive civil revolution of gangsta rap had reached a defining peak when popular mega-rappers "Biggie Smalls" Wallace and Tupac Shakur lost their lives in a confusing whirlwind of senseless violence. After their demise, the hip-hop music industry seemed to shed much of its angry weaponry for new artillery: *domination of the global marketplace*. As one writer said, "If the civil rights generation called for 'Jobs, Jobs, Jobs,' then the mantra for the hip-hop generation had become 'Business, Business, Business.'"[4] Additionally, as some gangsta rappers assimilated to some of the responsibilities of those in the establishment—like family, children, and home—they realized that the lyrics were antithetical to family values. In other words, they didn't want their own children listening to the profane, derogatory lyrics of their songs!

Black Enterprise magazine has done an excellent job keeping us informed of the burgeoning multimillion-dollar enterprise of hip-hop. In the early nineties, they featured industry players like Russell Simmons, the undisputed "Godfather of Hip-Hop," who used music as a springboard to reach urban youth and develop a new generation of consumers hungry for apparel, movies, magazines, politics, and products that reflected this new "flava." Simmons continues to create an international market for hip-hop consumerism through youth-culture advertising.

In 1999, this same magazine featured hip-hop moguls Sean "P Diddy" Combs (the rapper-cum-entrepreneur formerly known as "Puff Daddy") and Percy "Master P" Miller (father of popular young rapper Lil' Romeo). Both young men appear quite debonair—like high-profile businessmen—in their chocolate brown suits and conservative eyewear. These new entrepreneurs revealed how they took rap music and built a sector that could no longer be ignored by the business mainstream.

Hip-hop's bourgeoning economy has been sustained and developed by other key rap artists turned entrepreneurs like Jay-Z, Snoop Dogg, and Busta Rhymes—all multimillionaires. Last year, *Black Enterprise* featured the owners of Roc-A-Fella Enterprises, "a $300 million octopus with tentacles that extend into music, movies, and fashion."[5] Hip-hop is a multi-million dollar industry of global proportions.

The irony is that hip-hop is no longer a "black thang." According to *The Source,* a leading hip-hop magazine, white consumers purchase 70 percent of all rap and hip-hop music, and it has recently outsold both rock and country to become the nation's top-selling format of popular music. Hip-hop culture can be seen and heard just as easily in Paris, Belgrade, and Tokyo as in New York, Los Angeles, and Atlanta.

Age of Impact: The Undercurrent of Hip-Hop's Dominating Philosophy

In an article entitled "Hip-Hop Kingdom Come," William J. Brown, dean of the College of Communication and Benson P. Fraser, professor of communication at Regent University in Virginia Beach, Virginia, write about the enormous impact of this musical genre for *ChristianityToday.com*. "Hip-hop . . . it's not a homogeneous subculture but a diverse supraculture transcending ethnic, geographical and artistic boundaries," they contend. "Though hip-hop has achieved a secure place in popular culture, its colorful styles and poetic whimsy also come with a dark, disturbing element. For many parents and youth leaders, much of today's most popular rap/hip-hop music sets off moral alarms," Brown and Fraser surmise.[6]

These moral alarms flow out of the sound track of hip-hop's dominating philosophies: materialism (the love of money and things) and hedonism (the pursuit of self-pleasure), laced liberally with worldliness and sensuality. These are disturbing elements for a musical and cultural force that is dominating the planet in a manner akin to the Pied Piper, casting its intoxicating cadence over legions of youth and adults who blindly follow.

Like Brown, Fraser, and many others, I can hear a spiritual cry in some of the brazen lyrics belted out by rappers like DMX (Dark Man X). In his 1999 cut "Ready to Meet Him," he raps, "[T]he real war is to follow the law of the Lord/Lord, you left me stranded/And I don't know why/Told me to live my life/Now I'm ready to die."[7] Likewise, Ja Rule, in his song "Life Ain't a Game," declares, "Take my life, take my mind/Take my heart, take my soul/Take my cash, take it all/But save me."[8] As a mother and a minister, the plea for significance and redemption screams in these lyrics. Even though the music is mixed with a lot of nihilism and fatalism, a clear yearning for spiritual truth echoes through the vibes. And the adult Christian community must be willing and ready to respond appropriately in love.

When it comes to hip-hop, we've got to separate our disdain for the liquid content of the lyrics from our spiritual concern for the containers. It's not impossible for God to empty the content and pour in new wine! But if we despise the containers along with the content, we fail to display the redemptive power of the Gospel.

Age of Inspiration: Holy Hip-Hop Brings Fresh Wind

Whenever darkness and worldliness seem to prevail in a culture, God has a sovereign way of raising out of its midst a generation that will obey His voice and heed His call. Like Gideon and his army of three hundred (downsized from thirty-two thousand), God never needs a crowd to do His bidding, but seeks instead a faithful remnant who will walk upright and courageous despite the glitter and gold of the status quo.

A group of young rap artists known as the Cross Movement of Philadelphia represent part of this called-out remnant. These urban ministers are an independent rap group with their own record label (Cross Movement Records). They also operate a ministry organization (Cross Movement Ministries) with a mission to see that all who are influenced by hip-hop culture are presented with the Gospel of Jesus Christ. Some consider them among Christian hip-hop's finest contributors. To date they have produced four albums: *Heaven's Mentality* (1997), *House of Representatives* (1998), *Christology* (1999), and *Human Emergency* (2000).

I interviewed John Kevin Wells (aka "The Tonic"), who serves as president of Cross Movement Records; Brady Godwin Jr. (aka "The Phanatik"), a lyricist and vice president of Cross Movement Ministries; and Virgil Byrd (aka "Life"). The three talked candidly about the history of hip-hop, its rise and dominance in the culture, and their mission to rap exclusively for the kingdom of God—without compromise!

Each of these young men grew up steeped in secular hip-hop before giving their lives to Jesus Christ more than a decade ago. They know the language and the culture like the backs of their hands; but because their hearts have been changed, so has their message. Below, they provide a unique perspective on such issues as the immoral aspects of secular hip-hop; helpful tips for concerned parents of teens caught up in hip-hop culture; and explanations on why Christian hip-hop is so effective in winning this present generation to the Lord Jesus Christ. Here are some relevant insights on hip-hop culture from a few members of the Cross Movement:

GENERAL ANALYSIS ON HIP-HOP CULTURE:
"The amazing thing about hip-hop as an art form is its ability to give instruction and direction. Hip-hop at its core is about telling and teaching, feeling and informing. Young people are particularly needful of this." *Brady, "The Phanatik"*

"Hip-hop has basically been pirated! It didn't originate on an anti-God agenda. There are various types of rap known as 'Conscience Rap' or even an 'Islamic-Infused Rap,' that don't use bad language and negative words about women. None of that is used." *John, "The Tonic"*

"I would say that hip-hop has grown into its own today. It's one of the biggest voices in music genre. Everybody is endeared to it, from the church to corporate America. Everyone can identify with it, [is] affected by it, or knows someone who is. Hip-hop has massive crossover appeal and suddenly knows no boundaries. I would say that it's central to life—not just an urban thing anymore. Hip-hop has longevity and staying power." *Virgil, "Life"*

CROSSING OVER FROM SECULAR TO CHRISTIAN HIP-HOP:

"When we came to church we had on baggie jeans, a T-shirt, and a skullcap. Over time, God made us models from the inside out, because we never changed our dress or put on a suit. But we loved to study the Bible, pray for hours, and rhyme for the Lord. We were eager to tell God's side of the story and alert everyone to the fact that a movement had begun at the Cross that was still making its way across the land. The elders in our churches had to face the fact that we were true disciples of Jesus Christ. We didn't 'look or sound the part,' but were passionately leading others to the Lord, expounding the complexities of the Scriptures in clear terms, and, basically, doing the work of the ministry." *John, "The Tonic"*

THE IMMORAL ASPECTS OF SECULAR HIP-HOP:

"There are good and bad sides to hip-hop. On the bad side are those inherent messages that talk about violence, drugs, rebellion, and promiscuity. Underneath the surface, hip-hop has done a terrible thing. It has erased the shame of these things from the culture. Since the music and its messages are being pumped so consistently, people are desensitized by the consequences of their actions. When confronted with the issue of promiscuity, for example, a person will respond, 'Why is this wrong?' or 'Who says it's wrong?' The music sends a message to a generation that sin is okay and acceptable. This is the negative part of hip-hop. It's feeding a part of the sinful nature that was born separate from God. Really, it's feeding a monster!" *Brady, "The Phanatik"*

"Rock music promoted these same kinds of things—but rock went on to talk about different issues from time to time. With hip-hop, this is all there is to talk and sing about: money, rebellion, murder, self-worship, and humanism. These are the main messages that are being pumped." *John, "The Tonic"*

"Music becomes the *perfect pill* to get the message more potently into the bloodstream of a nation. The sad part is that hip-hop points us to the thing that we love most—ourselves—and gets us to buy into what we already want in our existing nature. This is the reason why it's so effective. Hip-hop points to the thing in us that is against God and says, 'That's okay!' This is very visible in the culture." *Brady, "The Phanatik"*

"Hip-hop basically got cancer, and part of it still has to be surgically removed. It's like a good apple with a big, brown rotten spot. You don't throw the whole apple away. You just cut out the bad part and enjoy the rest." *John, "The Tonic"*

AID FOR CONCERNED CHRISTIAN PARENTS:
"Since the message of [secular] hip-hop is so consuming, parents need to do their best to cut it out of their children's diets. If that is not possible, because it's literally everywhere, then parents will need to help their children understand the hearts of men according to the Bible. Kids will need to step up into what God says in His Word about His creation and what's going on in the human heart. Paul talks about all of these things in 2 Timothy 3. It's all laid out in the Book. Parents have got to bring this message home and help their kids understand the reality of sin and the fall of man. This is what secular hip-hop is really feeding into . . . the fallen nature of man. If we open up the Scriptures and review these things at home, this will become the most effective angle for combating the destructive elements of hip-hop. It will give parents the 'biggest leg up.'" *John, "The Tonic"*

"Because hip-hop is so sweeping, parents must also understand the fascination with this music and take the time to get educated on its history and philosophy. It's hard to combat something that you don't fully understand. The very thing that Christ died for is inflated in hip-hop . . . the sinful nature of man. But Christ died to redeem that nature. Hip-hop is attempting to 'woo' a deadness that Christ came to revive with His blood. Sin cannot be entertained; it must be eradicated, and only the Cross accomplishes that! Parents will have to put on a different pair of lenses to guard against the sweeping tide of secular hip-hop. And it's not just young people; a lot of adults are affected by hip-hop too—you'd be amazed!" *Virgil, "Life"*

DESCRIBING THE POWER OF MUSIC:
"Music is such an effective way of communicating history and philosophy. God even told Moses to put the deliverance of the children of Israel into song. Miriam sang their history after they crossed the Red Sea in order to seal into their memories what God had done. And they sang in each generation all that God had worked for them." *John, "The Tonic"*

"Hip-hop has this elegance and eloquence about it! Music is an essential communicator of morality. I like what Ravi Zacharias said: 'Let me write the songs of the nation; let someone else write their laws.' There is something about the power and persuasion of music that can impress a thought or communicate an ideal better than anything else." *Brady, "The Phanatik"*

KINGDOM BUILDING WITH CHRISTIAN HIP-HOP
"We have had problems trying to communicate the Gospel in the traditional church. Christians basically thought that hip-hop was *of* Satan, and not just something used *by* Satan." *Virgil, "Life"*

"We must be willing to grasp the 'technical terms' of theology to communicate truth to this culture. It's more than taking teens bowling, throwing a pizza party, or showing them Christian love. We must learn to take heavy and deep terms like *propitiation* and *atonement* and break them down so that even a baby could understand it. This culture needs a sound dose of theology, not human efforts with a Christian twist." *Brady, "The Phanatik"*

"We call what we do . . . Gospel hip-hop, Holy hip-hop, and Christian hip-hop. We keep the message centered on the atoning work of Christ and what He 'finished' on the cross. We challenge lifestyles. The message hasn't changed, just the method that we are using." *Virgil, "Life"*

"We're not here to tell anybody that their culture is wrong. We're here to represent the kingdom of God and to let them know that the 'broad way' leads to destruction, and you don't have to go that way. You can take the narrow way through a 'strait gate' that leads to life." *Brady, "The Phanatik"*

"Once we got saved, we thought we'd have to give up this art form in order to follow Jesus—leave the dark side and come over to the Christian side. But we started rapping about salvation and sanctification. That's a good part of hip-hop that we still admire; we could be who God made us to be and not something other people expected. Pure hip-hop can truly describe a love for God and a relationship with one another. It can be a useful tool and an evangelistic outreach. God said to us, 'Take it and use it to My glory.'" *John, "The Tonic"*[9]

Practical Aids for Parents of Hip-Hoppas

For a helpful parent's resource, visit www.parentguide.com, a site that addresses a variety of parenting issues, including wading through the mass of electronic mediums that influence children and teens. The movie, electronic game, music, cable, and broadcast television industries each have voluntarily developed clear and informative parental advisory systems to help families with advance information on the content of entertainment products. Parents will find that making use of such a rating system will aid them greatly in filtering undesirable influences away from their children. Additionally, there are other ways for parents to learn more about what their teens are listening to. Here's a few ways to get involved and stay connected.

HOST A HIP-HOP HUGGER. This is a time for your teen and his or her friends to hang out in the family room and school the adults on what's happening with hip-hop and what it's all about. Huggers get teens and parents conversing about one of the biggest influences in their lives. It should be a casual, fun-filled event similar to a roundtable or a "rap session." Teens should feel free to share openly and express their true feelings.

ESTABLISH A MONTHLY OR QUARTERLY II-T-3 FORUM. Using 2 Timothy 3, review and rate the newest music videos. Invite all the neighborhood hip-hoppas over for popcorn and punch and take a long, hard look at what's on BET, VH1, or MTV. You can spruce it up with review sheets and clipboards or keep it light and informal. Whatever your approach, be sure to use the Scriptures as the key "sounding board"!

READ *GOSPEL TODAY'S* "WORD ON THE STREETS." This column, written by college students Roland Hairston and Kimar Morris will provide you with an insider's view on the most popular recording artists in the industry today and how their lyrics and philosophy jive with biblical truth. The column is thought provoking and penetrating. For example, one column featured rap artist Ja Rule and his set of Jeffrey Atkins' Rules. His signature saying is tattooed to his chest, "Pain Is love." The student writers asked the poignant question, "If God is love (1 John 4:8, 16), and Ja Rule says that pain is love, then is God pain?" Their well-written commentary refocuses the reading on that eternal truth that God is love![10]

STAY ABREAST OF HIP-HOP CULTURE THROUGH SECULAR PERIODICALS. Read popular magazines like *The Source* and *Vibe,* whose entire mission is to showcase the ins and outs of hip-hop around the globe.

LIGHT UP THE COMMUNITY WITH A "CROSS MOVEMENT BLOCK PARTY." Play nothing but Jesus jams and invite some "sold-out teens," church members, and youth leaders to "kick it" with the kids. Administer tracts and share the Gospel.

BECOME FAMILIAR WITH UNDERCURRENT PHILOSOPHIES IN HIP-HOP CULTURE. Terms like hedonism (pursuit of self-pleasure), nihilism (rejection of all moral values), misogyny (hatred of women), misology (hatred of reason, argument, or enlightenment), secularism (concern for the temporal rather than the spiritual), and humanism (a continual applause for human achievement over the adoration and worship of God) are all reflected in hip-hop culture. Introduce your teens to these philosophies that certain aspects of hip-hop glorify but run counter to the Christian faith.

WRITE A PERSONAL RAP DURING FAMILY NIGHT. This activity can center on your personal family or some aspect of your faith. Give everyone a verse to memorize and sing. Be sure to add a nice beat to make it flow! Alternatively, let everyone write an individual piece to showcase where that person is in his/her life and faith.

PUT THE FAMILY HISTORY IN A RHYME. This will help teens and their siblings remember important people and dates that make up their family tree.

Final Thoughts: Power to the Parent

Since hip-hop culture apparently is here to stay, let's be intentional about making it part of a lifestyle that is pleasing to Christ. Parents, we can set the pace and help our teenagers express their creativity and still "keep it real" with God. So let me end this thing with my own little rap. For "the bottom line" in this life hasn't changed in two-thousand-plus years, and it never will:

A Parent's Eternal Rights
by Yolanda Powell

Tell me, what does it profit / you or me
To gain the whole wide world / and lose eternally
Gotta tell ya the truth / make it biblically plain
The Savior gave His life / He wasn't brutally slain
E'nuf of the dark side / and all the mess
'Cause sin and shame must take their rest
See, the true light has come / and He's shining bright
Baby, now is the time / to finally get it right!

Chorus:
So, come on / come on / come on
Take a walk with me / into eternity
Just come on / come on / come on
Take a walk with me into your destiny
I say now, come on / come on / come on
And let the Word of God set you totally free!

Household Operations: Organized Closets and a Full Fridge

I should have written an article entitled, "Confessions from the Family Room: Our Struggles with Household Maintenance and Management." With a husband, three boys and a 100-pound dog, our humble abode often resembled a pigsty! We created mounds of laundry and dirty dishes (which no one enjoys washing), and piles of excessive clutter. Often we needed a snowplow to clear a path through our family room. We had to buy a special chemical called Zap to handle the heavy-duty grime that resided in our bathroom. Our kitchen cupboards and fridge often resembled our gas tank and bank accounts—-empty and in need of being filled up and replenished. We always had more meetings, games, errands, and practices to schedule than should be allotted to one single family. Our household was running amok!

The only problem with publishing such an article is that I didn't have any "overcoming wisdom" to offer anyone.

No one wants to read about the obvious and familiar struggles of families without some "tried and true" solutions that will make a difference. I felt like a domestically impaired woman in every way. William kept telling me "maintenance, maintenance, maintenance." But his advice was easier said than done, because we didn't have a clear and workable system of teamwork. William was helpful in the kitchen with meals but had repeatedly warned, "I don't do bathrooms!" The boys washed dishes on their assigned weeks, but hardly lifted a finger to do much else without being coaxed and coerced. So, the bathrooms went through long periods of being untidy and disheveled. Sometimes the kitchen floor got mopped twice a week and sometimes not for two weeks! Of course, the majority of household organization and supervision fell on my shoulders. I desperately needed a consistent and creative way to keep a "tight ship" as they say in the Navy, with "all hands on deck!" The overall healthiness of my family depended on it!

You see, household organization is so important to the internal life of a family. It removes the strain and struggle of daily demands so that members can breathe easier, accomplish more, and live in a carefree atmosphere of unity and camaraderie. When organization is a stranger and cleanliness foreign, the family unit is unable to perform at its optimum. I recently read in a home management article that, "Every house has a voice." That's a fascinating reality. When I considered the "voice" of the Powell house at that point in our lives, it was loud and clamorous, and quite muddled and unclear. We desired to live in peace and order and yet our habits and activities kept creating a different picture.

When a household is not in order the members of a family are frazzled and divided in their focus and energies. Meals don't get cooked as needed; kids are late for school and practices; dogs don't get fed or walked on schedule; the lawn resembles a forest and the bills are repeatedly paid late! Everything moves either at a slow pace where nothing gets done on time or at in rapid rate where few things get done effectively—both of these extremes have a crippling effect on the family unit.

In this kind of ongoing disorder, emotions constantly flare and relationships are always at odds. A sense of strife and discord flows throughout the family and a spirit of self-preservation runs rampant like a contagious disease. Husbands and wives live at odds due to the stress of disorder; and children are frustrated with lack of continuity and clarity. The life of every family member is drastically affected by a lack of simple planning and organization. This reality ranges from a lack of clean underwear due to forgotten clothes washing dates to starving kids coming home from school to an empty fridge and bare cupboards by the ATM.

Handling the Money Madness

Finances are also ravished by disorganization and inattentiveness to detail. When normal household repairs and various fees are not addressed and paid in a timely manner, the family reserves or savings are made subject to the "tyranny of the urgent." Families end up having to "rob Peter to pay Paul" just to do what should have been done without penalty. For example, the ceaseless drip in the upstairs bathroom that was repeatedly ignored has now created severe water damage that requires $1,200 for new flooring. These are dollars that literally went down the drain! Only organization and good stewardship provides peace and order and saves time and money.

"We don't have a lot of money, but we've got a whole lot of love!" I've heard older family members recite these comforting words since I was a little girl. Yet, this phrase seemed simpler in the 50's and 60's than it does in the 21st century. Everything simply costs too much today! Between a host of regular expenses each month (including the mortgage and car notes), there's the ever rising costs of groceries, clothes, sneakers, haircuts and hairdos, lawn care, vet fees and dry-cleaning bills . . . not to mention the ever

expanding cost of a college education! Even with greater job opportunities, increased tax options and more disposable income, many families still struggle with the similar issues of "how to make ends meet" and move ahead financially.

So, whether we've got mo' money, lo' money or no money, we still need Jehovah Jireh (the God who Provides) to help us maneuver through the turbulent waters of money management. As African-American Christians, we must realize that our God is, indeed, Possessor of heaven and earth, and all that we have (both great and small) comes from Him.

For African-American families, the issue of household organization and financial management is a prime concern. We often battle in work settings that are extremely stressful, maneuver in social situations that are dehumanizing, and struggle consistently with "more month than money." Having to come home and fight clutter and chaos will put our health and sanity in jeopardy. Where can we relax at the end of the day if our homes are in turmoil? Isn't the privacy of our homes supposed to be the place we replenish our tired souls and rest our weary bodies? Home should be the one place on the planet where a semblance of peace abides. An orderly household is key to an orderly family. They fit like a hand in a glove.

Struggling With the "O" Word

My good friend Judy and I received a simultaneous one-word impression from the Lord: *Organization!* It came in various ways— over the radio, in the hair salon, in our personal Bible reading, and in our corporate prayer time together. Neither of us could deny that this was a strong, unceasing admonition from the Lord. It kept coming at us like a bulldozer everywhere we turned and it seemed to have megaphone power! The driving directive was clear: *Get organized, be disciplined, and set your house in order!*

"I just feel like something's going to happen," Judy said with a serious expression. "And when it does, we won't have time to get organized—we're going to have *be* organized! I don't know what's coming," she spoke with a puzzled look. "But it's as if we're going to be on the go and our homes will need to *already* be together when that time comes."

Judy's words were loud and clear but, in my opinion, her house was already together. She ran a beauty salon out of the basement of her home and both the exterior and interior was always immaculate. My house, however, was at the opposite end of the spectrum. It was a home in grave disorder!

Struggling To Strike A Balance

I knew the truth and so did the Lord! He didn't waste any time getting my full attention about my continuous lack of organization. So, one morning in that predawn hour between sleep and wakefulness, I heard a familiar phrase of Scripture echo in my conscience:

"You strain out a gnat but swallow a camel!"

The force of those words jolted me to a wide-eyed, sitting position and brought stinging indictment to my soul. I immediately recognized the verse from Matthew 23:24 (NIV) as harsh and searing words of hypocrisy that were hurled at the Pharisees by the Lord Jesus Himself. Some Bible scholars explain that this verse addresses the Jewish prohibition against eating anything that "swarms, crawls on its belly, walks on all fours, or has many feet," as outlined in Leviticus. The Pharisees would meticulously strain out the smallest unclean insect, like the gnat, with a cloth filter before drinking their water or wine. However, Jesus reproves them for being so willing to "swallow a camel," which is a large unclean animal. The Lord was using the power of exaggeration to illustrate the point of how much these men neglected the "more important matters" of justice, mercy, and faith in lieu of being diligent to pay their tithe of spices. Both were vital disciplines; yet their understanding of these spiritual requirements was extremely shallow. Without mincing words, Jesus showed them their spiritual error.

Unlike the Pharisee I had reversed my responsibilities. I was working hard on the "more important matters" of studying the Scriptures, fasting, and praying; but I had almost dismissed my less interesting duties of keeping the house in order. I, too, was neglectful, however, considering the physical organization of our home of little importance to my spiritual pursuits. Yet, just as the Lord told the Pharisees, He now told me, "These you ought to have done, without leaving the others undone." Somehow my gnats and camels weren't being handled properly either.

All of those small previous impressions concerning organization and discipline were suddenly flashing across a gigantic movie screen. Like Hollywood film producers, the Lord often uses the technique of "flashback" to help me see myself in different scenarios. Instantly, I could see in living color: the disheveled living room jam-packed with the boys' backpacks, Sampson's hair all over the place, and my school papers scattered about. Then there was the kitchen sink with yesterday's dishes still there; the soggy washcloths in the boys' bathtub half wrung and; and the mound of clothes strewn across the chaise lounge in the master bedroom. The searchlight of the Spirit of God was moving rapidly through my heart and illuminating our messy abode.

First the Natural, then the Spiritual

As the flick rolled on, the Lord seemed to talk in front of it for dramatic effect. He chastened me for having more spiritual prowess than natural muscle when it came to our home. "You cannot do one well and leave the other undone," He chided. "The natural reflects the spiritual and the spiritual fortifies the natural. They are two sides of the same coin." Paul's insights in 1 Corinthians 15:46 came racing to me, " . . . the spiritual is not first, but the natural, and afterward the spiritual."

What I failed to understand is the relationship between the natural and the spiritual. The matriarchs in my family were the Marthas of their day; they felt strongly that "Cleanliness is next to godliness!" And they spent all their time on natural order—making sure that beds were made and floors mopped and dinner prepared. In a quiet defiance, I was not going to be the kitchen help, but the "one who sat at the feet of Jesus and listened to His words." I wanted to be like Mary who "desired the better portion, which can never be taken away from her" (Read Luke 10: 18–42). But, I lacked balance in my approach and perspective. Jesus, however, had come to visit our home and set me straight!

Operation Organized to the Glory of God!

That very day I arose from my wet spot in the carpet to put the plan the Lord had showed me into action. Every piece of clutter had to go! If it had no pertinent use or function to the Powell family, it was bagged up as trash or advertised in the local *Penny Saver.* Every article of clothing that had not been worn in three months was given to the Goodwill. The instruction from on high was to "streamline," "discard," and "downsize." I was to make space and room for our new houseguest: Organization & Discipline. Room by room I worked diligently "like a mad woman" to restore order to our home. The boys' rooms were atrocious! They were too small for such a big mess! So, I removed bulky dressers, painted dingy walls, threw away broken toys "in Jesus name!" and created workstations complete with desks and shelves. Storage bins for boxing shorts, socks and T-shirts rolled under beds with ease. Other clothes were color-coded by plastic hangers and hung in the closet. The anthem of our mission became: *Organized to the Glory of God!*

All summer I communicated the will of the Father to my family with great resolve. "Our lives are on the line," I constantly reminded them. "I didn't get my orders from B. Smith or Martha

Stewart! This is a command from Almighty God and we must obey!" Some days we'd all be panting and sweating with exhaustion and I'd say, "Just a little more to go before quitting time." No project was complete until everything was cleaned up and returned to its proper place. Bad habits died hard, but we pressed past summer and into fall with a great deal of our household in order. Our goal was to be ready to put *Operation Organized to the Glory of God* into full swing by the Wednesday after Labor Day to coincide with our youngest son's return to school. With a few bruised egos and a little over budget we made it! The Powell Family had completed Phase I of the Operation (the removal of clutter, painting throughout, and minor decorating). Phase II has to do with interior and exterior beautification and major decorating and Phase III remodeling and expansion of the existing premises.

Because we live in a small brick ranch in a rural setting, I thought I could laze about. "No one will visit and it's just us," I reasoned. When company was expected, we all knew it, because "all hands were on deck" in a marathon of frenzied preparations. We were feverishly dusting, vacuuming, running, dashing, tossing and stuffing—trying to do weeks of work in a few hours.

What a sad testimony this was for any Christian family, to live beneath their privileges of natural and spiritual order; to not organize their home for their own benefit and enjoyment. When the atmosphere of peace and orderliness is set—who knows the good and exciting things that can happen spontaneously? It brings me joy to see William and the boys playing four-way chess in the living room or the five of us engaged in a game of Taboo at the dining room table. Organization provides the enormous blessing of "simply being" and the unexplainable peace of enjoying our orderly home together!

Today I even dream of teenagers in my kitchen making breakfast at 1 A.M., rather than hanging out in the Wal-Mart parking lot. I foresee couples fellowshipping in my living room around a warm cozy fire discussing ways to strengthen their marriages. I anticipate tons of women (saved and unsaved, older and younger) seated at my dining room table on Tuesday mornings for a neighborhood Bible study and brunch. Our homes should be central places of love and learning, giving and sharing, teaching and admonishing; and it should be a place of natural order and spiritual refreshment.

Diversities of Gifts & Divisions of Labor

Well, let's get down to the basics of creating household organization. Some say, *"There's men's work, women's work, and children's work. Now everybody jump to it!"* But our lives are not this cut and dry! Our household work is really determined by the diversity of our gifts: *whoever has the time, interest and ability!* Families would do better to divvy up the labor of the household based on the skills and abilities of its membership. Who should wash dishes and maintain the family laundry? Who should rotate the tires on the cars and take out the trash? Who does the daily cooking and the deep cleaning? How does the lawn get cut and the trees pruned? Does Mom do everything and everyone else live free? Families work well together and accomplish more when *everyone* is willing to pull some aspect of the heavy load.

As we consider trying to work within our families with more creativity and efficiency, I'd like you to ponder on the following "out of the routine" questions of household responsibility. I call it the "Is it Possible and Can it Possibly Be Points to Ponder." Read them aloud and reflect on the current status of your family:

- If a forty-year-old man can set up and synchronize the stereo set and the VCR for surround sound, can he learn to prepare a simple meal in the stove or microwave?

- Can a preschooler set the table for breakfast and dinner?

- Can a twelve-year-old who created a fantastic science project fix the box of Hamburger Helper for dinner and make a side salad?

- If a man can learn to sort laundry and read clothing care labels, can a woman learn to take the car in for regular check-ups? (And should she? Doesn't it all depend on who has the time, inclination, and skills rather than on social pressure and expectation?)

- Can three teenage boys who can operate expensive three-wheelers and dirt bikes cut the grass, bag trimmings, edge the lawn and sweep the driveway and sidewalk?

- Is it right to say that when a man cleans out the refrigerator and washes the dishes that he's helping? But when a woman does the same, it's her job?

- Is it right to say when a woman takes out the trash, she's helping? But when a man takes out the trash, it's his job?

- Can boys and men learn to put the toilet seat down and toilet paper on the dispenser?

- Can women and girls put the cap back on the toothpaste and clean hair out the bathroom sink?

- Can a teenage daughter learn to fill up the tank after using the family car?

- Is it possible for adolescents and teens to care for their own clothes (including washing drying and putting them away) and not let items pile up on the floor?

- Can family members share living space in a peaceful and considerate manner?

- Can a woman allow her husband and kids to cook meals several times a week with a grateful heart? And not try to get them to do it differently than they are capable or compelled?

- Can a household operate without hearing the words, "How come I have to do it? I did it last time!" Can members of a family become a team and work in unity together to keep the household running smoothly?

- Can three growing boys, a traveling minister mother, rational-thinking father, and one 100-pound dog sit down once a month for a family planning meeting or brainstorming session?

If our families are going to become the organized Christian centers that we desire, all of us are going to have to learn to take some lessons from the business industry and make them applicable in our troubled and chaotic households. Terms like "delegation," "team-building" "down-sizing," "outsourcing," and "simplification" are workable in families just like in corporations. Let's see how!

The Family Manager

Popular author and motivational speaker Kathy Peel was the first woman I'd ever heard to use the savvy and succinct term, "family manager." "What do we call a person who runs one (or several) departments in any kind of organization? Who's responsible for getting the right people and the right things, with the right tools at the right time, to the right place, with the right attitude? We call that person a manager," Peel writes.[1] African-American professional organizer Cheryl R. Carter agrees. "[Our] homes should be managed like a business with [the wife and mom] operating as the Chief Executive Officer (CEO) of quality control," Carter says. "In fact, the home can arguably be considered the best managed business in the world today."[2]

In her book *The Family Manager*, Peel gives women tons of workable solutions to help them fine-tune their families and organize their households. Her creed is one that connects managing moms around the globe:

The Family Manager's Creed

I oversee a small organization—
Where hundreds of decisions are made daily,
Where property and resources are managed,
Where health and nutritional needs are determined,
Where finances and futures are discussed and debated,
Where projects are planned and events are arranged,
Where transportation and scheduling are critical,
Where team building is a priority,
Where careers begin and end.
I oversee a small organization—
I am a Family Manager.[3]

Following the advice of experts like Peel and Carter, helped me understand that not only was I the "hub" in the middle of the household, but I was the catalyst for corporate change. The organization of my home didn't require that I do it all, but rather that I managed it all well. So, I began to modify and utilize four managerial skills in household management:

- *Delegating* tasks to the appropriate person (like getting Jeremy to clean and organize the hall closet).

- *Motivating* the troops and building a strong family team to work cooperatively on various projects (Jordan and

Jeremy have such good research and computer skills that I can have them pull together our summer vacation plans on a Caribbean cruise liner via the Internet. They'll look at all of the sites and finally write up several options with dates, cost, and activities and I'll be thoroughly informed and able to talk to William intelligently about our findings).

- *Simplifying* our complicated and hectic lives through "living more with less" via the process of downsizing and streamlining (e.g. giving used clothes to the needy, rotating seasonal clothes to storage, disposing of old junky items that crowd closets and garage space).

- *Outsourcing* the family's needs or activities (e.g. ironing, yard work, sewing/mending, pet grooming, etc.) to others who could perform the task better than we could individually or collectively. When extra money is not available, bartering may be an option. I often save our family budget a good bit by bartering services for personal items like hair care. When we lived in New York, I wrote advertising copy and did radio commercial voice-overs for my hair salon owner in lieu of paying her hefty hair care prices. It was a tremendous trade-off that benefited my family and me.

Whether you are a full-time homemaker, career woman, or single mother, the management system of the household is probably 90 to 100 percent your responsibility. So learning to delegate, motivate, simplify, and outsource will be to your advantage.

Turning Disorganization into Diligence

When a family has been as disorganized as we were, a step-by-step process is necessary to help get the household turned around and into full operation again. By the time things are really "crazy" and out of order hubby and children will be ready for someone to help pull them up from the Pit of Untidy & Trifling Living. So, you'll want to call a formal family meeting and begin working on a centralized plan that everyone will help draft and abide by. Here are eight strategic steps to walk you out of frustration and despair and into household peace and order:

- STEP #1: Stop the madness! Be open and honest with the Lord about your weaknesses and shortcomings and receive His forgiveness. Then ask the Organizer of the Universe to impart His supernatural aid for the task at hand and receive His sovereign help.

- STEP #2: Clear the air! Encourage family members to "air their differences" and pinpoint their frustrations about the way the family has functioned. Openly dialogue about breakdowns in schedules and in the execution of tasks. But don't just dwell on the negative. Talk about the times, projects, and events that worked well—when everyone worked together. Include discussions on being a "valued member of a great team." Encourage everyone to share.

- Step #3: Make a list! Define the areas of your household where delegation, teamwork, simplifying and outsourcing could be improved or implemented. It might be helpful to put the entire household into departments like: Food, Finances, Upcoming Events, etc. Plan how each area will be addressed and handled in the future. Remember that many of these decisions are based on our "diversities of gifts."

- Step #4: Write out a few rules! "The Family Rules of Order" is based on your new covenant to work together to create a happy and peaceful home life. Our rules have been changed and modified over the years, as the boys have gotten older. As Kathy Peel said, "House Rules . . . [are] like having a standard operating procedure manual for your home . . . a corporation wouldn't just let employees start a new job without some guidelines and without knowing some basic company policies."[4] I wholeheartedly agree. We expect our family to work hard and give 100 percent, but no one is clear about the rules or the rewards of such diligence.

Powell Family Rules of Order

1. We all must abide by the rules; they apply to everyone, including Mom and Dad.

2. No strife and bickering—that includes name-calling and put-downs.

3. Everyone is responsible for his or her own words and actions.

4. When someone asks for forgiveness, we must release them by saying, "I forgive you" and extending a kind hand and a warm heart.

5. Respect each other's space and their stuff.

6. Everyone will work diligently to keep our home peaceful, orderly, and clutter-free.

7. No lies! We commit to always speak the truth in love.

8. No tattling or telling on each other out of spite and ill-will.

9. Always remember that hard work is our friend.

10. Be willing to sacrifice and go an extra mile to serve one another.

◆ STEP # 5: Schedule Family Planning Time! It's stimulating and refreshing when families block out periods of time to plan their direction and organize their lives. These kinds of sessions can be held monthly, quarterly, or annually. Meeting to brainstorm and consider everyone's schedule and responsibilities is very empowering for individual family members. Everyone's agenda is important and every "small piece fits into the bigger picture."

◆ STEP #6: Implement a Decluttering and Quick Cleaning Plan immediately! Outlined below are two home maintenance strategies that can help you create a sense of household peace and order from day to day. And it's super simple for domestically challenged family managers like me.

O'Clocking the Clutter

Even before we can implement a weekly cleaning plan for the family, each room has to go through a decluttering process that will make the transition from disorganization to order smoother. Cheryl R. Carter, author of *Put Your House in Order: A Practical Guide for Bringing Peace and Order to your Home* and founder of Organize Your Life!, is "a self-avowed recovering messie" who like many of us have now been converted to the glory of God! "I must give you the first law of household organization," she writes. "Keep it simple. Less is more. Most of us have acquired more junk, papers, and stuff than we can possibly use in a lifetime. It clutters our lives."[5] We've found that the best place to begin the decluttering process is with the room closest to the entrance door. This will provide lots of positive reinforcement when family members or visitors enter and notice the remarkable change. "You must clutter each room before you can clean or organize it," Carter says. "It is a chore even the organized must undertake periodically. Think of it as pruning a beautiful plant to make it grow more beautiful."[6]

In order to tackle the clutter more efficiently, Carter has coined the phrase "o'clocking a room." During this strategic process you began systematically circling a room like the hands of a time clock. "Start decluttering at the 12 o'clock position; work in a circle and continue around the room until you arrive back at the 12 o'clock again," Carter instructs.[7] This strategy will keep you from running back and forth from room to room "like a chicken with your head cut off." O'clocking keeps a family manager and the entire team focused, detailed, and determined to complete one room at a time.

During this one-room process, you clear out junk draws, clear off tables, and straighten up disheveled items as you move along. According to Carter, it's important to have three large bags with you as you o'clock a room:

- A Throw-Away Bag—for items going straight to the trash

- A Give-Away Bag—for items designated for public charity or as blessings to extended family

- A Put-Away Bag—for items that need to be returned to their proper place

We are warned by this management consultant to be ruthless! "Throw it away, give it away or put it away," Carter strongly emphasizes. "But don't let the clutter stay!"[8] The serious family manager must be diligent in her desire to create a clutter-free atmosphere where Christ and each family member would be pleased to dwell.

The Quick Clean Plan

Once we've learned to "o'clock the clutter" it becomes easier to implement a "quick clean method" into the family's home life. It's easier to do a chore or two a day rather than let tasks accumulate and become overwhelming. With full schedules and undisciplined lives many of us often clean on a "catch-as-catch-can" basis. But it's always a wise idea to make a plan to address household tasks on a regular schedule and not a sporadic one. Our ad hoc plan has been adopted from a few sources including family matriarchs (like my mother and aunts) whose homes are always tidy and orderly, and tried and true management experts like Peel and Carter that I've encountered along the way. It's easy to adopt and adapt a system for those of you—who, like me—would rather be "out and about" on a Saturday than stuck in the house cleaning all day. So you're welcome to keep the adoption process alive and well—tweaking it until it's workable and productive for you and your family.

Your family team will need to commit (at least) one and one-half hours a week to thorough and concentrated cleaning in order to make this plan work properly. Again, being faithful to a quick clean schedule on a weekly basis will help to alleviate cleaning up all day on the weekends when the family should be out doing something enjoyable together.

The quick clean plan should be performed on each room in your household once a week (or daily as needed). Assign each capable member a certain area of the house to "quick clean!" It's always a lot of fun to set the kitchen timer and have everyone working simultaneously. If that's not possible, it helps to make copies of the checklist for each person to date, check off and sign when completed. They should be left in a central place for the family manager to review. This kind of accountability ensures that everyone knows exactly what he or she is responsible for and encourages each person to complete the task well. In this way, household maintenance becomes an ongoing and "official duty" that cannot be shirked or performed with half a heart.

With this smooth system, all parents have to do is supervise the troops and periodically reward their tidy efforts! At other times, you may have to encourage them to address the "heavy duty" tasks that should be tackled periodically. But let's see if we can't get the family jump-started with a workable "quick clean" before we move into "deep clean" mode. Here's how our household management system works from week to week:

QUICK CLEAN LIVING AREAS:

* Remove clutter

* Toss or recycle magazines and newspapers (discard all junk mail and file bills and receipts)

* Empty wastebaskets

* Clean glass, mirrors, and tabletops

* Dust furniture, pictures, and lamps

* Vacuum carpet or damp-mop floor

QUICK CLEAN KITCHEN:

* Remove clutter from table and countertops

* Clean and reorganize inside of refrigerator

* Spray sink and countertops with disinfectant

* Shine outside of small and large appliances

* Wipe down kitchen walls

- Disinfect trash can, replace liner

- Sweep floor and mop

QUICK CLEAN BATHROOMS:

- Remove clutter

- Spray and wipe tub/shower/toilet with heavy duty cleaning solutions (wipe all surfaces)

- Clean mirrors

- Reorganize linen closets and/or medicine cabinets

- Clean sink and shine faucets and chrome

- Empty wastebasket and deodorize

- Sweep floor and damp-mop

QUICK CLEAN BEDROOMS:

- Remove clutter

- Reorganize closet by hanging clothes and putting shoes away

- Straighten dresser drawers and put accessories away

- Sort clothing piles for dry-cleaning and laundry

- Clean mirrors

- Dust furniture, pictures, and lamps

♦ Strip and remake bed linen

♦ Vacuum carpet, sweep or dust-mop floors

As I stated, there are also heavy duty and deep cleaning chores that should be performed on a biweekly, monthly, quarterly, and yearly basis that require more time and concentration than the everyday maintenance tasks. They are discussed in various home management resources and should be added to the maintenance plan as your family becomes more astute at o'clocking your clutter (daily) and quick cleaning your home on a weekly basis. Happy organizing!

Organized for a Family Crisis

When my father died suddenly of a heart attack last year, my entire world shifted. I found myself in Atlanta for weeks at a time fulfilling my duty as the eldest daughter. Dad not only handled all of the finances and legal matters of his own household (leaving Mom without a clue for getting things done); but he was also steward over my great Aunt Lil's banking and real estate affairs (she's nearly ninety-years-old and homebound). So, it became my responsibility to help my two widows put their lives in order and rebound after the shock of Dad's sudden passing.

The irony of it all was a bit humorous. I was helping my mother and great-aunt organize their households while managing my own from afar. This was a tall order for a woman who had just learned to pay bills on time, calculate taxes, grocery shop consistently, and quick clean her house on a weekly basis. The Lord must get a nice chuckle out of seeing us thrown into such contrary circumstances. Yet, His grace is always sufficient. And I always appreciate the exchange of my weakness for His tremendous strength.

When I got the call in late October that Dad had passed away, I flew to Atlanta the very same day. But my house needed only a light sprucing, because of the fierce organization we had accomplished in early September. I was gone for seventeen days straight! William, the boys, and I returned home after the funeral and memorial services to have a quiet Thanksgiving and catch up on some needed rest. I took this time to reorganize my household before returning to Atlanta for an additional two weeks to address pressing business and legal matters. As the daily schedule was outlined (from food menus and clothing care to lawn maintenance and sports activities), I could only give thanks to the Everlasting Father! He had sufficiently prepared and exercised our family "for such a time as this!" Just as my friend Judy had prophesied six months prior, "we won't have time to get organized—we're going to have to be organized." And organized we were—to the glory of God!

Peace At Home . . . A Wonderful Change

Once we bring our homes under the subjection of Christ, we will find our hearts energetic and excited about life! There is some kind of connection between our homes and our hearts. You'll see it more clearly when all things are in their place, and a quiet feeling of order abides on your humble abode. Learning to die to old habits may take some time and lots of effort but it is worth it! When there is peace at home, you'll feel like you can go out and conquer the world for Christ!

PART FOUR

Our Cultural Heritage and Extended Relationships

Country Ribs and Revival at the Old Landmark

Young people just don't think serving God is important today," my eighty-year-old Uncle Richard exclaimed with a sad demeanor. "When we was growing up, everybody went to church and learned the lessons taught in the Holy Bible," he preached on with strong conviction. "We lived by that Book and learned to treat everybody right!" As we stood against the old farm fence where he farms tobacco and raises cattle, Uncle Richard talked passionately about the way things "use ta be." Thoughts of yesteryear must have pressed heavily on his mind that fall morning, because he talked of the past almost instantly as we greeted each other on our way to different chores. Nevertheless, his sense of nostalgia enraptured me, and I gave him my full attention—throwing in a polite "Yes, sir," and an occasional "That's right," as he reminisced.

"Back in the day, we always honored our parents and had respect for folks—whether it was our teachers, preachers, or anybody else," he continued with a strong voice. "The older people taught us to be respectful and stay humble—so we could be wise."

Uncle Richard's jetlike journey down memory lane was so juxtaposed to the present. As he compared and contrasted yesteryear with modern times, we both grew solemn and a bit downcast. "Today, young people act like they know everything and that life is gonna always be on their side," he said with the conviction of a church deacon. "They don't realize that we all have to meet our Maker one of these ole days. I try to tell 'em, but when they don't listen, I just pray for 'em. But Lord knows, I sho' miss the way things use ta be!" he said resolutely with a big sigh.

Ever since I can remember, the elders in our family have talked of "going back to the old landmark." As they recalled the past, many times their eyes would water, and they'd hum an old spiritual and rock awhile. Until this writing, I've always been left with a feeling of impossibility when I considered the concept of the old landmark. Such a place seemed inconceivable and so far removed. How could we ever find our way? Was it really possible to "go back"?

Doing the Sankofa!

Yes, connecting the past to the present is possible! And the riches and the treasures of the past can be rediscovered. We learn this truth from the flourishing coastal communities of West Africa. We have been given the valuable wisdom of the term *Sankofa,* which means to "go back and fetch that which was lost and move forward with it." There is a certain power in remembering former times and being fortified by their lessons in order to walk boldly into a new day. The wisdom of Sankofa is just one of the enduring symbols and philosophical concepts of the highly valued Adinkra, a hand-printed, hand-embroidered cloth designed by the Akan people of Ghana. There are more than five hundred design motifs in the repertoire, and several symbols are often combined to communicate complicated ideas and expressions. Sankofa is just one of the meaningful transcontinental traditions and experiences that unite Africa with its people of African descent in the Americas.

As African-Americans, we must boldly declare that we are "Africa's New World Children." Our ancestral lineage flows back to the continent of Africa, with its many ethnicities and tongues, and extends throughout the Diaspora. As a people, we have a derivation, a place of origin, a native homeland! Our roots stretch across the Atlantic Ocean, down into the Caribbean, and around the Seven Seas. These "ties that bind" can never be disclaimed or ignored. Everything about us—our internal makeup and external design—sings the melodies of African styles and influences. Our heritage must be reclaimed and forever settled in our hearts. Learning to do the Sankofa is described in African-American circles as "going back to the old landmark." Yet it's only possible to make this journey when we all understand what the old landmark really is and how we can recapture its timeless value in a modern era.

Defining the Old Landmark

Whenever we hear the term "old landmark" sung in a gospel song or hear its pleasing refrain in a Black history lecture, what are we really talking about? Is it descriptive of historic nostalgia and our return to a certain point in time? What is it that former generations possessed that we must "go back and fetch" or Sankofa? Honestly, the old landmark is one of those terms that begs for a clear, concise definition as we cascade through a new century. The surest place to garner an understanding is in the inspired Word of God, for within the pages of their tattered and torn King James Bibles the elders first understood and applied this important wisdom.

Like our forebears, you and I must open the Word of God and follow the advice of Job (8:8–10 NIV):

*"Ask the former generations and find out
what their fathers learned,
for we were born only yesterday and know nothing,
and our days on earth are but a shadow.
Will they not instruct you and tell you?
Will they not bring forth words from their understanding?"*

If we are going to recapture the power of the old landmark in a new millennium, we must follow the trails of our forebears and trace their steps back to former times. There must be a willingness on our part to receive their wisdom and instruction on how to revive our spiritual hunger and restore every major area of our lives. With all that has happened socially, economically, and religiously to the African-American family, we cannot wholly rely on contemporary solutions and directions. There must be a renewed reliance upon that solid and enduring foundation of faith that served our ancestors well, as they maintained an intimate relationship with God and a strong commitment to family.

"Do not remove the ancient landmark which your fathers have set." These words flow out of the Hebrew wisdom recorded in Proverbs 22:28. This verse specifically addresses the posting of stones to mark the boundaries of property or real estate; however, its larger meaning centers on public trust, justice, and the preservation of inheritance. Established landmarks determined how things would be done, recognized, and agreed upon by all members of a given group. They were *stones of faith* that clearly indicated how folks would work out civic issues and show respect for the property of others before an all-seeing, all-knowing God.

Although new generations would arise and eventually occupy the land, the markings and boundaries of life in the community were still to be honored and upheld. No changes allowed! Once a historic marking was established for how to do business, sell goods, or harvest crops, no young blood or newcomer could emerge and carelessly alter things. A *physical* landmark could not be transgressed or dismissed—not even by time or death. To do so was a grave violation.

The same holds true for *spiritual* landmarks of faith. God told His people in Hosea 5:10 that "the princes of Judah are like those who remove a landmark; I will pour out my wrath on them like water." God had erected mental markings, or spiritual boundaries, around His chosen people. His Holy Word was to be their landmark of conviction that helped them to discern right from wrong. The landmarks of His laws and commandments were established as guideposts to keep Israel on the straight and narrow way. When the ruling officials toyed with these boundaries, God was angered because His people were put in spiritual jeopardy and had become confused about His standards of holiness. They no longer knew how to conduct themselves in foreign lands.

Our African-American ancestors must have understood this, because they strived to maintain the ancient landmarks of righteousness, justice, and truth. These godly men and women strictly followed the Judeo-Christian markings that had been handed down through the years. These landmarks kept them on a safe and straight path. The landmarks caused them to cling to the Lord with fervency and self-abandonment. They learned to wait upon God and not lose heart. I can testify to this as I observed the elders in my own family.

My grandmother, Carmeta Ferguson White, was a God-fearing woman. She had a petite and delicate outward frame but strong intestinal fortitude. Everyone called her "Mama Carmeta" and respected her quiet confidence in God. Through her Christian experience, she learned to pray earnestly to the Lord and to quiet and comfort herself in His presence. When I was young, I often found my grandmother on her knees in dedicated prayer (just after making up her bed each morning). Her petitions were never spoken.

With face and hands bowed into the chenille spread, she tarried at her bedside for what seemed like hours. I'd often return repeatedly, peering in on her hallowed communiqué with the Lord. She was always in the same position—yielded and still, without an audible moan or groan, and no visible display of tears or doubt.

At other times, when I knew she was grappling with some area of pain or hardship (like the time her face and hands experienced second- and third-degree burns cooking at the school cafeteria where she worked), she'd simply sit quietly in a chair, eyes closed, rocking gently while humming a sweet serenade to Jesus. Her hands would move ever so slightly in unison to the beat. Mama Carmeta would remain in that place until the physical pain or inner storm subsided and her peace returned.

My grandmother's humbled posture is imprinted in my memory as a portrait of a faith-filled and consecrated woman. Recently, when I was thrown into an intense spiritual battle, I could literally feel my heart rolling back the scroll of time . . . taking me on a Sankofa journey . . . helping me to remember my grandmother's posture in similar moments of peril. Suddenly, I ceased fretting, quieted myself, and took on her spiritual instruction. The inner sanctuary of my heart opened up to the Lord, and I found myself rocking gently and humming softly to Jesus in the sweetest voice of faith I could muster. I was transported back to a familiar landmark of quietness that Grandma Carmeta had erected for me. There I found strength and solace. There I regained my spiritual bearings to move forth with confidence in God my Savior.

The *old landmark* represents the tried-and-true precepts of God's ways and His commands; it's a spiritual place of peace, power, and provision. As you discern the *old landmarks* erected by the elders of your family, you'll gain more spiritual direction and rediscover what our ancestors learned—*the old paths lead to a good way*. They never abandoned course; rather, they hungered for total deliverance.

A Determined Deliverance

As our ancestors clung to the ancient landmark of the Holy Writ and kept close to the old paths, I believe they forged covenants with the Lord to praise and worship Him regardless of all hardship and struggle. Our enslaved foreparents never accepted the view that God ordained their enslavement, nor that He had relegated us to a position of second-class citizenship. They were wise enough to recognize that God is an emancipator. He is the God of liberation. So they sang songs like "Didn't My God Deliver Daniel?" and "Why Not Us?" and "Let My People Go."

When Israel was in Egypt's Land, Let my people go;
Oppressed so hard they could not stand, Let my people go.
Go down, Moses, Way down in Egypt land
Tell ole Pharaoh, Let my people go!

The liberating influence of the Holy Bible soon enveloped our ancestors and soothed their anguished souls. They saw Egypt as the slavery plantation, Pharaoh as the white slave-owners, and Moses as a soon-coming deliverer who would rise up as God's mouthpiece and change agent.

As time passed and new generations were born, an even more aggressive stance was taken in singing spirituals like "Oh, Freedom" "Oh, freedom! Oh, freedom! Oh, freedom over me! An' befo' I'd be slave, I'll be buried in my grave, An' go home to my Lord an' be free."

With every ounce of faith they could muster, these chatteled human beings believed that God Almighty would hear their despairing cry, just as He had heard the ancient Israelites. They held strong that eventually He would part a similar "Red Sea" for their progeny to cross on dry ground. We are the offspring of the generations for which they fought, bled, cried, and labored in prayer. They died believing . . . envisioning a better life for us!

In his book *Free at Last? The Gospel in the African-American Experience*, author and theologian Carl Ellis provides a comparative analysis of the nation of Israel to African-Americans:

> *For four hundred years they had been oppressed. Their sense of history and destiny was all but wiped out. Their consciousness was blurred and distorted, their culture polluted with false values. Their knowledge of the one true God had been outgunned by a proliferation of man-made gods. Their sense of dignity had been overwhelmed by feelings of inferiority, feelings which came from the dehumanization inflicted by a racist society. The people felt forsaken by God. Yet God remained faithful. . . . .In fact, He was already implementing His eternal plan of salvation. In ten demonstrations of judgment, God broke the back of a king who used his technology to maintain a brutal system of slavery. God thus brought His people out of Egypt so that they might become a light to the nations. A goal . . . not [to] be achieved overnight. The people had to be prepared slowly through de-Egyptianization as they journeyed through the wilderness. God began to restore their culture, raising it to new heights through Moses and the law . . . A survey of Black history reveals that, like the children of Israel, we have had a four-hundred-year collective trauma from which we have yet to fully recover.[1]*

Consider for a moment the far-reaching effects of their faith. Almighty God has provided miraculous wonders for the African-American family down through the years. Despite modern changes, the African-American family is an open display of sheer wonder. As a people, we have persevered through the degradation of slavery, the drudgery of sharecropping, the despair of second-class citizenship, and the divisiveness of systemic racism. Despite these historical hardships, we entered the new millennium as *overcomers*.

But there is a distinct sound being lifted from the "great cloud of witnesses" (our grandfathers and mothers, great-aunts and uncles, mothers and fathers, godparents and in-laws, principals and school teachers, and countless others) who watch from the ramparts of heaven (Hebrews 12:1). They applaud our social progress, business achievements, political savvy, and economic developments; but they are saddened that too many have forgotten the "old paths" and lost their way in the long march toward Canaan, the land of promise. They seem to be saying, "Indeed, Jericho was a victory. Thank God that political walls have come falling down, but continue to set your eyes upon Canaan—the land that flows with milk and honey!" They are cheering us toward the spiritual nourishment that only Jesus Christ can provide. And they are hoping that we will not settle prematurely for natural goods and services and forfeit our rights to true (spiritual) riches. The words penned by James Weldon Johnson in our Negro National Anthem accurately express this sentiment: "Lest our hearts, drunk with the wine of the world, we forget Thee."

We can hasten the day of discovery by reviewing the plight of the African-American family in light of our great accomplishments and many strides! As we move closer to the "promised land" that Dr. Martin Luther King Jr. and others prophesied about, we can celebrate our awesome survival, while looking steadfastly at our family profile and future purpose.

The African-American Family: Preserved for a Purpose

Because of our proven ability to endure, the African-American family in Christ is uniquely poised with spiritual purpose and destiny. We are witnesses to the world and can speak boldly to the truth of how we made it over! Our historic pilgrimage clearly unleashes the power of perseverance. Yet there is one question that must be asked, "Why has God chosen to preserve us?" The African-American family in Christ has been preserved that we might bring forth the praises of Him who brought us out of darkness and into the marvelous light! We are to continually proclaim His goodness to the nations (and to other family groups both near and far). As we learned to "call on the name of the Lord" in our struggle for human dignity, the great God Almighty openly revealed Himself to us, just as He did to Moses in the cleft of the rock. Through everything (both bitter and sweet), we have become acquainted with Him through personal relationship and have found His nature to be good, loving, caring, gracious, and forgiving (see Exodus 34:5–7).

Recently, as I was praying for the African-American family, the Lord led me to study the Abrahamic covenant with a new pair of eyes. Turning to Genesis 12:1, I began to read about how God called Abram (whose name would later be changed to Abraham) out of Ur of the Chaldeans. The Lord was specific in telling Abram to leave his existing country, extended family, and the immediate members of his father's house. God promised to take him to a new land and there create a great nation through him. Furthermore, the Lord told Abram emphatically that He would bless him, cause his name to be great, and make him a blessing to others. God openly declared that He would bless those who blessed Abram and would curse those who cursed Abram. This was a covenant that no man in his right mind could refuse!

Then, as I read the Lord's final pronouncement over Abram I gasped, because the words literally danced on the page, "and in you all the families of the earth shall be blessed" (verse 3). I thought, *All the families of the earth? Does this include the African-American family, with our many heartaches and life pains? Yes, it does!* I had never seen this before. The African-American family in Christ could not be left out—literally, no family could be! This was a promise to "all the families of the earth" that believed in the God of Abraham, Isaac, and Jacob and accepted the lordship of Jesus Christ! I leaped all over the room praising the Lord for sustaining the African-American family through a never-failing promise of biblical blessing.

We are blessed by the covenant of promise and preservation that God decreed to Father Abraham. God took a people whom others despised and rejected, and He empowered us by His Holy Spirit to win against all odds! Now, in a twenty-first-century culture (where human effort wars against biblical truth), we must lift up the One who determined our deliverance and showed Himself strong on our behalf! As believers, we can confidently declare that the Sovereign Lord has unveiled His glory to the African-American family in Christ—and because of this, we worship Him in spirit and truth! Our "sphere of influence" must be enlarged to encompass those who need to be redeemed by the Lord our Savior. We have been preserved to boldly proclaim the saving power of Jesus Christ throughout the earth!

Departure from the Old Landmark

When we depart from the old landmark of faith, we begin a quest for identity and dignity outside of what God has written in His Word. The basis for human identity and dignity is outlined in the Holy Scriptures: "So God created man in his own image, in the image of God created he him; male and female created he them" (Genesis 1:27 KJV). Our identity and dignity is directly related to God the Father. We are somebody because God is Somebody! His image and likeness reflect beautifully through us as we yield to Christ.

The late Tom Skinner understood this quest well. He was a renowned evangelist and apostle to the African-American community. Tom, who grew up impoverished in the slums of Harlem, once led a gang called the Harlem Lords. He spent his formative years looting, rioting, and stealing. In his book *How Black Is the Gospel?* Tom sheds light on the relevance of Christianity in the midst of the African-American's quest for identity and dignity. "Those of us in Harlem knew we were black long before people came along advocating, 'Black Is Beautiful,' 'Black Power' and all the rest. . . . But I soon discovered that merely knowing I was black, even though I was convinced that black is beautiful, and all the rest, still did not help me discover altogether who I was."[2]

Tom was able to discover his true identity and grasp real dignity only after he met the Lord Jesus Christ. He echoes this in his own written testimony, "I have not had to negate my blackness in order to become a Christian; but rather, now that I am committed to Christ, it is God's desire to live His life through my 'redeemed blackness.' I'm God's son; I'm a member of the royal family of God . . . which means that I can now go out and face the world with a completely different attitude. Black is beautiful, but a lot more than that, a lot more beautiful, since Jesus Christ is living through it, and one of the things I have discovered is that Jesus looks great in black."[3]

I can remember listening to Tom speak numerous times while I was matriculating at Clark College in the late seventies and early eighties. He often talked of the security that came into his life when God began living in him as a black man. As a remarkable communicator of the Gospel, Tom always spoke passionately to our young, impressionable minds about our culture and its connection to our newly found faith in Christ. More than any other person, he enlarged my views that the Gospel had the tremendous ability to invade any culture with its life-changing truths and then empower that culture (without annihilating it) through the dignifying presence of the kingdom of God. I have never forgotten the things I learned from this awesome man of God.

Clearly, Tom understood that his security came from a personal relationship with the true and living God. A true relationship with God is the only thing that will unveil and fortify the essence of our personal identity and dignity—both individually and as a people. Our very lives are secure in the person of Jesus Christ. As Jesus Himself testified in John 17:3 (NIV) as He communed with the Father, "Now this is eternal life: that they may know you, the only true God, and Jesus Christ, whom you have sent." All emancipation and liberation (both now and forever) is ours in Jesus' name! Our history (past) and our quest (future) are secure in Christ alone.

Lest We Forget Thee

In Job 8:11–14 (NIV), we are given a word picture of what happens to those who forget God and depart from the *old landmark*. Initially, they wither and dry up because they have failed to drink from the living water that nourishes the soul. Before long, they become godless and are soon wiped from the face of the earth. This is because they chose not to rely on the true and living God but on something similar to a spider's web. Truly, there is a great penalty in forgetting God. Listen to this wisdom:

> *"Can papyrus grow tall where there is no marsh?*
> *Can reeds thrive without water?*
> *While still growing and uncut,*
> *they wither more quickly than grass.*
> *Such is the destiny of all who forget God;*
> *so perishes the hope of the godless.*
> *What he trusts in is fragile;*
> *what he relies on is a spider's web."*

In *Free at Last?* Ellis pulls readers into a humorous but pensive discourse about our belief in God. His quintessential pulpiteering style is thought provoking:

> *Moses must have been somewhat startled when God revealed his name as "I AM" (Exodus 3:14). God was saying that his existence is the most obvious and fundamental thing in human experience. There can be no IS without God's IS; and since IS is, God is, because God is IS. God here introduces himself as the very bedrock of all existence. Since all people experience existence*

itself, then all people automatically experience God's existence.[4]

Here, Ellis requires us to look down the long corridor of time to examine God's eternal vitae. He challenges the heart and mind of contemporary Christians in light of God's awesome acts of self-disclosure and revelation.

Even though we live in the age of information and can download almost anything at our fingertips from a personal computer, that doesn't mean that we've gotten too sophisticated for the basis of our existence. If we have evolved so brilliantly to believe that God is now reduced to a Higher Power who operates at our beck and call—or even worse, that He is a figment of our imagination born out of our stress and struggle—then we are in deep trouble. As Paul wrote in Hebrews 11:6:

Without faith it is impossible to please Him, for he who comes to God must believe that He is, and that He is a rewarder of those who diligently seek Him.

This is no time to forsake the true and living God who has revealed Himself in the Holy Scriptures and through African-American history. Of all people groups, we cannot afford to embrace contemporary debates on the existence of God, because simply, God *is!* This knowledge begins our quest to know God intimately and to appreciate our extended family.

13

Extended-Family Feasts

In the 1997 movie *Soul Food,* Sunday dinner at Big Mama's house brought familiar memories and mouthwatering grins to millions of African-American moviegoers. When the traditional menu of fried chicken and fish, collard greens, corn bread, potato salad, fried corn, sweet potato pie, and ice-cold tea flashed across the big screen, all of our five senses went into "slaphappy" motion.

Similar to the blockbuster flick, my recollections of Southern cooking always stir a feeling of wholeness and satisfaction deep within my soul. Even now, my mind's computer is uploading the scrumptious smells and tastes that defined my growing years. I can personally recall the lip-smacking, finger-licking delicacies that were prepared in our family's small, hot kitchen. Tasty items like Momma's cabbage greens, Uncle Ed's smoked turkey, Aunt Evelyn's sweet sausage dressing, Uncle Charlie's crab shallah,

Grandma Gladys's conch fritters, Aunt Irene's pigeon peas and rice, and Grandma White's jelly cake all make me "wanna holla." With a well-bred mixture of South Georgia country, Carolina Creole (aka geechee), Floridian coastal, and Bahamian Island spice, I thrived in the bountiful feasts prepared by extended family members—all full of eclectic cuisine.

Childhood Reflections

Indeed, every generation looks back with a special fondness on certain aspects of its childhood. Whether the setting was rural or urban, favorite memories are forever etched in the crevices of our minds. Most often, there are memories of special feasts like the Friday Night Fish Fry (casually held at Grandma Gladys's home) or the Soon-as-Church-Is-Over Dinner (hosted regularly at Grandma White's).

Warm recollections provide a sturdy path upon which we all can move forward. Truly, our past is a powerful part of who we are! Even now I can hear the continuous ringing of the doorbell, "O Happy Day" blaring in the background, and the cacophony of conversation filling our tiny living room like a marching band. In quiet moments, I remember and sometimes even laugh out loud.

From a child's perspective, there is nothing like extended family time—with smiling relatives piling in from across town and distant places, whirling casually from room to room. Everyone appears jam-packed, like sardines, and feeding feverishly off one another's energy. During these occasions, adults are less tense and parents more liberal. A quintessential joy and casualness fills the atmosphere. Tall bodies appear to have been snatched into another world of entertainment and adult conversation.

As a youngster, I remember these times vividly. There always seemed to be a deep sense of satisfaction in the air when my entire family was present. Even if there was a disagreement between

Mr. Jimmy and Miss Ocala (two of my parents' friends who always got into an argument), it seemed all right because we were all together.

During family feasts, my cousins and I got to do the forbidden things like jumping on the bed, telling scary stories with the lights off, and returning to the loaded buffet table to eat more than our stomachs could hold. We felt wonderfully mischievous as we whizzed through muttering crowds in perfect wonder and child's play. In the lateness of the hours, relatives and other adults were always more agreeable to whatever was asked. So cousins or best friends would even get to spend the night—a culminating height of extended family time! We'd wear oversized T-shirts to bed, play favorite board games with a flashlight, and giggle until the wee hours of the morning.

My memories of family gatherings are exhilarating; there's nothing quite comparable! Even today, recollections of extended family times are what inspire me to plan such occasions for the benefit of my own children. I want my sons to be able to lock away familiar fragrances, favorite delicacies, repeated songs, and hilarious playtimes—just like I did!

Committed to Family

Many African-American families still gather once a week for family meals of some sort. These are important times for keeping the extended family connected around plenty of food, lots of conversation, and loads of personal exchange. Even in the most divided family, a special occasion like a wedding, funeral, graduation, or baby christening brings out the faithfulness in everyone. No matter how much the new clothes, rented tuxedos, hotel rooms, or travel arrangements cost, everyone is willing (though with some complaint) to spend the cash or swipe the credit cards. Such sacrifices must be made, and everybody in the family knows it!

Then there are the more regular events like birthday parties, anniversary dinners, and family reunions. These special events bring aunts and uncles out of the woodwork and produce a slew of cousins whom no one is quite sure about. It's fun to see the family tree in full bloom and extending its branches "every-which-a-way." We've even heard of more than a few cases where third or fourth cousins, who were romantically inclined, discovered that they were related to one another during a family gathering! It's vitally important that we come together from time to time to learn about our lineage and linkage one to another.

Finally, the holidays create a spirit of celebration that also makes family members put aside their many differences. Everyone seems a little kinder and gentler as Thanksgiving, Christmas, and Kwanza finalize the year. When Resurrection Sunday (Easter), the Fourth of July, and Labor Day roll around, family members often call around to ask, "Anybody having anything?" There is an insatiable need to *just be together* and relish the company of those whom you know and love. All of this is done despite maddening activities like food preparation, furniture rearrangement, kitchen cleanup, and other late-night duties to return the house to normal.

These gatherings mark the growth and expansion of the extended family unit and offer opportunities for young and old, talkative and quiet, to spend quality time together. The extended family feast is still one of the African-American community's greatest assets—despite notions of dysfunction and disintegration. When we commit to this gathering time, the family is deeply strengthened and enlarged.

Family Times: Special Events

Family gatherings are like huge, unwrapped presents full of surprise and anticipation. On one hand, you never know what good news or great stories will be shared to enhance your life and understanding of the world! On the other hand, you always have to brace yourself for the resurfacing of past issues and exploding emotions—they simply come with the territory! Now that I'm an adult, I still feel that family gatherings are special events. We should plan big annual family reunions and not forsake small weekly get-togethers that include every age group. We should revive special times like Sunday dinners, Friday fish fries, Saturday picnics in the park, and backyard barbecues. Our homes should resonate with the happy sounds of extended family, close friends, and other adoptees that would benefit from an atmosphere brimming with such activity. During these times, we get to solve the world's problems, analyze the social issues of the day, make important plans for the future, and generally put in our two cents on the latest fad, flick, or figure in the news. You'll have to admit—you never come home quite the same after spending an afternoon or evening in the presence of your own family group. These times fortify something deep and unseen in the family—both immediate and far-reaching. I am convinced that a strong sense of personal belonging and self-identify is being fashioned and formed as we eat, talk, play, laugh, and even fuss together. Families that meet on a regular basis are making a huge investment in themselves, from elder to younger. In this atmosphere, two struggling groups are greatly enhanced. Elders are given opportunities to pass on wisdom and instruction while feeling needed and connected; and teens are encouraged to thrive and excel, while feeling supported and strengthened. We must have extended-family time!

Gathering Without Gaps

Historically, African-Americans have been blessed by a cross-generational family system where every member is esteemed, respected, and supported—no matter his or her *stage* in life. This tradition must continue into the new millennium, because generational gaps are a hindrance to goals of family unity and closeness.

I learned this from my friend Karla while my family was living in upstate New York. We were new transplants to town, so she always invited us over to family events she was hosting. I was particularly amazed to see her interaction with her teenage nieces. They'd hug her tight, sit on her lap, tell her all their love secrets, and welcome her intimate involvement in their lives. No gap existed and the door was wide open for the wisdom of one generation to flow easily into an emerging one. My desire for family times, minus the generational gaps, was forever sealed by her living example!

Families—across generations—should commit to being in one another's presence on a continual basis. We need to draw strength and courage from the family in which we were born. The good, bad, and ugly are realities of living in a fallen world. But such issues can be worked out and made better if we just stick together with tough love. If we are honest, every one of us is enriched and enlarged through self-sacrifice and being joined to others.

Maintaining Strong Family Ties

After the September 11 attacks on our country in 2001, many Americans became more sensitive and aware of the importance of maintaining strong family ties. In 9/11's aftermath, family members across the nation called to check on the well-being of relatives wherever they were and to reaffirm their love and care. The experience has shown that even if families fail us in some way, they're still the greatest influence in our lives. Lovers, children, friends, or even coworkers cannot replace severed family ties. A part of our soul and spirit is buried when family systems are not active and vibrant in our lives.

Psalm 68:6 affirms that "God sets the solitary in families; He brings out those who are bound into prosperity; but the rebellious dwell in a dry land." This is no time for "dissing" family and trying to make it alone. The Lord our God designed the family unit for the purpose of strength and personal development. It is within the midst of family imperfections that we are fashioned into better people. Our alcoholic uncle, fresh cousin, nosy aunt, hardheaded nephew, drug-addicted sister-in-law, and hot-to-trot niece all need us in their lives! Remember, God is the One who sets us in the family of His choosing. It's not a guessing game or an issue of misplaced identity. These folks are our relatives—no matter how they look, dress, talk, whine, or carry on in a crowd. The Word of God confirms that a solitary life is not the fullness of life. If we refuse and rebel against "familiness," we will literally "dwell in a dry land." We desperately need the waters of relationship that flow plentifully out of the family irrigation system.

Overall, it's really our active participation in family life that produces *true* celebration and personal wealth. We must not rebel against what God has ordained for our personal and spiritual development—the family organism is alive and well. It is an institution of God's own design!

Transforming a Family Feud

No one was born into a perfect family! As we live and grow together, issues will arise that shatter existing peace and darken happy days. All of a sudden, the family finds itself trying cautiously to cope with a feud that's as old as Methuselah or thrust headlong in the throes of a serious offense. The breach may exist between adult siblings, elderly relatives, snapping spouses, or "kissing" cousins; but somehow it infects the entire family system like poison.

As Christians, the Holy Scriptures minister to us a tremendous promise, "Great peace have they which love thy law: and nothing shall offend them" (Psalm 119:165 KJV). An offense is anything that causes us to stumble in our walk with God by casting a weight on our spirit and bringing trouble to our mind. It breaks our spiritual equilibrium, throws us off-kilter, and skews our perspective to the negative side of life. Yet here the psalmist gives us the key to living a peaceful life free of offense. It is parallel to what has been defined by our Savior as the greatest of all commandments: To love the Lord with all our heart and to love our neighbor (especially our family) as ourselves (Mark 12:28–31; Luke 10:27). This is whole law of God! We can walk in great peace when our hearts are insulated by these two great commandments.

Once we begin walking in covenant peace, God can use us to heal broken relationships, arrest a family feud, or minister the truths of offense to others. In countless cases, many feuds and offenses have long since passed, and only the vague and lingering stench of resentment clouds the atmosphere. And the internal situation is often pitched between two people or factions. We can become mediators of reconciliation within our family system by serving as a compassionate counselor or spiritual go-between. If you desire to stand in the gap and provide a Christian presence and some godly wisdom in this atmosphere, here are some steps you can take:

REFUSE TO BE TIMID AND WAIT. If your family is in the midst of a trial, begin working toward restoration immediately.

CHOOSE A NEUTRAL BUT COMFORTABLE PLACE TO MEET, SUCH AS YOUR HOME. Avoid public places like parks or restaurants where it's easy to create a dramatic scene or where one or both parties can easily walk away.

SET THE ATMOSPHERE FOR A PEACEFUL EXCHANGE. Say a brief prayer or read an appropriate Scripture or poetry piece to establish a positive setting.

SHARE HAPPIER DAYS AND MOMENTS. Remind both parties of a time when things were positive. Briefly take them down memory lane to whet their appetites for former days.

GET RIGHT TO THE POINT. Open up by reviewing the objectives of reconciliation and everyone's desire for mutual understanding and restored fellowship. Set a time limit of one hour for the exchange to help relieve the strain of the unknown. This will automatically relax both parties.

RESIST PLAYING FAVORITES OR TAKING SIDES. A good way to do this is to be transparent and simply say, "I am not here to take sides but to mediate a long overdue reconciliation between two people I love very much." Allow neither side to question your position of neutrality in the matter.

ESTABLISH A FEW CONSIDERATE "TALKING" RULES. Make sure that each side gets an opportunity to share viewpoints without interruption. Agree to conduct this time of reconciliation in a God-honoring and respectful manner.

ASK EACH SIDE TO REVIEW HOW THE CONFLICT BEGAN. Each side should be given the time needed to express his or her viewpoint without feeling rushed or intimidated.

REPHRASE THE INITIAL CONFLICT AND DISAGREEMENT. If the disagreement no longer makes sense, rephrasing can shed lots of light. For example, "Are you saying that at Christmas dinner seven years ago, she jokingly told everybody she walked in on Uncle Jim in the bathroom and you've been angry ever since?"

ASK EACH TO CONSIDER THE OTHER'S VIEWPOINT. Ask both to restate the other person's position in their own words. This becomes much easier to do once the dialogue is flowing and all of the initial quarreling has toned down. Then ask if they are willing to reconcile after having gained a better understanding of the situation.

HELP THEM LOOK AHEAD AND NOT BEHIND. Remind family members of the lateness of the hour. Life is short and tomorrow is not promised.

REVIEW SCRIPTURES ON FORGIVENESS AS A CLOSING POINT. Encourage both sides to seek reconciliation through the passport of forgiveness. Keep them in remembrance of God's words on forgiving others. Close in prayer despite the final outcome. If reconciliation was achieved (or at least begun), bless the Lord! If more work is required, thank God for the beginning of this reconciled relationship. Leave the time on a positive note. Sometimes relatives leave the formal setting without making amends but are drawn together in an informal atmosphere at another time. Restoration takes place naturally in this setting because the ground of their hearts was made open and pliable. So expect miraculous things to happen, even if they don't happen right away.

Once we have put feuding and offending behind us, we can joyfully enter times of greater fellowship together as an extended family unit. There are so many fun and exciting ways to come together for "family time."

Creative Ways to Be Together

We can add twenty-first-century flair to our family times and concentrate on developing new ways to have clean and contagious fun! Extended family times can center on:

PRAYING TOGETHER. Prayer is the proverbial glue that holds all-important elements together, and the extended family is no exception. Recently, lots of my family members, close friends, and church members were gathered at my parents' home following a funeral. We had cried much, hugged unceasingly, and eaten plenty when a call came in that one of my nephews had been involved in an accident. Before the phone hit the receiver, the room exploded in thunderous prayer! Not one person left the room, moved in hasty fear, or attempted to investigate the matter in the natural. With one accord, we simply bombarded heaven and took spiritual authority over his health and safety in intercessory prayer. It was so powerful and electrifying! I'd never experienced anything quite like it. We prayed with such faith and fervency that before the hour was up, little Charles came bouncing into the room with a bandaged hand (administered by the paramedics) and an angelic smile on his face. Being in one place with one accord had made a miraculous difference. A family that prays together can move heaven and earth and change the course of any circumstance. Some powerful ways to pray together would be to:

- Erect a special place of prayer in a room or closet of your home or in a serene spot in your yard (like in a garden or near a pond).

- Before the family is under attack or enduring the struggle of life-threatening dilemmas, host a "Family Prayer Block Party" in your basement. Encourage everyone to bring at least three requests that will be lifted up and three praise reports that will be celebrated!

- Keep a Quarterly Prayer Jar for each immediate family. Each time God answers prayer, place a reminder slip in the jar. Encourage family members to toss theirs in on a different-colored slip of paper, or appoint a family scribe to perform this task once a week. During family times, get-togethers, or prayer block parties, bring your jar along to share praise reports. As new quarters unfold, paste the "praise slips" in a Family Scrapbook of Prayer and pull it out from time to time to encourage one another and remember the hand of God on your lives.

PLAYING TOGETHER. When was the last time that your entire family (across generations) played a game of kick ball, challenged one another in a favorite board game, or spent the day at a state park basking in the sun and grilling various meats to perfection? Family play is critical, especially when times grow more sullen and serious. Despite the terrors that plague the planet, families must find playful ways to relieve increasing strain and build stronger unity. Our trampoline has become our family's newest toy, exercise gym, and therapy tool. Whenever there's a lot of tension going on, we always find ourselves jumping, sitting, or lying flat on this multidimensional contraption. By the end of this family playtime, everybody's giggling and too exhausted to be angry or disappointed about anything. We bought our trampoline used from advertising in our local *Penny Saver* paper; it has been the wisest *investment in family play* that we've ever made.

Some other fun ways to play together could be to:

- Spend an afternoon baking different batches of cookies to share with family, friends, or kids at the local community center. The fun part of the activity is to assign parts of the baking process to various members. The roles are rotated over several different batches. This can be done with out-of-town cousins or older relatives visiting for the holidays or a special occasion for extra fun and excitement!

- Go berry picking at a local grove or orchard, and return home to make special treats of berry pie, berry ice cream, berry popovers, berry Slurpee, and on and on! This is much more exciting than going shopping at the Wal-Mart superstore and it's a lot more interactive!

- Go fishing! Either take the family to a farm-raised catfish pond during the day (which is a lot easier for beginners), or go to an old community pier at night (which is usually very satisfying for veteran fisherman). Fishing is still a sport that affords a family the time and tranquil setting in which to hold meaningful conversation. So grab a few poles and cast the line!

- Spend an early Saturday morning antiquing. Take a caravan of cars from yard sales to estate sales to look for those diamonds in the rough. It's still true that one man's junk is another man's treasure, so coordinate the best places to visit, and get everyone stirred up to browse and shop. At noon, stop and have lunch at a favorite restaurant and talk about your new finds, bargaining strategies, and interesting observations. Be sure to take the entire family —that's what makes it so much fun!

PERFORMING TOGETHER. Our house is filled with verbal presentations, from skits and musical recitals to Scripture memorization and dramatic readings. The key is to become a consummate entertainer! Children young and old love to have adults entertain them. During these performing times, I've given an oration of Sojourner Truth's "Ain't I a Woman?" dramatized the "Gettysburg Address," read chapters from great classics, and interpreted favorite poems to create a love for words, language, and literature in my children, nieces, nephews, and other neighborhood kids. Once an adult kicks off a stage performance of any kind, young folks will be jumping to stand in the spotlight! We once performed a family play about how telling a small lie is really a big matter, from James 3:5: "Even so the tongue is a little member and boasts great things. See how great a forest a little fire kindles!" The boys performed a skit on how a little boy was beaten up and his backpack and bike burned by a bully because some mean-spirited kids decided to play a joke on him by starting a rumor. They acted out all the parts and showed great emotion. We all learned a lesson about the destructive potential of telling lies on others.

PLANNING TOGETHER. A family that plans together and enlists the involvement of all parties will experience the energy and power of *Ujima,* a Swahili term that is one of the seven principles of Kwanza, meaning "collective work and responsibility." This same concept is parallel to *Harambee,* another Swahili term that means "to get together and push." Ujima and Harambee are a call to unity and solidarity. When a family is planning a move, organizing a special occasion, experiencing a dilemma, or preparing to battle a huge trial, it's best to get everyone in a planning circle. This is essential because all aspects of the issue can be more effectively hashed out with the participation of everyone affected. Bad family planning, on the other hand, would be that directed by a single person and dictated to the group or carried out haphazardly by halfhearted members. During an effective planning meeting (or brainstorm session), everyone operates on the same playing field and is brought to the "planning board" to help generate creative ideas for addressing the issues at hand. One person is designated to write out the plan and make it visibly plain for all eyes to see. The plan manager is also a vital "cheerleader" and not a supervisor. He or she is responsible for keeping the members encouraged and inspired until the plan is successfully implemented.

PARENTING TOGETHER. "It takes a village to raise a child" has become an overused truth by now. Yet the reality of its words is unchanging and far-reaching. There are often times when a child will not take the advice of a parent, and a surrogate parent will need to step in and speak the same words with a different force of insight. This happened to my son Joseph last summer when he convinced William and me that he wanted to play football. He promised to maintain his grades, do his homework, fulfill his household chores, and meet all of his other responsibilities—if we would just let him play. Though we wondered how someone so disorganized could accomplish all of this, we happily shelled out all of the monies needed to grant his request.

As the later days of the August sun beat down upon the Junior Varsity (JV) team, Joseph grew more weary and worn. I pepped him up with calcium and vitamin B each morning before school and prayed a lot for his endurance. Finally, one afternoon he sat in his room—lethargic, undressed, and unwilling to attend practice. We were having a family time later that day at his Auntie Mia's, and he wanted to quit the team and stay home. "It's too hard; I just can't do it!" he reasoned unequivocally. I pleaded with Joseph spiritually and emotionally to hang in there. William followed with obvious disappointment. After a long while, we gave up. Obviously, it was no use; his will was too strong against ours. Silence filled the atmosphere and no compromise was in sight. William left the room, and my sister-in-law Mia, who just happened to stop by, suddenly entered the room. She whispered in my ear, "Go on to the car and give me five minutes." I don't know all that she said to her nephew that afternoon, but Joseph came out of the house with a mind to play football and he has never turned back. He girded up his mind and pushed his body into strenuous shape. His "parenting auntie" was able to challenge him in ways that his parents could not.

Keeping the Family Circle Enlarged

Historically, the African-American community has enlarged its borders and tents through opening our hearts and homes to abandoned children. It didn't matter whether they were family or not. The general consensus has always been that the child didn't ask to be born and should be given every chance to succeed at life, despite the situation. Unfortunately, this is not always the case today. As a family and a community, we sometimes have adopted an "us four, no more" mentality that is detrimental to preserving future generations. "Back in the day," as my children often say, it seemed that the African-American families housed and fed children from near and far who were in need. Orphaned black children were passed on to relatives to be raised "just like one of theirs," without concern for food and finances. If a student was attending a local college, he or she often had several meals at the homes of the local black families who would encourage his or her matriculation and become a "home away from home."

Jacquelyn Bailey Kidd, spokesperson for the National Association of Black Social Workers (BSW), recently participated in an on-line discussion with Black Entertainment Television's Web affiliate, BET.com. Her comments supported our feeling that changes have occurred within our community concerning children. "On any given day, 600,000 children are in the national foster care system. Our children [African-Americans] stay longer waiting for families. On any given day we would have 100,000 African-American children available for adoption."[1]

In a historical light, Ms. Kidd shared that as a community, we have taken children over the generations and not allowed them to go into foster care. "Children who were in need of families were just absorbed into the community. We didn't think of them as being adopted. We thought of it as 'so-and-so took in a child.'"[2]

According to Ms. Kidd, this casual system of "taking in children" was drastically changed by the invasion of crack cocaine, the creation of legislation around foster care, and the sheer numbers of children that mushroomed in the system. In a final analysis, Kidd observed that "the adoption system has placed a lot of barriers and challenges to African-American families who want to come forth and legally adopt."[3]

The commitment to leave this world a better place for the children should not be replaced with temporal concern about ourselves. The Christian family especially must find creative ways to create a Christian center in their homes as places of refuge for all of the many needy children around us.

Our friends James and Gloria have been a source of inspiration about parenting "needy kids." When their oldest son brought a friend home from church one Sunday afternoon, they had no idea he'd live with them on and off for the next several years. His immediate family lived on the opposite side of the country, but even with his relatives nearby James and Gloria became his unofficial guardians and spiritual lifeline. Even though he was a towering teenager, they counseled, corrected, and cuddled him— just as if he were their own. A strong sense of stability and security surrounded his life as this caring couple gave him solid direction during his misguided years.

How many of us are willing to open up our homes for the "long haul" to an adolescent or teen who simply needs to be connected to an "intact" family? It's an area of sacrifice that could make the difference between an abiding citizen and a convicted felon. We must learn to "lengthen our cords and enlarge our borders" (Isaiah 54:2–3) to receive the young and hurting in our family and community.

Today, the family circle is also being enlarged through "blended" families. My friend Kandie and her husband, Robert, are wonderful examples of this family challenge. The Lord sovereignly carved out their life paths and brought them to one another. They married after previous relationships had left them weary and disenchanted. Robert brought four children (three girls and one boy) to the union and Kandie brought two boys. Together they have raised seven children (the Lord blessed them with our godson, David Malik, after several years of marriage).

William and I have marveled at the work of God in the lives of their children. Kandie became a *real* mother to her three girls and has skillfully trained them in biblical womanhood. She has taught them to clean a house from top to bottom, dress like young ladies, organize their schoolwork, and have quiet time with God. Her influence in their lives has been life changing and significant. Robert has done likewise, instructing his four sons in manhood through the Christian life. They have watched their father provide for his family, worship Christ with a whole heart, and lead in

righteous living. The lives of these young men have been fortified by having a father who instructs them by precept and example to "follow me as I follow Christ."

The African-American community is enhanced by couples like
James and Gloria, and by the examples of Robert and Kandie, who
have availed themselves to raise and train children in a godly
household. Only time will truly tell their story better and return
unto them a harvest for all of their labor and sacrifice.

As a community of African-American believers, we can have
a tremendous influence on a life by bringing a child into our home
through one means or another. Whether it's via adoption, foster
care, surrogate parenting, volunteerism, or mentoring—there are
hundreds of children in our immediate families, neighborhoods,
church communities, or social service networks who need a
"home" and a place to be loved and supported by a caring family.
Jesus spoke emphatically to every generation, "Suffer little children,
and forbid them not, to come unto me: for of such is the kingdom of heaven" (Matthew 19:14 KJV).

Extending the family circle can be easy. You simply open your
eyes and ears to see and hear the desperate cries of the children
all around you. They can be seen and felt everywhere and reconnect to the power and wisdom of family elders. Let's keep the family circle enlarged.

14

The Elders' Lifetime Tribute and Awards Banquet

The African-American family is a viable unit supported on the strong and capable shoulders of its elders, including mamas and daddies, grandmammas and papas, great-aunts and uncles, godmothers and fathers, older cousins, and adopted saints. Many of our aged relatives have carried the family literally upon their broad backs and in many ways have helped to preserve the family's existence through their tireless dedication of lifetime service. Without complaint, these patriarchs and matriarchs have cooked mouthwatering meals when we were hungry, nursed us when we were sick, cautioned us against wrong crowds and forbidden places, and prayed us back into the fold when we abandoned the God of our youth. With eagle eyes by the day and owl vision by night, they have guided us over the pitfalls of living in a fallen world laden with unforeseeable traps and snares. We have not always listened and learned from their many years of intuitive foresight, but we have always been blessed when we have.

As we reflect upon the contributions of our family elders, we will notice that these are the faithful folks who have given their lives for the healthy survival of the family. They have counseled the distraught in times of confusion, financed educations on low-paying wages, mortgaged homes to bail out the foolish, and bombarded heaven with urgent tears of mercy for the rebellious. Without these human bulwarks, we would be aimlessly adrift, oblivious to our own potential and purpose in this life. God has personally raised and groomed these *strong anchors* to stabilize our young and restless souls. Where would we really be if it were not for their "labor of love" and untiring sacrifices? One of the main ways that any family advances is by following in the well-charted footprints of its older members.

Gray Hairs, Glory, and God

The Bible refers to this special group of elders as the "gray head" generation. Proverbs 16:31 (KJV) records that "the hoary head is a crown of glory, if it be found in the way of righteousness." The Hebrew word for *hoary* simply means "old age; to have silver hairs or be gray headed." Those who have achieved this visible status are to be applauded for their personal achievement. To be gray haired and righteous is a notable lifetime achievement that is worthy of double honor and glory! The Lord certainly applauds these elders. When He was handing down various laws and commandments for Moses to relay to the children of Israel (Leviticus 19:32), He spoke emphatically: "You shall rise before the gray headed and honor the presence of an old man, and fear your God: I am the Lord."

God instructed the younger members of the congregation to stand up when an older person entered their presence as a way of showing reverence and submission to God. This spiritual discipline should be revisited in modern times, especially in communities of color. When we were young, every adult member in our neighborhood was referred to as sir, ma'am, Mr., or Mrs. First names were nearly taboo unless preceded by a Miss or Mister. Respect for all adults was enforced with vigor. We didn't quite understand then that by acknowledging older citizens and family members we were giving direct respect to God Almighty. This invisible connection between our elders and the Lord is mind-boggling to me as I contemplate the Leviticus reference. Here the Lord Himself reveals the significance of having gray hairs and commands us to salute and honor our elders at *all* times.

At a recent gathering, the Powell family enjoyed the rhythmic sounds and powerful choreo-movement of Africa. Our cousin Tony Powell leads an African dance troupe in the D.C. area and brings the teachings and customs of the Motherland to the Mid-Atlantic. In the spirit of African culture, he asked those who were sixty-five and older to come to the middle of the floor for a sort of "tribal" recognition. The faces of our elders shone with effervescent joy and wonder as they each stated their name and age and shared a little about themselves. We all rose to applaud and esteem them highly; and I marveled at the power of this simple yet grand display of honor. At the end, Cousin Tony pronounced a blessing upon them and evoked a special prayer. This awesome ceremony was life changing and empowering for everyone present—both young and old. Just think about it—the ever-watching God of heaven receives the highest glory when we acknowledge our elders in this way.

A Celebration of Honor for a Senior VIP

Last year I was involved in a heart-stirring celebration given by my dear girlfriend Charlotte for her sixty-eight-year-old father. Deacon Beedle has battled diabetes, prostate cancer, and kidney failure for many years. He's been sick unto death at times, and yet he looks like a wise man in his forties, with a handsome head of gray hair and matching beard. God has raised him up and preserved his life through various bouts of illness. He has indeed "lived in the way of the righteous," serving both his family and church with dedicated wisdom and commitment for over forty years. When his wife of fourteen years died suddenly, he was left with four children to raise. But he never tired of his responsibility as a loving father and servant.

I can recall Charlotte telling me how her father "stayed on his knees in prayer" for hours, praying for his children and other matters in the church and community. Now a hoary-headed saint of distinguished honor, Charlotte wanted to herald the crown of glory that graced his life. "I want to celebrate my daddy's life and accomplishments while the blood is still running warm in his veins," she said passionately. "I refuse to have family come to a funeral and celebrate his life once he's gone on to be with the Lord! We need to have this celebration of life while he's still here with us!" And what a celebration they had!

More than one hundred family members, close friends, and church members filled the decorated sanctuary of red roses for "A Celebration of Fatherhood for Deacon Willie R. Beedle Sr." His grandchildren read original poems, played musical instruments, and performed interpretive dance; and his children (all gifted singers) belted out many of his favorite hymns and songs.

I was asked to speak briefly on fatherhood and felt led of the Lord to talk about the "Lovesick Father" in Jesus' parable of the prodigal son. Little did any of us know that Deacon Beedle's estranged son (of nearly thirty years) had agreed to come and brought all of his children and their children, many of whom had never seen their grandfather! It was a moving time of forgiveness and flowing tears, happiness and healing hugs, redemption and restored relationships. Celebrating the life of this one elder had far-reaching and eternal ramifications. We all were moved and deeply inspired!

Grandparents Are Grand

My mother and father are *Grand* parents! They were present each time I gave birth to one of their grandsons. The many miles between us seemed no barrier at all even though they resided in south Florida, and we lived in either Atlanta, Georgia, or Jackson, Mississippi, during all three deliveries. Despite the distance, our boys have fostered a close and intimate relationship with their grandparents. With the use of video recorders, tons of letters and cards, and the information superhighway, they are never too far away. During a special time in our lives, my parents even resided with us for a while, creating an even stronger bond between these two generations. I have felt more than "showered" with blessings from my parents' commitment to their grandchildren and have experienced an outpouring of love!

When we relocated to southern Maryland, the boys were in close proximity to William's parents in the District of Columbia. It has been a special joy to have them around for holidays, birthdays, sports events, and school assemblies. The wonder that grandparents are able to work in the lives of their grandchilden is awe-inspiring. I have wondered at their ability to calm fears, create excitement, and reconstruct bad attitudes.

Both sets of grandparents have received high marks from the Powell boys. They admire their grandparents and enjoy spending time with them. There are no generation gaps in the relationship between these guys and their grands. Issues of the heart that would take me all day to discern and defuse, our parents can hash out in nearly twenty minutes from start to finish! They have a knack for relating their insights and experiences with great passion while maintaining a nonjudgmental and nonthreatening presence. Our teen boys welcome their input and respect their opinions because of their "cool and collected" demeanor. Of course, their willingness to pay top price for any tennis shoe or name-brand item on the market may also have something to do with it! My sons know that when they really want a big-ticket item, Nana and Granddaddy White or Grandma and Grandpa Macon are the true source of their supply.

My mother-in-law and I shared a deep chuckle the first summer that the boys went to a faraway camp for two weeks. I was so proud of all the T-shirts and shorts I was able to find at the local Goodwill. The clothes were in good condition, the sizes were perfect, and the prices right! But the following day, Grandma and Grandpa took the boys to a nearby mall to finish their camp list. Designer shirts and jeans filled shopping bags, with sparkling tennis rackets to match! On the phone that evening, I expressed our delight and gratitude to them both. "The boys are really grateful for the new things you all bought," I said with great excitement. "They are?" my mother-in-law replied meekly. "Yep! They knew I'd gone downtown, so they were really rejoicing when y'all went *uptown!*" We laughed hysterically.

Grandpa and Grandma Macon have been so generous to their grandchildren that all of them *really* believe that their grandparents are secretly rich and have an inconspicuous money tree growing in their locked basement. Whenever anyone in the family gets something new, all the kids honestly believe that their grandparents paid for it! One time, when my sister-in-law and her husband, who live in Cleveland, brought a new car, our niece Blair was so excited and thankful that she ran in the house and called her grandparents in D.C. There she was on the telephone, saying, "Thanks, Grandma and Grandpa, for our new car!" We all had a royal chuckle on that one! Years later, however, when Blair turned eighteen, Grandma Jean sent her eighteen presents for her birthday—one for every year of life! How can their grandchildren resist such an outpouring of specialness? I bless God for the generous liberality of the Macons!

On other ocassions, Nana and Granddaddy White have done the same sorts of things! When Joseph turned fifteen, my parents sent four boxes by United Parcel Service and two by U.S.

priority mail! Each day leading up to his birthday, a box was left on our doorstep. To me it seemed a bit much, but this is just how my parents celebrate birthdays, and there's no changing them at this age.

Following a family breakfast, Joseph was allowed to opened his boxes, not just presents! To our surprise, Mom and Dad had wrapped gifts for the entire family, even Sampson the dog! We were overwhelmed with their outpouring of thoughtfulness. One box was filled with party goods and snack foods fit for a grand party! Joseph didn't seem bothered that we all had received gifts on this special day. Our house was filled with special merriment as each of us tore into bows and wrapping paper and stepped on tons of packing peanuts. It was truly Christmas in April! Jeremy and Jordan also have had similar outpourings by both sets of grandparents. Both the Whites and Macons give with deep humility and boundless joy. The boys couldn't have designed better grandparents on a computer software program!

Defining the "Grand" Parent

What is a grandparent? Is it all about money and gifts? I don't think so. There is another more powerful element at work in these seasoned parents. I call it the element of "cool, collected confidence." The areas in which William and I struggle as parents, our folks seem to glide through with arresting ease and familiarity.

The secret weapon of any grandparent is broad knowledge about this "young and restless" generation. With enormous skill and insight, these aged individuals have unraveled the whole rope of child-rearing tactics and understand the potency of time. Having competed in the game of parenting before, grandparents are familiar with the entire playbook. And they are convinced that right or wrong, good or bad, all things will work together for good. While first-time parents pull their hair out in anxiety, the veteran grandparent remarks confidently, "This too shall pass."

It's a measure of having "been there and done that" in every way. After years of trial and error, and a slew of triumphs and mishaps, I've observed that grandparents are well acquainted with the three Ts of strategic parenting: timing, technique, and tenderness. They seem to know that:

+ all children eventually grow into adults and leave home one way or another, so there's no need to depair;

+ all children are unique individuals that require a creative and varied approach; and

+ many children will make you tense and tough, but a tender talk or touch can win them over.

Simply put, a grandparent is a veteran parent possessing grand qualities and effective know-how that causes the lives of their offspring to be enhanced a thousand times! This is what makes grandparents such special people.

An Ode to a Good Ol' Grandma

The strength of any family system lies in the dedication and commitment of its elders—those who give untiringly of themselves to ensure that the rest of the family members have what they need. In the African-American family, grandmothers especially should be applauded for their enormous labor of love on behalf of their children, grandchildren, great-grands, nieces, and nephews. These women, many functioning as female heads of household, have struggled to raise and rear strong and successful children. Grandmothers are the true gatekeepers of the community. Their prayers have kept a race of people from being consumed by drugs, violence, prostitution, and prison. They have parented their own children, their children's children, and other people's children on limited resources and with minor complaint.

The first time I heard Kirk Franklin's CD, *The Rebirth of Kirk Franklin,* I wept like a baby. The introduction is a dramatic rendition of the early days of his life as his young mother thrust him into his grandmother's arms in the wee hours of the morning and ran off into the darkness. That night Ms. Gertrude, who raised her grandson, prayed a prophetic prayer over young Kirk's soul that kept him through the lowest days and darkest nights of his life and career. While listening to her simple, heart-felt prayer, I was overwhelmed with the power of a maternal figure.

When we lived in Alabama during the late nineties, there was a particular song that filled the gospel radio airwaves. The DJ played it religiously as an introduction to his morning show. It was entitled "Mama 'em" (read: Mama and them). The words to the song were dedicated to all the mothers who singularly help the family to survive and advance. The specialness of this family matriarch is encased in the catch-all phrase "Mama 'em." Everything starts with Mama, and everybody else is added on as an afterthought! She is deeply admired and single-handedly represents a group or community of people. "Mama 'em" is a hilarious truth that has stark realities in the African-American community. Even in families like my own, where two parents are present, my children still single me out to soothe wounds, acquire funds, check assignments, and offer up prayers!

The reality of this role spreads to my mother and was true of both my grandmothers . . . all of these women could be affectionately called Mama 'em! They always seemed to be the ones that we went to in times of trouble. The spirit of comfort and relief that they offered was a source of great strength. One pastor friend of ours refers to the woman as characteristic of the Holy Spirit— full of wisdom, comfort, compassion, and truth. On the other hand, the man is designed to express the characteristics of the Father—full of power, authority, might, and sovereign rule. Perhaps there is deep insight in this comparison.

Whether they are tough and strong or meek and mild, grand-mothers have given their backbone to ensure the family's success. Their daily sacrifice and lifetime service should be continually applauded and rewarded. We can all chime in with gospel record-ing artist Shirley Caesar as she sings her signature love song with tear-filled eyes, "I remember Mama!"

A Regal Crown for Grandfathers

Even though mothers and grandmothers receive great appre-ciation from their offspring, there is a quieter but equal place reserved exclusively for grandfathers. These patriarchs receive a lot of praise and esteem from watching their seed multiply and increase. Grandfathers are electrified that their lineage has been extended and lengthened by their grands and great-grands. King Solomon was able to look down the annals of time and write in Proverbs 17:6 (KJV), "Children's children are the crown of old men. . . ." A lot of hope and insight is etched in this verse for the African-American family. Solomon's wisdom provides us with a secret key to unlock the restoration of our community. If God's Word declares that older men are truly crowned by the presence and proliferation of their grandchildren, then this is a message we must herald with great diligence.

I recall one mother who talked of her seven-year-old son's crav-ing for male companionship and the brief relationship he'd had with his grandfather until the elderly man passed away. Her story is one many woman can relate to. "George minded my father," she recalled. "When my father was there, I would have no problem with him. When my father went, that's when my son went." It's clear that a significant part of a child's self-worth and perspec-tive on life is tied to positive relationships with parents and grand-parents.

Children in our urban centers are angry and frustrated because something is missing! And often it's a father, grandfather, uncle, or other surrogate male figure who could perform in that vital part in a child's life—to establish discipline, offer advice, and set protective boundaries around them.

When William was relocated out of state for a six-month period, I was so fortunate to have my parents reside with us and "make up the hedge." The bonding between my father and his three grandsons opened an entirely new world of understanding for me. Their relationship was more intense and developed than any other. Some nights they would stay up late and play Monopoly until the wee hours of the morning, building financial empires. During other times these four men would huddle in protracted conversation, telling tall tales and sharing deep secrets. I could only watch from a distance. Their camaraderie seemed almost sacred, as if Dad was pouring "familiness" into their loins, and they were wrapping unforeseeable strength around his heart. At one point, I looked at this grandfather in the midst of his heritage, and he appeared taller and wiser than I had ever noticed before. He looked almost regal with an esoteric crown sitting upon his short afro. Without doubt, Joseph, Jeremy, and Jordan had fulfilled the Scriptures and had ceremonially crowned Dad with his greatest asset of pride and joy: children's children!

Family Traditions and Teachings of the Elders

As we seek to nurture and revitalize our family units, we must re-create caring communities where every member is supported. More and more it seems that many African-American families have lost the art of transferring their traditions and teachings from one generation to the next. Grandparents can play a special role in helping younger generations realize who they are, where they come from, and what it will take to make a personal difference in a changing world. Here are a few ideas to get you started:

- Get together to develop a mission and vision for the family.

- Lay out the family tree on a huge poster board and tell stories about each relative.

- Stay connected with weekly talk times, either on the telephone or in person.

- Bring the Sunday Soon-as-Church-Is-Over Dinner or Friday Night Fish Fry alive again with extended family and friends.

- Celebrate Christmas and Kwanza together as lasting traditions of spiritual and cultural enrichment.

- Begin a family collection of black memorabilia, such as stamps, dolls, trucks, or pins—anything that everyone can share in!

- Make a family album for each child.

- Host a class on social etiquette and good grooming.

- Buy stocks and bonds for grandchildren (at Christmas and birthdays) in addition to other gifts.

- Celebrate a major milestone in your family's history each year.

- Take grandkids on extended trips to expose them to the larger world.

- Create a large support system.

- Make your home a part of a centralized learning network full of books, maps, and videos.

The Indelible Mark of an Elder's Life

I was raised with my right eye constantly upon two strong elders in my family: my maternal grandmother, Gladys Killingsworth Goss, and my paternal grandfather, Edward Julius White Sr. From the earliest days of my life, these two people left a special mark on my life that is undeniable.

Grandma Gladys was dear to my heart. I loved her so and followed her everywhere she went. She was among my first caretakers and took responsibility for training me in social etiquette. I can remember being swiftly chided once for taking a quarter from a stranger. "You give that right back!" she snapped. "Don't ever take nothing that you haven't earned!" In my mind's eye, Grandma Gladys was the proudest African-American woman I'd ever met. Even as I write these lines, she seems larger than life to me. So confident and surefooted, she always walked with her head up, like she knew where she was going. Who could possibly turn her in a different direction?

We traveled all across America by bus, train, and even plane (before most of our other family members). Grandma earned a good salary as head cook at the Palm Beach *Post Times* and was well respected in our town. She lived her life to the fullest and encouraged all of her grandchildren to do the same. "Life's too short to be bored," she'd contend. "Get out and do something exciting with yourself," she would say enthusiastically.

After a heart-wrenching divorce from T. C. Killingsworth in her younger years and the death of her second husband, James Goss, in her later life, my grandmother became a liberated woman and a staunch Republican. She had strong opinions about all kinds of issues, from welfare to Watergate. She dressed with eccentric flair and was always draped in the newest styles of costume jewelry. I admired her independent spirit and sense of adventure.

My mother and I often chuckle over our favorite sayings and doings of this great woman. "I was afraid of Momma right up to the time she died," my own mother once confided in me. "That woman put the fear of God down in her children, and it never lifted during her entire lifetime!" Making a difference and leaving your mark!—this is part of the legacy that her life inspired in me.

I never had a close relationship with Granddaddy White but loved and admired him from a distance. Getting too close would have seemed fatal somehow. My grandfather was a large man with an ominous presence. Over six feet tall, he walked softly but carried a big stick! And everybody knew it! He maintained a formal disposition from sunup to sundown and had no time for "casual talk and foolish jesting." On Sundays after church when my grandmother chatted a bit too long with the ladies from the Willing Workers Club, Granddaddy White just tooted his horn once, and if she didn't come then, Grandma Carmeta would have to find herself a ride home!

My grandfather lived his whole life on a strict diet of sameness. He bought the same groceries each week, including chicken, rice, and peas for Sunday dinner! His only treat was an occasional Little Debbie raisin cake. He wore the same color khakis, white shirt, and brown shoes during the week, and a black or gray suit on Sundays. I have never seen my grandfather or any of the other men in his generation wearing shorts or a T-shirt. Such "dress down" items were never considered in their code of dress.

My grandfather was a self-made man. He left his home in Marianna, Florida, when he was about ten years old and worked his way down to Palm Beach County by doing odd jobs along the way. Although he never finished school, he became a wise and enterprising businessman. In the early fifties, he started his own company, White's Collection Agency, and began collecting rent payments on rental properties for wealthy landlords in the North.

Edward Julius White Sr. had the very first home office I had ever seen. He had converted his front porch into a collection office where clients could come and pay their weekly rent. It had a huge desk, an enormous typewriter, and lots of file cabinets. Everything was black or steel gray and designed in that bulky, hard style of the 1940s. A clashing sofa and chair were lined up on separate walls. It was clearly a place of "business." If any of the grand-children were caught playing in his office, we'd be swiftly whipped with Granddaddy White's brown leather belt that we called "Big Bertha"! Even though we did cross the line of forbidden terri-tory occasionally, we were all careful not to get caught.

My grandfather was never intimate or emotionally available, but I found his strength of character and sense of solid direction to be remarkable. He put four sons through college and paid cash for his oldest grandchild's first car (a used 1972 Subaru, which I loved!). We all considered him the "Money Man" and were blessed by his untiring work ethic and ability to save for a "rainy day." Granddaddy White was goal oriented before the term was popu-lar, and dedicated to his dreams. Most of all, he had a single vision to excel and succeed—against the odds. This was the endearing mark that he left on my life. I learned from him that tenacity and hard work make all the difference!

The A-to-Z Wisdom of the Elders

Over the years, many of my family elders and other saints in the church have shared pearls of wisdom with William and me, or with other friends and family, that are worth remembering and sharing. When times are really difficult, or situations in the family are stir-crazy, the elders can still speak as we recall their life-giving wisdom:

- ◆ A—Always put God first!

- ◆ B—Be consistent in everything you say and do. Don't be wishy-washy!

- ◆ C—Child, you come from good stock! Of course you can make it!

- D—Dreams may be delayed, but they are not denied. Don't let your dreams die!

- E—Every child of God must cry sometime, but behind every dark cloud is a bright sunshine.

- F—Forget all those things behind and press toward the high mark of God in Jesus Christ.

- G—God can make a way out of no way! Hear me what I say!

- H—He may not come when you want Him, but He's always right on time!

- I—I will look to the hills from whence cometh my help; my help comes from the Lord!

- J—Just keep on living . . . you'll see that thing turn around.

- K—Keep on keepin' on! We've come this far by faith, leaning on the Lord!

- L—Life is tough, but God is good!

- M—Make hard work your friend!

- N—Nothing ever goes into a tight fist and nothing ever come out. Everyone has something to give.

- O—O, magnify the Lord with me, and let us exalt His name together!

- P—Perk up, child! Where there's a will, there's a way!

- Q—Quench not the Spirit! And let the Lord lead you forth!

- R—Riches and fame won't ever replace peace and joy!

- S—Sometimes up, sometimes down, sometimes almost leveled to the ground!

- T—This too shall pass!

- U—Use the common sense that the good Lord gave you!

- V—Victory is yours, if you want it!

- W—When someone gives you a stone, give them bread. God is watching and He will bless you!

- X—eXamine your own self first!

- Y—You can, if you think you can!

- Z—Zero tolerance will be paid for foolishness!

The contribution elders make is in passing on their lessons. In this way, every member of the family is given a picture of the legacy and the history to help carry on the family values.

Passing On
Family Legacies

Each generation is built on the legacy and foundation laid by the preceding generation. Our mandate to families goes beyond class, status, education, and income. From the projects to the penthouse, each of us must commit to equip our children with a heritage that will empower them to compete and achieve in the global market. Beyond the latest toys, sneakers, and video games, we must provide cultural and spiritual connections for our children and grandchildren that are strong and unfading.

From the family unit, we are to emerge empowered and enabled to take a bold stand in the world. Schools facilitate, churches undergird, and neighbors support—but the legacy of "passing on" articles of wealth and words of wisdom must have its beginning and maintenance within the family system. It is vital that we pass on our tangible keepsakes, cultural traditions, oral stories, material inheritance, and spiritual heritage from one generation to the next. This five-fold legacy can enrich the lives of families, keep traditions and mores alive, and establish an eternal flame in the hearts of each member.

Tangible Keepsakes

Every family has a few special keepsakes that are cherished by its members. Keepsakes are those treasures resurrected from Grandma's attic, collectibles purchased at an estate sale, or what-nots with strong sentimental value. These special pieces can be "passed on" to chosen offspring who will commit to maintain the item's history during their lifetime and make plans for its preservation once they are gone.

My house has quiet touches of such keepsakes that have remained in my care either after the passing of my elders or that were given to me as gifts by living relatives. These pieces gracefully kindle childhood memories and keep me in rememberance of family members. In my cabinets are choice pieces of porcelain, pottery, and "cut glass" that my mother used to serve holiday meals during my growing years. On my desk lies my Granddaddy White's delicate 1902 *A.M.E. Hymnal.* Encased in antique frames are Grandma Carmeta's black-and-white photos of family and close friends taken in the forties and fifties. Lacing our shelves are old books and first editions that were handed down from my Uncle George and Aunt Lil's massive library. In my jewelry box are vintage brooches, hatpins, and earrings from my Great-Aunt Irene's Fifth Avenue collection (circa 1920s). Precious what-nots so dear to my Grandma Gladys are placed about my living room.

In 1997 I coauthored a book entitled *From Darkness to Light: A Modern Guide to Recapturing Historical Riches* with Alabama auctioneer LaCheryl Cillie.[1] We wanted to provide the African-American community with a resource to help our folks, in particular, to preserve family keepsakes and collectibles and to understand auctions and estate sales. It was a fascinating writing project that helped me discover the importance of reflecting on days gone by. Up until that time, I was a "modern girl" who had little regard for the "old-fashioned" things stored in the closets and cupboards of the past. Like most contemporary African-Americans, Grandmother's worn things and the overly used artifacts of my senior kinfolk often found themselves carted off to the local Goodwill or tossed in a trash heap for collection.

As a twenty-first-century woman, I wanted the new glitzy items instead. But I came to realize that our past should not be discarded so easily and forgotten. Family keepsakes are a part of our makeup and can help us maintain our focus on the things that are really important: *like preserving family memories.* Recapturing historical riches (whether cultural, material, or spiritual) can often define our future and bring us to our destiny. We have learned this valuable lesson from the West African Adinkra symbol Sankofa, which means "to go back and fetch that which was lost and to move forward with it!" Our past is an indelible part of our future.

So, let's reminisce for a moment and take a walk down memory lane. Can you see that big potbellied stove, pure black skillet, or cast-iron teakettle nestled in the kitchen of yesteryear? How about those perfectly folded handkerchiefs and cool cotton dresses of the 1950s? Have you forgotten items like parasols, flour sacks, butter churns, doilies, and weather vanes?

Can you recall the scrub board and clothesline (long before sculptured nails, washing machines, and dryers)? How about when telephone numbers included letters (ours was TE-2-2723)? Remember when older men drove a work car during the week and maintained their shiny one for Sunday go to meeting? How about when grown folks continually referred to their childhood friends as classmates? Has it been so long ago that homemade biscuits and baked sweet potatoes were as popular as hamburgers and French fries? Can you ever forget when hand-churned ice cream and freshly baked tea cakes were a regular dessert? Times have surely changed, but the pieces that defined our family's existence and our "growing-up years" must be preserved.

Cultural Traditions

In America, our mosaic of African-Caribbean-West Indian influences reveal themselves in grand expressions, from Juneteenth and Black History Month Celebrations to the Annual Black Family Reunion Day and Kwanza festivities. Our history in this country is rooted with "overcoming" accomplishments and bourgeoning success. Therefore, our children must know the history of the Civil Rights Movement, study the Harlem Renaissance, sing the Negro National Anthem, and relish the accomplishments of black history makers. This is a cultural legacy too rich and flavorful to throw into a melting pot of colorless ideals. I like what Joyce Ladner, author of *Timeless Values for African-American Family*, said: "Even though values are like the color of water . . . black values add a flavor that is rich and deep."[2] The cultural values and traditions of African-Americans are flavorful indeed. Our "color" and "spice" add specialness to the whole of American culture. In the areas of music, dance, and the arts, the expressions of black people have been extraordinary and significant.

Perhaps that is why my father and his friends were so tenacious about organizing the first "Afro-Arts Festival" in the early seventies. They desperately wanted my generation to know our cultural richness. It was the "best thing since sliced bread," as my grandmother Gladys used to say. The African dancers, gospel singers, painters, storytellers, and jazz musicians set our collective soul on fire! From early morning to late night, the African-American community of West Palm Beach was both enlightened and entertained. We didn't know that so much creative power and artistic flair dwelled within our midst. From the toddlers to the senior citizens, everyone participated, showcasing their talents and abilities. It was life-enchancing in every way.

The Afro-Arts Festival became a cultural tradition in our community, and soon others in various sections of south Florida began hosting similar events. A new day of self-expression and creative energy was dawning in communities of color.

After I married and began a family, my father was instrumental in making sure that our boys knew their history. During summer visits he took them to African-American museums and festivals to expose them to the cultural traditions that graced their lives and community. And when the video camera emerged, he invested in one to create "black history" videos for his grandsons. On many he chronicled various events relative to black life and culture; on others he taped segments from television shows and documentaries for them to study and learn from.

Recently Joseph, our oldest son, got into a civil debate in class about slavery and the Emancipation Proclamation. His teacher and many of the students seemed perplexed at his broad-based knowledge on the subject matter. "How do you know all of this?" they asked. "Because my parents and grandparents taught me my history!" he retorted boldly. Every African-American child should be equipped with this cultural knowledge and understanding. As the saying goes, "Those who do not know their history are destined to repeat it."

Oral Stories

Alex Haley, the famous author of *Roots*, was able to document his family geneology and write a historic *Saga of an American Family* that moved a nation to tears of repentence over slavery. This was possible because his grandmother and great-grandmother maintained an oral tradition with their offspring. They passed on the "spoken word" and orally preserved stories that have become family treasures. If the African-American family is going to thrive and grow strong in the twenty-first century, this deliberate and intentional practice of passing on cultural and spiritual inheritance must be preserved. Passing down stories is an excellent tool for maintaining the vital history of the family.

How well I know this firsthand. My sister Cheryl and I became familiar with our family history through the repeated and well-told stories of my great-aunt, Irene Ferguson Leary. Even though she was often mean and moody and could whip out a powerful tongue-lashing, we always ventured into her bedroom on Saturday mornings and Sunday afternoons to be enthralled by her stories of the past. We were uniquely blessed because Aunt Irene lived with us and was always accessible for a good story.

Her father and our great grandfather, Prince Alfred Ferguson, was of Bahamian decent. In the early 1920s, he led his wife, Frances, and their five children to the southern coast of Florida in pursuit of better work opportunities and a brighter future for his offspring. My great-grandfather and his descendants helped to establish a strong Negro community in West Palm Beach, known as Pleasant City. Many of the major streets have names like Cheerful, Contentment, and Beautiful. The Fergusons owned the corner grocery store, ran the local barbershop, organized Negro schools, and helped to establish St. Paul A.M.E. Church. Their financial prosperity enabled them to buy property and build a close-knit family homestead in America.

Aunt Irene always talked admirably of my great-uncle Bill, who bought the first shiny black car the family had ever seen. It was a triumphant purchase for the entire community. Seeing Uncle Bill riding down Cheerful Avenue gave everyone a sense of prosperity and hope that things were changing and getting better for Negro citizens.

She also made our great-grandmother Frances come alive in our hearts and minds. According to Aunt Irene, her mother was a wonderful seamstress and a first-class candy maker. In graphic detail, she described how Mama Frances boiled the sugary solutions to perfection to make peppermint balls. She often handled the hot mass in her strong hands before forming the small candies on wax paper, laying in the delicate red stripes. These handmade candies were then sold at the family's corner store as a "sweet tooth" favorite of the entire community.

Cheryl and I always sat intrigued and spellbound by Aunt Irene's dramatic storytelling skills and passionate memories of her childhood. As she talked of our family's pioneering and industrious spirit, we were inspired to make similar contributions to the world. So much of who we are today in the areas of business and community development flows out of this oral tradition.

Material Inheritance

Many families have family heirlooms, antique cars or furnishings, and rare possessions that have been preserved for several generations. Others have acquired new pieces in recent years that they want to see handled with understanding and care; and a few just have dreams of one day leaving real estate, businesses, and other kinds of material wealth to their children. The Scriptures encourage this and remind us that "a good man leaves an inheritance to his children's children." (Proverbs 13:22) So, whatever we do, the mandate is clear: *to leave an inheritance to your children and grandchildren!*

Historically, however, many African-American families have failed to designate a *specific child* for a *particular possession or aspect* of the family inheritance. All too often, we have failed to leave a last will and testament that adequately outlines our wishes and desires. Or we generally scribble "share and share alike" in a parting note. Some erect a formal will but leave personal property like a home, automobile, or dining room set "to be split six ways." This is an unfortunate request that causes unnecessary family feuds and distressful hardships among grieving siblings and other family members.

A wiser way to impart material wealth and inheritance to

succeeding generations is through a legal document written in a narrative format that does the following:

- clearly identifies a specific family member and tells why that person was chosen as steward over a particular possession, and

- cites the specific item, detailing its original price and owner (if possible), historic background, and current worth.

These decisions should be made based only on the following criteria:

- years of observation,

- fair assessments of character and integrity,

- a working knowledge of each family member's personal interests, hobbies, and giftedness, and much prayer!

Here is an example of how a family heirloom or inheritance can be wisely detailed and transferred in narrative form from one generation to the next:

My granddaughter, Mary Ann Brown Hall, will receive the Steinway piano, circa 1887, that has been in the Brown family for five generations. The piano was purchased by Anna Mae Brown Williams in 1910 for $28. She served as a dedicated music teacher and educator at the Hillside Methodist Church in West Alton until her death in 1963. On August 15, 1990, the Steinway piano was appraised by Pettyway Appraisals for $21,000. Documentation is enclosed. A monetary gift of $5,000 is attached herewith to be used to restore the piano's physical beauty and to

make any minor repairs. Mary Ann has been chosen as the fam-
ily steward over this musical inheritance because of her intense
love for music, faithfulness to keep the 'beat' at family gather-
ings, and overall accomplishments in music theory and apprecia-
tion at Lowell High School. Mary Ann, it is my prayer that you
will enjoy this historic treasure for many years and at the end of
your days pass it on to the family member of your choosing.
May the Lord use this piano as a reminder of your musical call-
ing and sober responsibility to keep the melody of this family
alive and well. With Love and Admiration, Momma Katherine.

In order to provide your offspring with the appropriate inheritance, you should ask yourself thought-provoking questions like:

- Of my three sons, which has demonstrated the best financial responsibility in this family?

- Which of the children will cherish these old quilts and
  tell their stories?

- Who will be able to uproot and move into the family
  home and be responsible for its upkeep?

- Does my grandchild have an interest in antique cars, or is
  he into modern vehicles?

- Would the family bed that was used by several generations be used and appreciated more by my granddaughter
  or my niece?

- Which of the children would benefit most from these
  stocks and bonds and continue to invest wisely in them?
  Or should I establish a trust fund of some sort for them
  all?

- ◆ Of my three daughters, who can best serve as a wise and fair executor of this estate?

- ◆ Does my nephew have the interest and ability to run this company and expand its vision?

This kind of diligent and objective analysis will benefit the entire family. Your children will know that you have given serious consideration to their inheritance. Disagreements and disappointments may still arise, but your wishes will be clearly delineated. You will have successfully accomplished one of the most important parental duties of your lifetime—passing on the inheritance. Ultimately, they will respect your desires, see the wisdom of your choices, and ensure that your requests are fulfilled.

Spiritual Heritage

In uncertain times like these, African-American families in Christ must be diligent to communicate a spiritual heritage to all their members. Young children and growing teens must have a clear, realistic understanding of faith. What is it that we really believe? Why is church so important? How come we celebrate Communion in this way? What is the purpose of tithes and offerings? Do prayer and fasting really accomplish anything? These are general questions that should be acknowledged with simple and heartfelt responses that are thorough and Bible based. Such questions become more complex as our children mature and encounter life's hardships. Yet our answers are vital to their growth and maturation in spiritual things. As the great evangelist Tom Skinner once said: "If Christ is the answer, what are the questions?" Our children need to know that Christ is the answer to all of life's toughest questions and challenges.

The psalmist in Psalm 78:1–4 (NIV) writes in a pleading tone of exhortation about passing on our faith and understanding of God to the next generation. Listen to his words:

O my people, hear my teaching; listen to the words of my mouth.
I will open my mouth in parables, I will utter hidden things from
things of old—what we have heard and known, what our fathers
have told us. We will not hide them from their children; we will
tell the next generation the praiseworthy deeds of the LORD, his
power, and wonders he has done.

Too often our children grow up spiritually malnourished, with
puny faith and a small anchor to sustain them through the
inevitable storms of life. We risk leaving them spiritually vulnerable simply because parents, grandparents, aunts, and uncles fail
to transfer the "data of the divine" to our progeny. However, they
need to know about such things as sexual purity, money management, forgiving others, forming a personal relationship with
the Lord, walking in business integrity, being faithful over a few
things, and finishing the assignment given regardless of the difficulty. These are issues of life on which God, in His Word, has
already given us instruction. We do our children a great disservice
when we gain the victory in God and don't tell the testimony at
home around the dinner table; or we mess up in our walk with
Christ and don't feel it's important enough to confess in family
prayer. Passing on our spiritual faith means making our children
privy to the blessings and the benefits, as well as the pains and
pitfalls!

Psalm 78:5–7 (KJV) further clarifies the call to "pass it on": "He
commanded our fathers, that they should make them known to
their children: that the generation to come might know them, even
the children which should be born; who should arise and declare
them to their children: that they might set their hope in God,
and not forget the works of God, but keep his commandments."

This is why we strongly advocate family nights, informal Bible
discussions, family prayer times, and personal devotions—all held
at home! Our children need to see us "walk out" our Christianity
in the dailiness of life and culture. They need to be able to voice

their frustrations and their unbelief, ask their questions, and share their thoughts. In turn, as parents we need to become increasingly transparent in this way and not shirk from telling the good, the bad, and the ugly!

As much as I love my grandparents, life was too stiff and formal for any kind of family discussions on the Bible. Religious talk was reserved for Sunday school, and too few discussions about it ever flowed into the rest of the week. Even during church services, those were listening times. If one had questions, this was not the forum to ask! We've come a long way, and I bless God for the changes in times and seasons. With a new century staring back at us, as Christian parents we must not lower our eyes. Instead, we should lift our voices and say something spiritually significant to our children—lest they are destroyed for the lack of knowledge! How desperately they need a clear understanding of the invisible, omnipotent God!

When Kizzy was born to Kunte Kinte in Alex Haley's *Roots*, Kunte took his day-old infant daughter out under the midnight sky and lifted her to the heavens. In his native Mandinka tongue, he spoke to her this spiritual truth: *"Behold, the only thing greater than yourself!"* How much our modern children need a well-communicated spiritual heritage!

Our children must encounter the great "I AM" and become personally acquainted with the "God of our weary years, God of our silent tears." They must become intimately acquainted with the One who has blessed and kept the African-American family "through many dangers, toils, and snares."

Furthermore, our children must understand why Jesus Christ gave His life on an old rugged cross for the sins of the world. The power of grace and mercy must become relevant and personal to a generation of churchgoing young people who shrug their shoulders indifferently at the message of Good News.

Finally, our children must grasp the urgency of the times and connect biblical truth to every social trend that they are experiencing in the present culture—from music and fashion to drugs and violence. The Gospel can touch every generation with eternal stealth and might. It's our responsibility as disciples to "make the case" and bridge the connections. The confidence of our children will grow and expand when they realize that the God of past generations is also their God! He is the same yesterday, today, and forever!

I recently read that the Bible refers to the term *generations* more than two hundred times, repeatedly underscoring the responsibility of the older generation to guide and instruct the younger. In an article entitled "From Generation to Generation: Discover the Biblical Mandate for Investing in the New Generation," author Fred Wevodau wrote, "Authentic faith must be transmitted personally from one generation to another if it is to live on."[3] He challenged adult Christians with an impending dilemma: that new and emerging generations lack a long-term history of God's power and provision. "We must envision it for them, drawing upon our own stories and those of Scripture," he exhorted.[4] Our children simply want to see someone whose life demonstrates that Christianity is "all that!" They are really assessing whether this Gospel has real answers to hard questions. They want living examples of kingdom life that will provoke them to follow us as we follow Christ. Our stories and testimonies display the power of the Gospel to redeem our mistakes and brokenness. Our faith can ignite their hope, if we will only pass on the torch!

A Final Exhortation

As a Christ-centered African-American family, we have been challenged to preserve special keepsakes, share oral stories about the family's history, establish cultural traditions that can be enjoyed by succeeding generations, wisely designate specific stewards of the material assets, and impart our faith to the next generation with real-life transparency. Our elders must be applauded for their wise and visionary leadership in helping transfer our meaningful legacies into the hands of ready offspring.

God requires that generations flow into one another, strengthening and sustaining every member as we go. In this way, we advance the greatest and most fundamental institution on the planet: *the family!* So, pass it on and be blessed. As you do, remember that the family is precious and valuable to God. There is still much work to do. Let's get busy repairing the walls of our lives!

Epilogue:
The Nehemiah
Challenge

The plight of African-Americans is so similar to that of the Jews during the time of Nehemiah. The walls of real peace, protection, and praise have been burned down all around us. We have lived in the "rubbish" and fear of broken communities, second-class citizenship, and unequal opportunities for so very long. We know within ourselves that we are a vibrant people, but so few acknowledge it! Those who pass by the exterior of our lives remark at the horror of our plight—the violence, drugs, low wages, unceasing racism . . . the list is long and visible. But few have truly sought the King of Kings and Lord of Lords on how to rebuild the walls, repair the breach, and restore lost honor!

Nehemiah was similarly distraught over the conditions of the remnant left in Jerusalem after the city was destroyed at the hands of King Nebuchadnezzar. Even though

Nehemiah held a prestigious position as cupbearer to the king of Persia, he was determined to take a leave of absence and begin the important work of rebuilding the walls of God's holy and historic city.

Many detractors tried to distract Nehemiah from his dedication. There were enemies within and without who attempted to hinder the work of restoration. But Nehemiah refused to be drawn into their trickery. He emphatically stated, "I am doing a great work and I cannot come down."

We are inspired by the dedication of Nehemiah. As John Perkins, pioneer of the Christian community development movement, would say, "He saw a felt need," and he moved swiftly to rebuild and make up the hedge. During times when the work was threatened by outside forces, Nehemiah wrote, "I stationed men in the lowest parts of the space behind the . . . exposed places [in the wall] . . . and I stationed the people in families . . ." (Nehemiah 4:13 NASB). This servant of God called families to work and fight to restore their own city and secure their own dwellings. And when the workers became afraid from agitators and mockers, he consoled them saying, "Do not be afraid . . . remember the Lord who is great and awesome, and fight for your brothers, your sons, your daughters, your wives, and your houses" (Nehemiah 4:14 NASB).

It is much the same today! Many pass by the ruins of our lives every day, and few openly display compassion and concern. On one side, masses languish in the rubbish of poverty and disenfranchisement at the urban core. Thousands of families are economically victimized, socially isolated, and spiritually malnourished. On the other side, many middle- and upper-class African-American families are also needy. They experience spiritual deficiency as a result of their individual struggles to attain material success. So, regardless of class or status, the walls of our vast and diverse community are in need of repair.

The good news is that repairing and rebuilding is not impossible. We believe that the "spirit of Nehemiah" is upon African-

Americans in Christ. It is we who are chosen and approved to rebuild the spiritual city of God and repair every breach in the wall of God's first institution—the family. Hidden within our trials and testimonies, talents and resources, positions and ministries are the blessings needed to complete this work successfully. These resources simply need to be excavated and put to good use.

As William and I have surveyed the walls that surround the African-American community, our prognosis is twofold. We need spiritual nourishment and community strengthening! And our hands are ready to work! African-American families must be stationed at certain portions of the wall to work on the internal and external repairs that are needed. That means that no vulnerable spot within our territory would be left unattended or unguarded. Some families could adopt a black child. Other family stations could include community and political involvement, substance abuse prevention, education and literacy training, closing the digital divide, monitoring media images, fighting against systemic racism, preserving the arts, or many other noble endeavors. Whether our efforts are targeted toward eradicating negative influences or reinforcing positive outlets and involvements, there are so many places in which families may serve. It's a big work, but the Lord is with us! He will strengthen our hands and bless our efforts to restore His wall.

Truly, the key to restoration in the African-American community lies with each family. Revival will be realized as we respect ourselves, understand and follow God's direction for our path, place trust in one another, and revive an old-fashioned, uncompromising faith in God. We must be families united before we can be communities reclaimed.

This is the vision. Will you covenant with us to become a part of the Nehemiah Challenge? Will you commit your family to a place of responsibility at the wall? Without you, a vital part of the wall remains irreparable and exposed.

We humbly ask you to take on the Nehemiah Challenge and

to meet us at the wall. With the Holy Spirit directing us, together we can repair our families and rebuild our communities. No greater work lies before us!

Please let us know how you are interested in implementing the Nehemiah Challenge in your own family and community. We stand ready to assist you with intercessory prayer and resource support.

William and Yolanda Powell
Oracles and Utterance, Incorporated
c/o Soul Food & Living Water
P. O. Box 1214
Huntingtown, MD 20639-1214
thepowells@oraclesofgod.com
www.oraclesofgod.com

End Notes

CHAPTER 4

1. Oswald Chambers, *My Utmost for His Highest* (Grand Rapids: Discovery House, 1935), 1.

2. "Sweet Surrender," *Discipleship Journal*, January/February 2002, 49.

3. Ibid., 51.

CHAPTER 5

1. Derek Prince, *The Marriage Covenant* (Fort Lauderdale, Fla.: Derek Prince Ministries, 1978), 23–24.

2. Al Janssen, *The Marriage Masterpiece* (Wheaton, Ill.: Tyndale, 2001), 179–180.

3. Ibid., 180.

CHAPTER 6

1. Taken from http://www.gospelcom.net/rbc/ds/q0504/point2.html (Kurt DeHann, *What Does God Expect of a Man?*).

2. Stuart Scott, *The Exemplary Husband* (Bemidji, Minn.: Focus Publishing, 2000), 97.

3. Ibid., 129.

CHAPTER 7

1. Emalyn Spencer, *A Woman That Feareth the Lord* (Montgomery, Ala.: Presbyterian Church in America, Committee for Christian Education and Publications), 1–2.

CHAPTER 8

1. Yolanda Powell, "You've Got the Power," *Urban Family Magazine,* Winter/1994, 22–23.

2. Dr. Ben Carson's life story is described in his book, *Think Big: Unleashing Your Potential for Excellence* (Grand Rapids: Zondervan, 1992).

3. Charles R. Swindoll, *You and Your Child* (Nashville: Nelson, 1990), 41.

CHAPTER 9

1. Yolanda Powell, "How to Help Your Youngsters Choose Right Over Wrong," *Urban Family Magazine,* Winter/1993, 8–9.

2. Dean and Grace Merrill, *Together at Home* (Pamona, Calif.: Focus on the Family, 1985).

3. Ibid., 161–162.

4. Ibid., 83–84.

5. Giles Wilkerson Wiles and Waldo W. Braden, eds., *Public Speaking: Principles and Practice,* 2nd ed. (New York: Harper & Row, 1963), 538.

6. Ibid.

CHAPTER 10

1. Excerpt by Alan Light, *The VIBE History of Hip Hop,* VIBE, October 1999, 121.

2. Carl F. Ellis, Jr. *Free at Last? The Gospel in the African-American Experience,* 2nd ed. (Downers Grove, Ill.: InterVarsity, 1996), 182.

3. Carter Harris, "Eternal Gangsta," *VIBE,* October 1999, 119.

4. Eds., "About This Issue" *Black Enterprise,* May 2002, 17.

5. Alan Hughes, "Hip-Hop Economy," *Black Enterprise,* May 2002, 70.

6. William J. Brown and Benson P. Fraser, "Hip-Hop Kingdom Come," http://www.christianitytoday.com/ct/2001/001/4.48.html

7. Ibid.

8. Ibid.

9. From a personal interview with the Cross Movement.

10. Roland Hairston and Kimar Morris, "God is Pain?" *Gospel Today,* May/June 2002, 64.

CHAPTER 11

1. Kathy Peel, *The Family Manager* (Dallas: Word Publishing, 1996), xix.

2. Cheryl R. Carter, *Putting Your Home in Order* (Long Island, New York: Jehonadah Communications, 2002), 7.

3. Peel, *The Family Manager,* xix.

4. Ibid., 46.

5. Carter, *Putting Your Home in Order,* 23.

6. Ibid., 26.

7. Ibid., 25.

8. Ibid., 24.

CHAPTER 12

1. Carl F. Ellis Jr., *Free at Last? The Gospel in the African-American Experience,* 2nd ed. (Downers Grove, Ill.: InterVarsity, 1996), 13–14.

2. Tom Skinner, *How Black Is the Gospel?* (Philadelphia: A. J. Holman, 1970), 65.

3. Ibid, 74.

4. Ellis, *Free at Last?* 158.

CHAPTER 13

1. From an interview with Jacquelyn Bailey Kidd on the BET Web site.

2. Ibid.

3. Ibid.

CHAPTER 15

1. LaCheryl B. Cillie and Yolanda White Powell, *From Darkness to Light: A Modern Guide to Recapturing Historical Riches* (Birmingham, Ala.: Creative Inspirations, 1997), 180.

2. Joyce Ladner, *Timeless Values for the African-American Family* (New York: John Wiley & Sons, 1998), 45.

3. Fred Wevodau, "From Generation to Generation: Discover the Biblical Mandate for Investing in the New Generation," *Discipleship Journal*, May/June 2002, 34.

4. Ibid.

The Negro National Anthem

Lift every voice and sing
Till earth and heaven ring,
Ring with the harmonies of Liberty;
Let our rejoicing rise
High as the listening skies,
Let it resound loud as the rolling sea.
Sing a song full of the faith that the dark past has taught us,
Sing a song full of the hope that the present has brought us,
Facing the rising sun of our new day begun
Let us march on till victory is won.

So begins the Black National Anthem, by James Weldon Johnson in 1900. Lift Every Voice is the name of the joint imprint of The Institute for Black Family Development and Moody Publishers, a division of the Moody Bible Institute.

Our vision is to advance the cause of Christ through publishing African-American Christians who educate, edify, and disciple Christians in the church community through quality books written for African-Americans.

The Institute for Black Family Development is a national Christian organization. It offers degreed and non-degreed training nationally and internationally to established and emerging leaders from churches and Christian organizations. To learn more about The Institute for Black Family Development write us at:

The Institute for Black Family Development
15151 Faust
Detroit, MI 48223

FOCUS ON THE FAMILY®

Welcome to the Family!

Whether you received this book as a gift, borrowed it from
a friend, or purchased it yourself, we're glad you read it! It's just
one of the many helpful, insightful, and encouraging
resources produced by Focus on the Family.

In fact, that's what Focus on the Family is all about—providing inspiration, information, and biblically based advice to people in all stages of life.

It began in 1977 with the vision of one man, Dr. James Dobson, a licensed
psychologist and author of 16 best-selling books on marriage, parenting,
and family. Alarmed by the societal, political, and economic pressures
that were threatening the existence of the American family, Dr. Dobson
founded Focus on the Family with one employee—an assistant—
and a once-a-week radio broadcast, aired on only 36 stations.

Now an international organization, Focus on the Family is dedicated
to preserving Judeo-Christian values and strengthening the family
through more than 70 different ministries, including eight separate
daily radio broadcasts; television public service announcements;
10 publications; and a steady series of books and award-winning
films and videos for people of all ages and interests.

Recognizing the needs of, as well as the sacrifices and important
contributions made by, such diverse groups as educators, physicians,
attorneys, crisis pregnancy center staff, and single parents,
Focus on the Family offers specific outreaches to uphold and
minister to these individuals, too. And it's all done for one purpose,
and one purpose only: to encourage and strengthen individuals
and families through the life-changing message of Jesus Christ.

• • •

For more information about the ministry, or if we can be of help to your
family, simply write to Focus on the Family, Colorado Springs, CO 80995
or call 1-800-A-FAMILY (1-800-232-6459). Friends in Canada may write
Focus on the Family, P.O. Box 9800, Stn. Terminal, Vancouver, B.C. V6B 4G3.
or call 1-800-661-9800. Visit our Web site—www.family.org—
to learn more about Focus on the Family or to find out if
there is an associate office in your country.

We'd love to hear from you!

Building Bridges—Strengthening Families

It's difficult to find biblically based family resources. Focus on the Family recognizes this need and is committed to partnering with African-American pastors, churches and communities to transmit biblical values and honor cultural traditions.

Find 10 ingredients for happy marriages in this paperback, along with practical guidelines for enhancing intimacy, communication and romance.

Choose the right public school, establish student- and parent-teacher connections and safeguard your child's faith using the practical help in this paperback.

This comprehensive, best-selling guide walks parents through a clear, concise plan for building everyday faith in their children ages 8 to 12.

Succeed in the parent-teen relationship with the advice and techniques in this hardcover while guiding your teens into adults who love and serve the Lord.

Prepare for the responsibility of caring for an elderly person with this comprehensive hardcover that provides information and support for the utmost in quality elder care.

•　•　•

Look for these special books in your Christian bookstore. To request a copy, call 1-800-932-9123, fax 1-719-548-4654, e-mail *sales@family.org* or write to Focus on the Family, Sales Department, P.O. Box 15379, Colorado Springs, CO 80935-4654.

Visit our Web site (www.family.org) to learn more about the ministry or find out if there is a Focus on the Family office in your country.

MOODY
PUBLISHERS

THE NAME YOU CAN TRUST

SOUL FOOD AND LIVING WATER TEAM

ACQUIRING EDITOR:
Cynthia Ballenger

COPY EDITOR:
Shana Murph, Focus on the Family

BACK COVER COPY:
Stephanie Pugh

COVER DESIGN:
Solid Roxx Media

INTERIOR DESIGN AND ILLUSTRATIONS:
Ragont Design

PRINTING AND BINDING:
Quebecor World Book Services

The typeface for the text of this book is
Berkeley